W9-BSO-698

WILLIAM DEAN HOWELLS

The Friendly Eye

Books by EDWARD WAGENKNECHT
Published by Oxford University Press

NATHANIEL HAWTHORNE: Man and Writer (1961)
WASHINGTON IRVING: Moderation Displayed (1962)
EDGAR ALLAN POE: The Man Behind the Legend (1963)
HARRIET BEECHER STOWE: The Known and the Unknown (1965)
HENRY WADSWORTH LONGFELLOW: Portrait of an American Humanist (1966)
JOHN GREENLEAF WHITTIER: A Portrait in Paradox (1967)
WILLIAM DEAN HOWELLS: The Friendly Eye (1969)

CHAUCER: Modern Essays in Criticism (1959)
edited by Edward Wagenknecht

Courtesy, Houghton Library
Harvard University

WILLIAM DEAN HOWELLS

The Friendly Eye

EDWARD WAGENKNECHT

The kindlier view of any man is apt to be the truer view.
WDH, 1887

818.
4
Howells

NEW YORK   OXFORD UNIVERSITY PRESS   1969

FINKELSTEIN
MEMORIAL LIBRARY
SPRING VALLEY, N. Y.

70-05917

Copyright © 1969 by Edward Wagenknecht
Library of Congress Catalogue Card Number: 70–83055
Printed in the United States of America

To my first grandson
GEORGE ROBERT WAGENKNECHT
son of Robert Edward Wagenknecht
and Therese Mueller Wagenknecht

Born March 21, 1968
Springfield, Illinois

PREFACE

In the Preface to *Nathaniel Hawthorne, Man and Writer*, which was the first book in the series in which this is the seventh, I wrote these words:

This book is neither a chronological biography nor a critical study, though it contains much information about Hawthorne's life and works. It is simply a study of Hawthorne's character and personality, based on his writings, his letters and journals, and on all that has been written about him. It uses the methods of Gamaliel Bradford and Sainte-Beuve. It should be judged entirely by the author's success or failure in understanding Nathaniel Hawthorne as a human being and his ability or lack of it to share this understanding with his readers. All other considerations are irrelevant.

Despite its name, psychography has nothing to do with psychoanalysis. Neither is a psychograph an essay, though persons imperfectly acquainted with the English language have so described it. It is the very hallmark of the essay that it is tentative, personal, and partial. The psychographer seeks to establish traits and characteristics by the citation of evidence which can be checked by other investigators and which, if he has used his findings properly, can be overthrown only by the citation of fresh evidence. In his investigations

and in the presentation of his findings, the psychographer is bound
by the same laws and standards which govern the chronological biographer, but his organization is different and his aim is more specialized.

All this applies to all the other books in this series, including
this one, quite as much as it does to the Hawthorne.

The novelist's grandsons, William White Howells and John
Noyes Mead Howells, gave me permission to quote from Howells's unpublished letters and from Mildred Howells's *Life in Letters of William Dean Howells*, copyrighted, 1928, by Doubleday,
Doran & Company, Inc., copyright renewed 1956 by the Estate
of Mildred Howells. None of this material should be reproduced
from my pages without permission.

At Harvard's Houghton Library, Dr. W. H. Bond and the
Howells Committee made the Howells Papers available to me,
and Professor Kennth S. Lynn generously allowed me access to
many materials he might have reserved for his own exclusive use.
As usual, Miss Carolyn Jakeman and her assistants in the Houghton
Reading Room have left me in their debt for many kindnesses.

Professors George Arms and E. H. Cady, both involved in the
preparation of the "Selected Edition" of Howells which is now
under way, not only encouraged me to write this book, but both
have read my manuscript and made many valuable suggestions.

Professor William M. Gibson kindly lent me photostats of some
of Howells's early contributions to Ohio papers.

I am very grateful to all these persons.

I should also like to say a word concerning the organization of
this book. In most of my recent studies in psychography, I have
prefixed the text with a biographical summary. It will be noted
that in this book, the preliminary section, much longer than
usual, is called "Howells's Life and Reading." Though this may
look odd, I believe it to be quite in harmony with my subject.
"To give an account of one's reading," wrote Howells, "is in
some sort to give an account of one's life." He also said that read-

ing was the only activity in which he could discern continuity in his life. Obviously, then, the influence of his reading upon his writing, his thinking, and his doing was profound. Like the overture to an opera, this introductory section will, I hope, be found striking many motifs which will hereafter be developed more elaborately in these pages, thus preparing the mind of the reader to encounter them.

In his utopian romances, Howells called the Altrurian, the fully developed ethical man toward whom he hoped American civilization might aspire, "Mr. Homos," and he called his American host, the novelist to whom he gave some of his own characteristics, "Mr. Twelvemough." Though I am well aware that Mr. Twelvemough was a less substantial writer than Howells himself, I have ventured to borrow his name for my first chapter, which deals with Howells's actual writing.

But Howells also theorized, almost legislated, about writing. He was called "the Dean of American writers," and he exercised great influence (and aroused great antagonism) among readers and writers both. I have, therefore, called my second chapter "Mr. Dean."

Yet he was not a writing machine; he was a man; he had many non-literary human relationships and interests. My third chapter, which views him in connection with the more personal of these, I have called "Mr. Papa," while the fourth, which deals more with matters of public interest, is "Mr. American." Finally, in the last chapter we come to Howells as a moral, ethical, and religious being, and for this I could find no more appropriate name than "Mr. Homos."

Howells is one of the few writers whom we have not agreed to call by the name he preferred to use. Nearly all his title pages read either "William D. Howells" or "W. D. Howells." Professor Gibson published his brief but valuable study of him in the "University of Minnesota Pamphlets on American Writers" as *William D. Howells*, and the "Selected Edition" is coming out as the work of "W. D. Howells." Yet nobody ever thinks or speaks of him as anything except "William Dean Howells," and I, too, have kept this form as having established itself through usage, though I must confess I do so with a certain twinge of conscience.

I have consistently italicized book titles even when writers from whom I quote have quoted them. I have used the conventional three dots to indicate omissions *within* my quotations, but I have generally avoided them at the beginning and the end of a quotation. Since I quote what I need, and only what I need, to illustrate the point under consideration, and never pretend to be quoting the entire passage, I do not see what purpose the use of such dots would serve.

Edward Wagenknecht

West Newton, Massachusetts
May 1969

CONTENTS

WILLIAM DEAN HOWELLS

The Friendly Eye

HOWELLS'S LIFE AND READING

William Dean Howells was born, March 1, 1837, at Martin's Ferry, Belmont County, Ohio. Except for an English grandmother, the forebears of his father, William Cooper Howells, were wholly Welsh; except for her Irish father, those of his mother, Mary Dean Howells, were entirely German. The religious background was Quaker and Swedenborgian, with heavy infusions of frontier Methodism, free thought, and other elements, but with Swedenborgianism predominating. There were eight children.

Howells's situation was peculiar in that, though he had very little formal education and was even more a child of the frontier than Mark Twain,[1] he grew up in a household intensely devoted to literature and was a slave to print as far back as he could remember. He went to work in the print shop at six or younger. He could never recall how he learned to set type. As far back as he could go, he had always known how to set type, and his first attempts at literary composition were made at the typecase without the intermediary of pen-and-ink. As a child he could set his thousand ems a day between seven in the morning and two in the afternoon, though he also knew what it meant to sit up late for the final telegraphic despatches and then get up at four or five to deliver the morning papers.

His father had every virtue except that of being a good provider; his mother seems never to have been guilty of anything worse than an occasional flare of Irish temper. In 1840, when William Cooper Howells bought the Hamilton *Intelligencer*, the family moved to that town. In 1844 J. Y. Scammon sounded him out on the possibility of coming to Chicago to edit the *Journal*, but nothing came of that; five years later he acquired the Dayton *Transcript*. In 1851 he became clerk of the House of the Ohio legislature, with his son a compositor on the *Ohio State Journal*, and the next year they all moved to Ashtabula upon the father's becoming editor of the *Sentinel*, which was moved, six months later, to Jefferson, where the Howells family at last stayed put for many years, and where a much-modified paper still remains as the Jefferson *Gazette*. For a number of years, William Dean Howells wrote extensively for the *Sentinel*, the Cincinnati *Gazette*, the *Ohio State Journal*, and other papers; in 1857 he was the Columbus correspondent of the *Gazette*.

His first publication between covers was *Poems of Two Friends*, written in collaboration with John J. Piatt, and published in Columbus by Follett, Foster and Company on December 23, 1859, but dated 1860. In January 1860 he first "made" *The Atlantic Monthly* with a Heine-like poem called "Andenken," and that same year he made his first trip east, establishing contacts which were to endure through the rest of their lifetimes with a rather astonishing number of the Boston literati. For his campaign life of Lincoln, he was rewarded, in September 1861, by being appointed United States consul at Venice. Here, since the position was largely a sinecure, he spent the four years of the Civil War in scholarship and literary study; in 1862, at Paris, he married Elinor G. Mead, of Brattleboro, Vermont, whom he had met at Columbus in 1860. During this period he accumulated the materials for *Modern Italian Poets*, a pioneering study, not published until 1887, and also wrote the substance of one of his most successful books, *Venetian Life*, which, having been rejected by the *Atlantic*, made its serial appearance in the Boston *Daily Advertiser* and in book form in 1866. In 1864 Lowell had taken him into *The North American Review*; he considered this the turning-point of his life, signalizing his switch from verse to prose. His first child, Winifred, was born in Venice, December 17, 1863. His only son, John Mead Howells, was born August 14, 1868, a second daughter, Mildred, September 26, 1872. Winifred died on March 3, 1889, which was the great sorrow of her father's life. Both his other children long outlived him.

Upon his return to America in 1865, Howells was first employed in New York, under E. L. Godkin, on *The Nation*, but in 1866 he came to Boston, where he settled in Cambridge and became assistant to James T. Fields on *The Atlantic Monthly*. He was editor in fact considerably before he was editor in name, but the name came in 1871,[2] and he held the post until 1881, when he resigned, not only because he was tired of what, as he did it, had been very demanding work, but because Houghton and Osgood had split, and Howells did not wish to be involved in the disagreement.

Disregarding the purely experimental (and aborted) serial, "The Independent Candidate" (1854–55), Howells's first novel was "Geoffrey Winter," written in the 'fifties, rejected by a number of publishers in the 'sixties, and extant only in the manuscript at the Houghton Library. *Suburban Sketches* (1871) are just that —not stories; the first published novel, *Their Wedding Journey* (1872), developed out of Howells's travels and travel-papers. With this work he had found his way, and his career mounted steadily through *A Modern Instance* (1882) and others to *The Rise of Silas Lapham* (1885).[3]

In January 1886 he began writing the "Editor's Study" in *Harper's Magazine*, but did not make his final removal to New York until 1891. With considerable reluctance he had accepted a university lectureship at Harvard in 1869–71 and had delivered a series of Lowell Lectures in 1870, and in 1899 he was to undertake a successful but most uncomfortable lecture tour of the Middle West, but he declined proferred professorships at Union College, Washington University, Johns Hopkins, and finally the Smith Professorship at Harvard, which both Longfellow and Lowell had held. Harvard gave him an M.A. as early as 1867; Litt.D.'s were forthcoming from Yale, Columbia, and Oxford, and an

L.H.D. from Princeton; in 1909 he was named an Honorary Foreign Fellow of the Royal Society of Literature.

In 1887 Howells revealed his keen social consciousness by
speaking out in defense of the "Chicago Anarchists," who had
been condemned to hang for killings they were not even suspected
of having committed. This was the period when Tolstoy was
furnishing him with his ideal of what a writer should be, and he
tried to modify his type of novel accordingly; *The Minister's
Charge* (1887), *Annie Kilburn* (1889), *A Hazard of New Fortunes* (1890), *The Quality of Mercy* (1892) and *The World of
Chance* (1893) are the works which show his sociological interests most clearly. Thereafter he returned to his own brand of
social comedy, now characteristically infused with a larger
amount of psychology, but continued to agitate for social change
in his non-fiction writings. At the turn of the century, he was an
outstanding opponent of the Spanish-American War.

In 1892 his last "Study" appeared. For four months he tried
to co-edit *Cosmopolitan*, which John Brisben Walker wished to
build into both a literary achievement and a distinguished organ
of social protest, but despite their sympathy with each other's
aims, the two men found it impossible to work together. In 1900
Howells began writing the "Editor's Easy Chair" for *Harper's
Magazine*, which he continued until his death.

In 1908 he was elected first president of the American Academy
of Arts and Letters, and in 1910 he lost both his wife and his
closest friend, Mark Twain. In 1915 he was awarded the Academy's Gold Medal for Fiction, which was thereafter named for
him. He died in New York on May 11, 1920.

II

Howells's devotion to reading, in the frontier environment in
which he grew up, was less anomalous than it may seem. He was
born into a reading family, and the year he lived in a log cabin
the walls were covered with a paper whose whole first page was
taken up with a story which, being continued within, "tantalized

us forever with fruitless conjecture as to the fate of the hero and heroine." The Ashtabula *Sentinel*, while Howells was close to it, gave literature the preference over news, and, at one time or another, reprinted most of the popular writers of the day.[4] His mother loved poetry and sang the songs of Burns and Moore of a summer afternoon; the first book he could remember his father reading aloud was *Lalla Roohk*. His own first reading was in history—Goldsmith's *Greece* and *Rome*, at nine. *Don Quixote*, "the most wonderful and delightful book in the world," he read over and over without realizing that it was a novel, and though he could not share his father's passion for *Knickerbocker's History of New York*, Irving still remained "the first of American writers in ease and grace." "What a lot I read, how much I knew," he wrote Charles Eliot Norton in 1907, "before I was twenty!"

He loved narratives of adventure and exploration, and a book about Greek and Roman mythology made the old gods and heroes his friends forever, but he was at first less impressed by *The Arabian Nights* than by what he afterwards considered the wretched stories in the *Gesta Romanorum*. Though he was already making verses himself, he preferred to read prose and could not, at the outset, make much of Byron or Cowper. Later he read "The Deserted Village" and became very fond of Pope's "Pastorals." Later, too, he read Pope's translation of the *Odyssey*. The *Iliad* he thought tiresome and noisy, preferring *The Battle of the Frogs and the Mice* to either of the greater works, and he confessed that he had never read the *Aeneid* as late as when he wrote *My Literary Passions*. It was not until he came to Longfellow and Tennyson that he read long poems without fatigue, and even when he wrote *A Boy's Town*, he thought poetry should be "a flavor, a spice, a sweet, a delicate relish in the high banquet of literature, and never a chief dish."

Howells's intellectual interests, though not wholly confined to language and literature, certainly centered there. "I was gifted in spelling, geography, and reading," he tells us in *Years of My Youth*, "but arithmetic was not for me." He would probably have done better than he did with science had it been taught to any extent in the schools of his youth; in *Italian Journeys* he records his boredom over the geological specimens which a museum keeper insisted on showing him. He was fascinated by Mars, but this was a literary and imaginative matter; when du Maurier's *The Martians* was announced, he had "the promise of pretty nearly all I could ask for in the way of mystical delight." But "I could touch science at Cambridge," he writes, "only on its literary and social side, of course, and my meetings with Agassiz were not many."

He did better with William James and John Fiske, who were scientists after a fashion but whose interests lay closer to his own, and he professed a certain fondness for books on medicine and the popular sciences, "perhaps because they too are part of the human story." As an *Atlantic* editor, he did not scorn scientific articles, and Harry Hayden Clark has shown that both his critical principles and his notions about the social order were affected by scientific methodology. Though he had no great interest in science, he respected its findings and never showed any disposition to "deny the facts."

When Daniel Coit Gilman offered Howells a chair at Johns Hopkins in 1882, the novelist wrote:

I have a literary use of Spanish, French, German, and Italian, and I have some knowledge of the literature and literary history of those languages; but I have not a *scholarly* acquaintance with them, and could not write any of them correctly, not even Italian. Greek literature I know only by translation, and not fully; under *peine forte et dure*, I might read Latin. As to English literature, why of course I know it in a sort of way, but rather in the order and degree of preference than thoroughly and systematically. And I do not know even our own language scientifically,—that is from the Anglo-Saxon up; and I might often be unable to give a philological reason for the faith that was in me.

This summary understates rather than overstates. Howells's interest as linguist was in the modern languages, yet he tells us that he learned enough Greek to read a chapter in the New Testament or one of Anacreon's odes, and as editor of the *Atlantic* he was proud of having detected errors in Sumner's Latin. One letter to his sister Aurelia seems to imply that he had a conversational knowledge of Welsh.

For a man who had educated himself through voracious miscellaneous reading, he was a linguistic phenomenon; once, as a boy, he was studying five languages simultaneously. And though the professorships offered him came too late to make it at all practicable for an established writer to accept them, he was tempted. His considered judgment was that "I might have had the making . . . of a professor in me, but it is now too late to inquire practically. . . ."

His approach to language study was nothing if not unorthodox, for he cared little about the science of the matter and was not much interested in learning to speak or to write. What he really wanted to do was to be able to read the literature and imitate the literary forms. Though he got farther with Italian than with any of the other tongues, he began with Spanish, being attracted by *Don Quixote* and Longfellow's play, *The Spanish Student*, and his father gave him a Spanish grammar before he had even learned that there were parts of speech in English. Though he knew little enough Italian when he arrived in Venice, he soon became proficient enough not only to converse with the gondoliers but even to understand the difficult dialect of Goldoni's plays, and when he came to Cambridge, he was accepted as a member of the Italianate circle which moved around Longfellow when he was translating *The Divine Comedy*. His *Atlantic* reviews of Norton's translation of *La Vita Nuova*, and T. W. Parsons's of the "Inferno" show knowledge not only of Italian but also of Latin and the Anglo-Saxon element in English.

He was translating from both Spanish and German in the Ashtabula *Sentinel* as early as 1855, and it seems odd that he never visited Spain until 1911, taking lessons in the language to prepare for the trip. His passion for Heine led him to German, and he read with a German tutor some of the literature that Basil March of *A Hazard of New Fortunes* read with old Lindau in his youth. Howells must have come to read German with considerable ease, since he translated a Venetian handbook from the German, and his *Atlantic* reviews of translations from German literature show that he knew exactly what he was talking about.[5] When, through his interest in Abraham Cahan and others, he finally approached Yiddish, he found that as soon as it was printed in German rather than Hebrew characters, he could read it, and this set him wondering whether New York "jargon" would ultimately become to English what Yiddish was to German. Testimony as to his competence with spoken German is somewhat uncertain however. As early as 1861 he looked forward to reaching the German frontier and "the honest, good *sprache*." But it was much later that he said his German "consisted chiefly of good-will," being "sadly perplexed in the genders and the order of the verbs; with me the verb will seldom wait, as it should in German, to the end." When he attended Carl Schurz's funeral in 1906 he could neither hear the address that was given in English nor understand the one that was in German.

Though French was not wholly neglected during the early years, he seems to have had much less interest in it. At least he felt the need of undertaking "a severe campaign against the French language" when he was in Switzerland. Between September 24 and November 12 he apparently made considerable progress, since he then reported himself able "to go about and talk with people" and to "pry bits of information out of a great many who don't suspect it."

Howells's reading in foreign literatures was impressive, though not always done in the original language. The classics were not very important to him. As a child he was made more familiar with Swedenborg than with the Bible, though he knew the latter well enough to make effective literary reference to it when necessary, as when Silas Lapham's ordeal is compared to Jacob's wrestling with the angel.

His Italian reading has been so well studied by James Woodress in *Howells in Italy* that only paraphrase is possible. Of the older classics—Dante, Petrarch, Tasso, etc.—only Dante seems to have

meant much to him, and one is amazed when, in 1902, he writes
Norton that he has never really read the "Purgatorio" till now.[6]
He thought Castiglione's *Courtier* an incomparable book which
"succeeded in teaching his countryman every gentlemanly grace
but virtue," while Casanova gave "much information about things
that had best not be known." *Modern Italian Poets* shows wide
reading of the Romantic poets and dramatists of 1770–1870, and
very capable translations from their work, but Howells became
progressively less interested in these writers, and none of them
appear in *My Literary Passions*.[7] A more lasting influence was that
of Goldoni, whom he preferred to Molière, and who may have
had some influence upon his realism. For many years, Manzoni's
I Promessi Sposi (*The Betrothed*) was the only important Italian
novel for him, but in 1881 he "boomed" Verga's *I Malavoglia* and
introduced the English translation which Harpers published as
The House by the Medlar-Tree.

Young Howells was very Germanophilic, but except for Heine,
whose lyrics he imitated and whose *Reisebilder* probably influenced his travel writing, he seems cold in his judgments of German literature. As translator, imitator, and reviewer, Betts finds
Howells "one of the most important intermediaries for Heine in
America," [8] but he finally turned against the poet on the ground
that "he did me evil both in my heart and in my literature." He
quotes Goethe significantly in *An Imperative Duty*,[9] and Betts
calls *The Minister's Charge* a Goethean novel. Howells himself
at least once called *Wilhelm Meister* one of his favorite novels,
but speaking generally he had no love for Goethe, seeing in him
the apotheosis of a Romantic cult which glorified selfish egoism
and "exploitation of a supposed genius, by all means fair and foul,"
and which affected many great writers even outside Germany, including Byron, Carlyle, and Ibsen. He was not enthusiastic about
Schiller either, but he tried to be fair to both writers: " 'The great
Goethe and the good Schiller' they remain; and yet . . . there
was something good in Goethe and something great in Schiller."
German fiction in general he thought "horribly second class."

Among modern German dramatists he speaks of Hauptmann and Sudermann (Betts credits him with the first American critique of Sudermann), and he says, "I do not suppose there is any man now living who has forgotten so many plays of Kotzebue." [10]

The only French writers Howells treated in *My Literary Passions* are Zola and Flaubert, who may best be considered later in connection with the discussion of his critical principles. He read many others however. He enjoyed Daudet but disliked de Maupassant for what he thought his brutality and deliberate uncleanliness. As late as 1917 he enjoyed Froissart. In the *Christmas Every Day* stories he made one of the boys a devotee of Jules Verne.

He fell in love with Erckmann-Chatrian (especially *L'Ami Fritz*) in 1870, when John Fiske brought him their novels to read when he was ill and could not sleep. He praised Mistral's *Mirèio* as possessing a "true naïveté of expression" which showed up Morris and Rossetti as hopelessly artificial. He greatly admired Sainte-Beuve as a critic, and though at first he had grave reservations about Taine, he seems later to have become more receptive to his ideas. He enjoyed the Belgian dramatist Maeterlinck but manifested a strange and settled antagonism toward Rostand which will fall to be considered elsewhere.

Fiction for Howells achieved its apotheosis with the great Russian novelists, of whom he finally crowned Tolstoy king, though it took him some time to convince himself that anybody could be better than Turgenev. About Dostoevsky he says comparatively little. After Tolstoy's death, he was inclined to award primacy to the Spaniards, especially Benito Pérez Galdós, Armando Palacio Valdés, and Vicente Blasco-Ibáñez, whom, at the very end of his life, he considered the greatest living novelist.[11] His enthusiasm for Spanish literature was not wholly confined to the modern period however. He did not care much for Lope de Vega, and he seems rather to have overlooked Calderón, but he called *Lazarillo de Tormes* "one of the most delightful books in the world." It seems odd that, rejecting Emerson's judgment that Shakespeare was "only the master of the revels," he should have gone out of his way to add that the statement would probably have been just if it had been made of his beloved Cervantes.

III

But of course most of Howells's reading was in English and American literature. Except for Shakespeare and a few other Elizabethans, the only early English writers he refers to are Chaucer, Gower, Milton, Bunyan, and Dryden. Though he gave Chaucer a few pages in *My Literary Passions* he knew very little about him. He spells Spenser "Spencer" and calls his poetry duller than the Presidents' messages before Theodore Roosevelt. He took the title *Stops of Various Quills* from "Lycidas," and his reference to the "austere Calvinistic religiosity" of *Paradise Lost* was perhaps a somewhat less unpardonable "boner" in 1902 than it would be today.

His familiarity with Shakespeare is attested first by the large number of titles derived from his plays—*A Modern Instance*, *The Quality of Mercy*, *The Undiscovered Country*, *Fennel and Rue*, and the rest. Scraps of Shakespearean phrase are often quoted in the body of the novels also. The fireplace at Belmont had an inscription from *The Merchant of Venice* about having come from Venice "as far as Belmont." *A Hazard of New Fortunes* refers on the surface to Basil March's hazard in leaving Boston for New York, which was considerably less serious a matter than the hazard Shakespeare had in mind in *King John*, but other, more critical hazards emerge in this novel also.

Howells once admitted "a certain impatience with the most noble speeches in *Hamlet* and the most beautiful in *Romeo and Juliet* because they were so long as to delay the emotion they were meant to provoke." Yet

When the curtain rises on the opening scene of *Hamlet*, or *Macbeth*, or *Romeo and Juliet*, a thrill goes through one as if at the behest of a supreme authority, and one marvels that while such plays still speak a living language, any other plays can be represented.

This is a playgoer's, rather than a reader's, delight, and Howells is not very profound when he sees *Hamlet* as " 'a prolongation of sketches,' studying now one phase and now another of the same irresolute temperament, without necessary sequence and without final unity of effect." In *My Literary Passions* he tells us that while his youth knew well that there was "poor stuff" in Shakespeare, and that "the persons and positions were often preposterous," he preferred Shakespeare's women to real women, and that "there was a supreme moment, once, when I found myself saying that the creation of Shakespeare was as great as the creation of a planet." Yet he admits that he never read quite all the plays, and when he thanks Hamilton Wright Mabie for his review of *The Seen and Unseen at Stratford-on-Avon*—("You must know how I value such words from such a Shakespearean as you")—he is either indulging in shameless flattery or else he did not know much about Shakespearean scholarship. On the other hand, I think there is considerable penetration in his own portrayal of Shakespeare in the Stratford book, which is marred only by what seems to have been a lifelong prejudice against Queen Elizabeth.[12]

Howells's urbane temper made the eighteenth century congenial to him, and he read in it extensively, both in youth and in age. Burke's essay on the sublime and beautiful influenced his thinking, and it was Goldsmith who inspired his saying that "the adoration which a young writer has for a great one is truly a passion passing the love of women." He gave Ossian a place in *My Literary Passions*, and in *New Leaf Mills* Thomson's *Seasons* is quoted in frontier Ohio. Burns he seems not to have cared for until he heard George MacDonald read him. He was fond of Crabbe and thought of working up Ohio life in something like his spirit. Pope he first worshipped, then, disillusioned by his private character, despised, "but now I am not sorry for the love, and I am very sorry for the despite." In *London Films* he calls "The Rape of the Lock" "the most exquisite artificial flower" on "the deep-rooted stem" of English poetry, but he never read it until a few years before he wrote *My Literary Passions*.

He has an interesting comment on Johnson and Boswell. "The

chief of biographers" had "lived his way through the stupid disdain of generations of critics." Yet his book

is the work of a commonplace man about a writer singularly uninspired in his poetry, obtuse in his sense of beauty and of art, mistaken in his political economy, narrow and intolerant in his religon, mechanical in his morality, servile in his theories of society; one who is no longer read now in his unwieldy and pedantic prose, and has been wholly superseded even as a lexicographer, but who is present here in the largeness of his heart, vastly and simply human; no poet, no critic, no philosopher, no savant, by the fine modern tests, but somehow immensely a man: a warm, huge bulk, living, breathing, not to say snoring, and simply biographied to enduring fame.

But Howells never read *Rasselas* until 1915, when he wrote about it for the "Easy Chair."

Among the eighteenth-century novelists Howells had nothing significant to say about either Fielding or Smollett. *Tristram Shandy* he was "slowly plowing through" in 1915. Even *A Sentimental Journey*, though not as bad, was "nasty." But Mrs. Radcliffe fares surprisingly well for a romanticist in *Heroines of Fiction*, and there is an excellent essay on Richardson,[13] occasioned by William Lyon Phelps's edition of his works. He had a true appreciation of Defoe. The influence of *Robinson Crusoe* is obvious in *A Woman's Reason*, where Robert Fenton is wrecked on a coral atoll. In view of Howells's general reputation for prudery, it is interesting that he should have recommended *Moll Flanders* both for its excellent style and its insight into human nature.

Among the Romantic poets, Howells did not pretend to have liked Wordsworth except in parts. The immortality ode is quoted at some length in *The Shadow of a Dream*. The only reference to Coleridge worth noting is Colville's amusing statement concerning Mrs. Amsden in *Indian Summer*: "That old lady has marked me for her prey: I can see it in her glittering eyeglass." He calls Keats "a poet whose work will last as long as our literature," but he says little about him. Byron gets the most attention, but Howells certainly did not admire him. Though he had a "few hours of maturity," he was "undoubtedly guilty of sin against the light which was in him," and the beauties of *Don Juan* shine "through the shimmer of its putrescence."

Tennyson is the only Victorian poet who gets a whole chapter in *My Literary Passions*, and, like Longfellow, he is often referred to in the novels also, as when Ellen Kenton is reminded by her ocean voyage of "the cold-white, heavy, plunging foam" in "The Dream of Fair Women," as the title is erroneously quoted. He has much more fault to find with Tennyson than with Longfellow, however, and by 1886 he thought his best work behind him. Altrurian women remind Eveleth Strange of Tennyson's girls in *The Princess*, but Howells had not read all of *In Memoriam* even when he wrote *My Literary Passions*.

Of Browning's work he seems really to have relished only *The Ring and the Book*. Even when he reread it in 1914, he still thought it a great poem. But he had no use for such late work as *The Red Cotton Night-Cap Country*, *The Inn Album*, or *Asolando*. Of the first of these he criticizes both its art and its morals, declaring that it might just as well have been called "The Man in the Moon, or Ding-Dong Bell." The story was "so told as to bring out its worst with a far-reaching unseemliness for which the manure-heap affords the proper imagery of 'dung' and 'devil's dung.'" Apparently the poet "lay in wait, and, lest any small twinkling or glimmer of meaning should reach his reader, sprang out and popped a fresh parenthesis on the offending chink that let it through." Yet when he reviewed Mrs. Sutherland Orr's biography, though he still suspected Browning of being basically simple and even undistinguished, he also called him "the deepest if not the loftiest voice of our time." Browning must have been hurt by some of these comments if he ever saw them: he enjoyed *The Lady of the Aroostook*, and he read some of Howells's poems at Moncure D. Conway's request, praising them rather heartily, especially "The Pilot's Story."

The early work of Rossetti and William Morris was severely handled too, neither being given credit for much technical competence. "The Defence of Guinevere" was objectionable because of its "anti-modernity," but since "The Haystack in the Floods" left Howells's nerves on edge, Morris was all wrong when he was realistic too. He did not like the prose any better and lambasted *Love Is Enough* for "its inexorable dreariness, its unrelenting lengthiness, and serious vacuity." All in all, he thought Morris's wallpapers much superior to his poetry. Later, however, he seems to have responded more warmly to some of Morris's poems, and he valued him as a social prophet, who may, indeed, have had a certain influence upon himself. He quotes from "The Blessed Damozel" in "Though One Rose from the Dead," and James Thomson's "The City of Dreadful Night" is spoken of in *An Open-Eyed Conspiracy*. In later years he admired Masefield with reservations, and he thought "The Listeners" by Walter de la Mare "the best and sheerest bit of weirdness in the world."

Among the Victorian novelists, Howells had far more to say of Dickens than of any other, but for reasons which will later appear, I prefer to discuss his treatment of both Dickens and Stevenson in another connection. As late as 1913, he spoke of Scott as one of the writers of the past who had never died, but, though he considered him a better stylist in verse than in prose, he was always highly critical of him, and he seems to have agreed with Mark Twain that Scott contributed to the development of that feudal ideal in the South which produced the Civil War. Howells had his "great tradition" in English fiction before Leavis, and Defoe, Richardson, Goldsmith, Fanny Burney, Maria Edgeworth, and Jane Austen were enrolled in it; Scott, on the other hand, was the prince of "effectism," a humorist and a humanist whom it was easier to love as a man than respect as an artist. Howells admired the character-drawing of both Jeanie and Effie Deans, and he rightly regarded the Scottish stories as superior to the mediaeval romances, but he saw only melodrama in Meg Merrilies. Ivanhoe's Rowena was "passionless" and "traitless," and because Rebecca lacked "inconsistency" and "variation," she lacked "the soul of feminine ideality also." His warmest praise was reserved for Lucy Ashton and *The Bride of Lammermoor*.

"The dear, the divine, the only Jane Austen herself" was

Howells's favorite English novelist, the most accomplished artist, and the only one completely free from the sentimentalities and melodramatic contrivances that have defaced English fiction in general. (*Pride and Prejudice* was her greatest novel, *Persuasion* her poorest.) One would expect a Janeite to admire Trollope also, "who was most like her in simple honesty and instinctive truth," but Trollope went whoring after false gods when he modeled himself upon Thackeray, "standing about in his scene, talking it over with his hands in his pockets, interrupting the action, and spoiling the illusion in which alone the truth of art resides." When Trollope's book on Thackeray was published in 1879, Howells flayed it—"as entirely idle and valueless a disquisition as any we know," common in ideas and awkward in expression. He was shocked that a man like Trollope should "talk down" to a man like Thackeray, and wondered whether he were addressing himself to young people or to the feeble-minded. Howells did not really come to Trollope until he was fifty, when he "came to him almost with a rush."

He was a greater painter of manners than Thackeray because he was neither a sentimentalist or a caricaturist; and he was of a more convincing imagination than Dickens because he knew and employed the probable facts in the case and kept himself free of all fantastic contrivances.

Perhaps Howells was put off from Trollope by the fact that he disliked him personally—"a thoroughly hateful person," he calls him to Brander Matthews even when praising him as an artist.

The criticism of Thackeray clearly came under the head of chastening what one loves. Howells recognized that Thackeray was at heart essayist, not novelist (why, then, was he so hard on him for his tendency to commentary?).[14]

He could not often hold his hand; when he painted a saint, he wanted to paint 'Saint' all over the halo; and when he did a devil, he thought it well to tag his forked tail with a label proclaiming his demoniacal quality.

Aside from this, his most serious criticism of Thackeray is identical with Dickens's: Thackeray "put on a fine literary air of being above his business; he talked of fiction as fable-land, when he ought to have known and proclaimed it as the very home of truth." Nevertheless he was a great writer, distinguished especially for his portraits of women. Though he considered *Vanity Fair* Thackeray's poorest novel, Howells thought Becky Sharp a greater achievement than Beatrix Esmond, the real depth of whose characterization he seems to have missed. He believed *Pendennis* the greatest novel (though he also calls *Barry Lyndon* "the farthest reach of a great talent"), and he saw no faults in the infuriating Laura Bell. On the contrary, she has "a high and wise soul," is "a most generous as well as most sensible creature . . . just and fine and real." He cannot ignore her cruelty to Fanny Bolton, but he calls it the result of "ignorant purity" and "almost a necessary evil." In fact, almost everything Thackeray did was "masterly" and "inestimably precious," and Howells preferred his "rinsings" —such as *Philip*—to "the fulness and prime spirit of many a famous tap we could name." Yet here again we see the incurable desultoriness of Howells's reading (which may well have been one of the factors which enabled him to preserve his zest unbroken to the end), for he tells us that he never read *The Virginians* through.

After Jane Austen's, the greatest talent in English fiction was George Eliot's, and Howells even grants that it was "a talent of vastly wider and deeper range" than Jane's "and of a far more serious import." Even in such a work as *The Spanish Gypsy*, where she proved herself no poet, she still mustered "grandeur" of conception. Howells must have been pleased when Henry James called *A Modern Instance* "the Yankee *Romola*."

Yet Howells also recognized all George Eliot's faults—her technical fault of intruding into her stories "Thackeray-esquely" and her moral fault of pursuing "some of her women with a rancor as perceptible as her fondness for others." He thought her more successful in commending Rosamond Vincy and Hetty Sorrel to our dislike than Romola and Mary Garth to our admiration. *Romola* and *Middlemarch* are the George Eliot novels most often referred to in Howells's fiction, the latter in the discussions between Tom Corey and the Lapham girls, the former in *The Minister's Charge*, *Indian Summer*, and *An Imperative Duty*. Mrs. Bowen and her daughter look up the *Romola* sites in Florence, and Mrs. Meredith's obsession with problems of conscience in *Romola* shows that Howells realized that even noble fiction can exercise a debauching effect over weak minds.

In his youth, Howells thought Bulwer-Lytton "brilliant and profound"; in his maturity he found him "solemnly empty" and "impossibly unimportant." He was often superior toward Charles Reade, on moral and aesthetic grounds alike, yet he found his female characters superior to those of both Dickens and Thackeray. He gave Charlotte Brontë the credit she deserves for having created the pure but passionate heroine, but he is impercipient in dealing with Emily Brontë's "lawless" heroine, and he thought *Wuthering Heights* badly told. "Seldom has a romance been worse contrived, both as to generals and particulars, but the essentials are all there, and the book has a tremendous vitality." Amazingly, he thought "the telepathy and presentiment which play a part in *Jane Eyre*" more effectively handled than the supernaturalism in *Wuthering Heights*.

Though Howells was slow in coming to Hardy, his final estimate of him was very high (the fullest account is Carl J. Weber's in *Hardy in America*, 1946). At times he seems to have overestimated *Jude the Obscure*, rather at the expense of works in which Hardy's "light and color" are much stronger. When he reviewed Mrs. Fiske's production of *Tess of the D'Urbervilles* in 1897, he stated that *Tess* was the only Hardy novel he had not read. He did read it before publishing *Heroines of Fiction* (1901), but he can hardly be said fully to have appreciated its merits, for he complains of "dregs of pagan earthiness" and finds Tess one woman in the first part of the book and another in the second.

On the other hand, he was able to get through only one novel by Meredith—*Beauchamp's Career*—and he says he never read a novel by either Blackmore or Stevenson! He praised Mark Rutherford for his realism, and he once confessed a weakness for Ouida,[15] though he nowhere wrote anything about her. I suppose he must also be said to have had a weakness for George du Maurier, whose *Peter Ibbetson* was "a miracle" which possessed "every grace, every beauty, every charm" short of the supreme truth to be found in the very greatest fiction. Many, too, would now feel that he greatly overestimated Mrs. Humphry Ward, whom he tended at times to place with Hardy and George Eliot, though he admitted her lack of humor and her "ejaculatory" and "suspiratory" style.

Howells considered Gibbon the greatest of historians, and in youth at least he was very fond of both Macaulay and De Quincey. He considered Ruskin a "great writer and even greater genius" but not a great critic, and of course he had no sympathy with what he considered his mediaeval social ideals. With "that antic satyr" Carlyle he was much less *en rapport*. "Carlyle loves a tyrant; and if the tyrant is a ruffian and a bully, and especially a German, there are hardly any lengths to which that historian will not go in praise of him." He wondered how Americans could be quite so wanting in sweetness and light as Arnold found them and yet still respond so warmly to Arnold's own expression of these qualities. Pater's book, *The Renaissance*, drew a mixed review, and Howells accused Pater of being "attributive" in his famous interpretation of the "Mona Lisa." This was the "vice" which Ruskin invented.

Among the younger contemporary British writers Kipling and Bernard Shaw draw most attention. He recognized Kipling's talent at the outset, though he was put off by his "swagger" and his imperialism; once he speaks scornfully of "the Rider Haggards and the Rudyard Kiplings of the day." Kipling admired him greatly, and after they became acquainted Howells could not avoid being influenced by this. Though he disliked *Fanny's First Play* as much as he enjoyed *Arms and the Man*, he calls Shaw "my daily, my nightly joy." He admired Arnold Bennett in his realistic novels, but did not do nearly so well on Conrad. *Almayer's Folly* is the only Conrad novel I can find he reviewed, and he knew nothing whatever about him when he read it, believing him to be an Englishman. "It seemed to me that the circumstance was all mighty good, but I felt that I was allowed to imagine it too much for myself. I longed for greater explicitness and downrightness in the author." He admired Leonard Merrick and Archibald Marshall, both of whom he discussed at some length, and he once brackets Eden Phillpotts with Hardy. In the Wells canon he preferred *Love and Mr. Lewisham* to *Kipps*. He thought very highly of *The House with the Green Shutters* (1903) by George Douglas and the early death of the writer was a personal grief.

Among English books out of the main stream I will mention only a few. *Through the Looking Glass* is referred to in *A Hazard of New Fortunes*, where the name of the paper March edits, *Every Other Week*, makes his wife think of "jam yesterday and jam tomorrow, but never jam today." Howells admired the poetry of Alexander Smith, and in *Indian Summer* Colville reflects on the one-time popularity of *Dreamthrop* (1863) and remembers that he had once preferred Smith to Shakespeare. He was also very fond of the *Epistolae Ho-Elianae (Familiar Letters)* by James Howell, and there is a humorous letter to his brother Joe in which he describes himself as their author during a previous incarnation.[16]

IV

For Howells American literature was largely contemporary literature, in considerable measure even literature written by personal friends; it is a little surprising to find him discussing Cotton Mather or *The Day of Doom*. At his seventy-fifth birthday, he presented his credentials impressively:

. . . if I missed the personal acquaintance of Cooper and Irving and Poe and Prescott I was personally acquainted with all the others in whom the story of American literature sums itself. I knew Hawthorne and Emerson and Walt Whitman; I knew Longfellow and Holmes and Whittier and Lowell; I knew Bryant and Bancroft and Motley; I knew Harriet Beecher Stowe and Julia Ward Howe; I knew Artemus Ward and Stockton and Mark Twain; I knew Parkman and Fiske.

Howells's admiration for the standard writers of the New England "flowering" was very warm, though, unlike many of their admirers, he was well aware of their limitations. Though there is at least one passage in which he seems to place Emerson ahead of him, Longfellow was undoubtedly the poet he read with the greatest relish, and though he was much closer to Lowell personally, he can hardly be said to have reacted more warmly toward him. "All men I have known, besides, have had some foible . . . or some meanness, or pettiness, or bitterness; but Longfellow had none, nor the suggestion of any." As for the poetry, it was all good, in "conception, diction, music . . . and who else will ever give us the like?" Longfellow, indeed, was "one of the most perfect artists who ever lived since those of the Greek Anthology," and "in many, if not in most regards, the first living poet in the English tongue." When he died it was

awful to think of his lying there in the beautiful old house which he seemed to fill with his goodness. I can't reconcile myself to his death. I had the sad and curious fortune to ring at the door and ask how he was almost at the moment he died.[17]

On Poe, Howells is a most unsatisfactory critic, not because he ranges himself with the enemy but because he so persistently blows both hot and cold. In 1887 he wrote that Poe had great talent but that his "perversity, arrogance, and wilfulness" made it impossible to take him seriously as a critic, while as a craftsman he was disabled by his own "mechanical ideal." In 1901 he declared in one and the same article that Poe was outmoded, his influence no longer being a force in American literature, and that it was "perversely possible that his name will lead all the rest when our immortals are duly marshalled for the long descent of time." But his most elaborate consideration of Poe came in the centenary article of 1909,[18] where he praises "To Helen" and "The Haunted Palace" but rejects "Annabel Lee," and declares that no "good magazine" would print Poe's stories today, after which he admits that this is no fair criterion, since our theater managers would not accept Shakespeare either.

Poe is subtle, but he is not delicate; he is mysterious, but he is not mystical. Where he attempts to put on the mystical, as in his studies of mesmeric experience, he is still grossly material, for all his recondite incidents.

Yet, though he lacked both imagination and sincerity, he was "an old-fashioned master," and to condemn his work without "the greatest reserves" (as Henry James did) was to condemn oneself.

After long misprizing him I have come to see him in his pathos, as a prodigal of wasted powers, the victim of cruel circumstances, of inherent evil propensities, with a certain majesty of nature inalienable in his moral squalor.

Compared to the other great New England writers, Emerson seemed cold when Howells met him on his first trip to New England (incidentally Emerson rather snubbed him when he mentioned Poe, first not recognizing the name and then dismissing him as "the jingle man"). When Howells was editor of the *Atlantic*, Emerson was one of his touchiest contributors, behaving on at least one occasion much like a spoiled prima donna. Nevertheless Howells rated Emerson very high.

Next after Lincoln there are reasons why he should have wider and fuller recognition than almost any other American, for he interpreted the American spirit in homely images and instances as poetically true to it as the point and pith of Lowell's stories were humorously true to it. Emerson talked in tropes, and Lowell in parables, as all America still talks.[19]

There is comparatively little on Whittier, whom Howells found "rather inconversible, though I am sure he had a kindness for me" (as a matter of fact, he wanted Howells as his biographer). As a poet, Whittier's besetting sin was didacticism. Oliver Wendell Holmes, a devoted friend, gets a whole chapter in *Literary Friends and Acquaintance*, but there is no close evaluation of his work. Though Howells's close relationship with Lowell not only bridged the generation gap but survived some important differences of opinion, the younger man still felt that Lowell was "too much of a poet to be a perfect critic" and too much of a critic to be a perfect poet. On the first count, "he had wings that lifted him into the air when he ought to be running along the ground"; on the other, his erudition "could not always keep itself from overweighting his literature." When Howells accepted "The Cathedral" for the *Atlantic*, he regarded it as one of the finest American poems; later he thought somewhat less highly of it. He also recognized the extraordinary complexity of Lowell's character which has baffled so many interpreters and frustrated so many attempts at evaluation.

Howells's personal contact with Whitman was pleasant ("he gave me the sense of a sweet and true soul"), but he had no love for his poetry, though he came to think somewhat better of it in later years.[20] In 1860 he was not sure whether Whitman was sublime or beastly but inclined, clearly, toward the latter view. Five years later, he got on somewhat better with *Drum-Taps*—at least he was no longer compelled to hold his nose—but he still did not think Whitman was supplying poetry "in a portable shape." His thoughts were "intangible," his method "artificial," his effect "unspeakably inartistic," and the total result, therefore, a failure. Howells seems now to have felt that Whitman's method was better suited to music than to literature, since it produced "the same inarticulate feeling as that which dwells in music." For literary art, which "cannot employ itself with things in embryo," this is not enough. It requires expression, not mere suggestion. "The method of talking to one's self in rhythmic and ecstatic prose" results at last in having "only the devil for a listener," that is, "the devil of reasonless, hopeless, all-defying egotism." In 1876 he substantially restated this impression of Whitman (which was shared by such different critics as Lafcadio Hearn and Sir Edmund Gosse): Whitman "is much such a poet as a summer morning is, or an alarm of fire, or some unpleasant smell which he would personally prefer to prayer," which last comparison is surely one of the few really mean things that Howells ever said.

Twelve years later, in 1888, on the other hand, we find him citing Whitman along with Keats as exemplifying "the same divine art" of poetry, and the very next year, reviewing *November Boughs*, he declares that "for the poet the long fight is over; he rests his cause with what he has done; and we think no one now would like to consider the result without respect, without deference, even if one cannot approach it with entire submission." But even in 1891 Howells's capitulation was not complete. Whitman was eager to seize and embrace beauty, but he often failed; "the divine loveliness eludes him, and leaves only a 'muddy vesture of decay' in his grasp."

Melville's *Battle-Pieces* (1867) drew a severe review from Howells on the ground that, not having felt what he described, Melville could not hope to move others. He decisively rejected Sidney Lanier's "Corn" when it was offered to him for the *Atlantic* at the beginning of that poet's career, and thereafter so studiously avoided mentioning him as almost to suggest that his conscience troubled him in the matter.[21] On the other hand, he did himself proud on Emily Dickinson, declaring of the original Todd-Higginson collection that "if nothing else had come out of our life but this strange poetry we should feel that in the work of Emily Dickinson America, or New England rather, had made a distinctive addition to the literature of the world, and could not be left out of any record of it." Certainly he paid Emily a supreme tribute when, in a letter to Mark Twain, he quoted her as a means of expressing the inexpressible anguish he experienced upon visiting his own daughter's grave. He is fair enough to Joaquin Miller when he recognizes "a true dramatic and descriptive faculty amidst a dreadful prolixity and chasmal vacancies," but one can hardly say the same of Richard Watson Gilder, in whose first collection, *The New Day*, he found "an over-athletic, almost carnal imagery"! He was generous to Thomas Bailey Aldrich, though he thought "Judith and Holofernes" too Tennysonian, and he appreciated William Vaughn Moody, though thinking him at times too finespun. He greatly admired the Canadian poet, Archibald Lampman. He received Edwin Markham's "The Man with the Hoe" warmly because of its passion and passionate social consciousness, and most contemporary critics would say that he greatly over-estimated James Whitcomb Riley, whom he praised in season and out of season and visited when he came to Indianapolis on his lecture tour. He admits that Riley's homeliness sometimes caused the "thin academic skin" to crawl upon his "critical body," but he also says that the Hoosier "has more perfectly mastered his instrument than any writer of dialect verse since Lowell, and I do not know why one should not frankly place him with Lowell as equally master in that kind." Toward the end of his life, Howells also often professed his "unfeigned admiration" for the newspaper poet Walt Mason, whom he would have been sorry to miss reading "for a single day out of the six."

When the "New Poetry" revival came along, just before World War I, Howells was reasonably cautious yet hospitable and discriminating. He found it to be "very largely, if not mostly, of an egoistic quality; to be private-spirited rather than public-spirited, to be overmuch an inquiry into the poet's psychical symptoms and less a concern for the commonweal," all of which led him to conclude that "we had better not expect too much from our young poetry . . . but do our best to enjoy it." He calls both Edgar Lee Masters's *Spoon River Anthology* and Amy Lowell's *Sword Blades and Poppy Seeds* "shredded prose," though he finds something to praise in each. He liked "The Klondike" in Edwin Arlington Robinson's *Captain Craig* volume, and found a "fine, manly *go*" in it, but this did not make him finish the book—"life is *so* short, and art is *so* long." He did better on Vachel Lindsay's *Booth* collection, which, he said, "makes the heart leap" and "abounds in rhymes that thrill and gladden one," and he was at his best on Robert Frost's *A Boy's Will* and *North of Boston*, which he found "very genuinely and unaffectedly expressive of rustic New England, and of its deeps as well as its shallows." Here was the quality of Sarah Orne Jewett, Mary E. Wilkins Freeman, and Alice Brown "finding metrical utterance." "Amidst the often striving and straining of the new poetry, here is the old poetry as young as ever; and new only in extending the bounds of sympathy through the recorded to the unrecorded knowledge of humanity."

Among American fictionists, Howells did not care much more for Cooper than Mark Twain did, but he was very enthusiastic about Hawthorne, whom he ranked with Jane Austen for "perfection of form." The forest scene in *The Scarlet Letter* could be equalled, he thought, "only in some of the profoundly impassioned pages of the Russian novelists who, casting aside all the common adjuncts of art, reveal us to ourselves in the appeal from their own naked souls." But his realistic bias comes out clearly in his choice of *The Blithedale Romance* as the finest of Hawthorne's long stories. Its influence upon *The Undiscovered Country* is obvious, and in *The World of Chance* Ray compares one character to Coverdale and another to Hollingsworth. *The Landlord at Lion's Head* derives in part from "The Great Stone Face," which is referred to in it. James Langbrith connects the fascination which the memory of his father holds for him with what he has read in Hawthorne about "the Puritan type," but the problem and atmosphere of *The Son of Royal Langbrith* suggest Melville quite as much as Hawthorne, especially the Melville of *Pierre*, though I have no evidence that Howells read this book.[22]

He wavers somewhat on *Uncle Tom's Cabin*, but in some moods he was ready to call it "perhaps our chief fiction." [23] He objected to the "gasping and shuddering" style of Elizabeth Stuart Phelps. As early as 1872 he took DeForest's *Kate Beaumont* and *Miss Ravenel's Conversion* (to which he oddly adds the much inferior *Overland*) as "strong proof that we are not so much lacking in an American novelist as in a public to recognize him." He admired Frank R. Stockton, whose *Rudder Grange* he spoke of affectionately in the addendum to *Their Wedding Journey*, and he was very enthusiastic about *The Grandissimes* by George W. Cable. "It is a noble and beautiful book, including all the range of tragedy and comedy; and it made my heart warm towards you while I had the blackest envy in it." He would not even grant, as many felt, that the book was "faulty and confused in construction."

Howells was very enthusiastic about the short story, which he regarded as distinctively an American form. He thought that the vast variety and range of American life necessitated specialization, making American fiction deep, not, like the English, broad. In 1875 he seemed to feel that Bret Harte was growing slovenly in his workmanship, but after his death in 1902, he called him "one of the most refined and delicate of artists," who used crude materials "with the exquisite perfection of a poet." He was always enthusiastic about Sarah Orne Jewett and about Charles Egbert Craddock (Mary N. Murfree), whom, on at least one occasion, he put ahead of all other women then writing fiction. Bellamy's *Looking Backward* interested him as a utopian document, but he reserved most of his critical praise for the author's short stories of the supernatural which he held almost if not quite worthy to stand beside Hawthorne's.

Among his younger American contemporaries, Booth Tarkington was the one who was most like Howells, and certainly nobody appreciated Howells more. But though Howells highly praised Tarkington's work, Tarkington seems to have needed him much less than he was needed by such writers as Harold Frederic, Brand Whitlock, Hamlin Garland, Stephen Crane, and Frank Norris. He praised Crane very warmly,[24] but he seems to have regarded Norris even more highly.

He died in the flower of his years, and has bereft us of a hope in fiction which no other now promises fully to restore. . . . he was in the divine secret of the supreme artists; he saw what was before him, with the things in their organic relations, and he made life live.[25]

It must now seem odd to many that he should have placed *Maggie* far ahead of *The Red Badge of Courage*.

He wrote much, and warmly, of Henry B. Fuller, Robert Herrick, and Edith Wyatt of the Chicago school. He admired Edith Wharton, but, at the outset at least, thought her too much an imitator of James. It is disappointing to find him silent on Willa Cather. He praised George Schock's Pennsylvania Dutch story,

Hearts Courageous, but I have found nothing about Elsie Sing-master's accomplished work in the same field. Like Mark Twain, he greatly admired George Ade, particularly in *Artie* and *Pink March*.[26] He was very enthusiastic about William Allen White's novel, *In Our Town*, and he praised Kathleen Norris for her labors "in the Tolstoyan faith of making Truth alone her hero," not being "afraid to find beauty every where, not only in the gardened spaces, but in the wind-grown alleys of life." Only "the greatest masters, the Russians" were her superiors in method.[27]

Mark Twain and Henry James were, by all means, Howells's favorites—and his closest friends—among his American con-temporaries, and it was his considered opinion that Mark Twain was the greatest humorist since Shakespeare and Cervantes with the possible exception of Heine. He began blowing the horn for him when he reviewed *The Innocents Abroad* for the *Atlantic*, which was a daring thing to do, not only because the book at-tacked so many contemporary gentilities, but also because the *Innocents* was a "subscription" book, and "subscription" books, which were not sold by the book stores, but hawked from door to door in cheap and gaudy format, by salesmen only one step up from the pedlars of snake oil at medicine shows, were not sup-posed to be literature. As *Atlantic* editor, Howells printed Mark Twain, and encouraged him to develop the best side of his talent; sometimes he referred to him even in his own novels; as friend and literary adviser, he ended his services only with Clemens's death. Though Howells was himself a child of the frontier, he was never unaware of his friend's shortcomings, either as a writer or as a man, but he tolerated and forgave everything of which he could not approve because he knew that the man's heart was sound and fine and that the gift which possessed him was genius. "There are many words of his that I should like to blot, because they grate upon my nerves, or offend my taste, but there is nothing that I could desire unsaid because it is untrue or ungenerous."

Howells's specific judgments of Mark Twain's work are not always quite those of modern critics. He had trouble with Huck Finn's willingness to go to hell over Nigger Jim, for example.

"Perhaps this is one of the places where the author comes too near speaking for his creation; but much might be said in favor of the risk he runs, and for what it achieves it was richly worth taking." Few today would make quite the coupling Howells makes when he writes:

I like *Huck Finn*, as I like *The Prince and the Pauper*, for the reality in it. Both books have their machinery, and I have about the same pleasure in making believe with the author that the town drunkard's son could tell his story, as I have in supposing that the king's son could change places with the beggar's and see England from the beggar's point of view. Both lose in probability through their final possibility, and it is when the author puts his story quite beyond the range of possibility, that he wins for it a measure of probabilty equal to that which he loses when he demands less of the imagination. For some such reason as this, none of his romances seems to me so great as the *Connecticut Yankee at King Arthur's Court*.

Howells seems never to have wavered as to the *Yankee's* supremacy. After *The Mysterious Stranger* had finished its serial course in 1917 he wrote:

The human predicament, as Mark Twain sees it in his wonderful story of *The Mysterious Stranger*, is such as apparently to turn our beloved humorist to a satirist without hope and without faith. The old tenderness for suffering, the old indignation with wrong is there. He is still at his best in these, but the laughter has died out of it all. He cannot promise himself or us any escape from the infamies and atrocities which form our conditioning here, as he could in the story of *A Connecticut Yankee in King Arthur's Court*.[28]

To James, Howells was more important as an editor than he was to Mark Twain but much less so as an adviser. Howells considered James "one of the greatest masters of fiction who ever lived," and he never tired of proclaiming this, though James, who found it difficult to say anything without qualifying it, and then qualifying the qualifications, blew both hot and cold on him. In 1919 Howells wrote:

I am much older than you, and I shall soon be in my eightieth year; but I have looked to you as my senior in so many important things. You have greatly and nobly lived for brave as well as beautiful things, and your name and fame are dear to all who honor such things.

Howells put both *The Bostonians* and *The Princess Casamassima* higher in the James canon than the tendency is to place them today, for he calls the former "one of the masterpieces of all fiction," and when the *Princess* appeared, he hailed it as James's greatest novel and incomparably the finest fiction of the year. He was overwhelmed with admiration for *The Tragic Muse*, even when reading it serially after his daughter's death. In view of the recent, generally silly debate over "The Turn of the Screw," it is interesting to note what he wrote James when it appeared: "the thing has interested me beyond any ghost story I ever read. Perhaps you think this is not saying much; but the kind is one that I am fond of, and I mean a lot of praise." One of his few reservations seems to have been entered in connection with *The Awkward Age*, which defeated him when he tried to read it serially.[29]

Howells read for delight: "I believe I have never got any good from a book that I did not read merely because I wanted to read it. I think this may be applied to anything a person does." As late as 1893 he writes that when he reads "a strong faithful book by a new author," he feels "the potentialities of life revived" for him. Nevertheless his reading-times knew their ebb and flow. "The paper and the ink had a certain odor which was sweeter to me than all the perfumes of Araby," he writes of certain books of his youth. "The look of the type took me more than the glance of a girl, and I had a fever of longing to know the heart of the book, which was like a lover's passion." When he became an editor, this delight extended itself to all the preparatory stages of publication, and when, in his old age, he found old volumes falling apart, he felt that his library was turning into a cemetery. On the other hand, he had no interest in rare books or beautiful bindings, and he once declared that except for works of reference what he possessed had been assembled haphazardly.

If Kitty Ellison, of *A Chance Acquaintance,* is in any sense representative of her creator, Howells read with absorption also, for he tells us that "a trance . . . came upon her at the touch of a book." This does not mean that he was never appalled at the bulk of what demanded to be read, for he speaks of it, and considers such short cuts as anthologies of great poems to help solve the problem. Sometimes his critical principles got in the way of what he might otherwise have enjoyed, though he was not quite without Mark Twain's relish of "hogwash." As late as 1903 he was devoted to serials:

. . . we spend our hour or half-hour with it, and then go contentedly about our business, with a little glimmer on our way of

The light that never was on sea or land.

We find ourselves thinking of those interesting people we met in the January number; and if they grow somewhat vague and uncertain by the time we meet them in the February number, we pull ourselves together. . . .

He adds that memories of the serialization of such great novels as *Bleak House, The Newcomes, Griffith Gaunt, Daniel Deronda,* and *Uncle Tom's Cabin* rank with "some of the happiest hours of the past."

His favorite reading, like his favorite writing, was undoubtedly fiction, though in the beginning he says he did not differentiate between fiction and fact. Autobiography came next; indeed, if you were to take him at face value, you would have to place it first, for it

has a charm which passes that of all other kinds of reading; it has almost the relish of the gossip we talk about our friends; and whoever chooses its form for his inventions is sure to pre-possess us, and if then he can give his incidents and characters the simple order and air of actual occurrences and people, it does not matter much what they are—his success is assured.

He enjoyed many non-fiction books—John Burroughs, for example—and once he wrote his father that he had seldom enjoyed anything so much as John Woolman's journal. But when he gave his lecture on "Novel-Writing and Novel-Reading," he declared for fiction:

I do not despise other kinds of reading. I like history, I like biography, I like poetry, I like drama, I like metaphysics; but I suspect that if I could be got to tell the whole truth, it would appear that I liked all these in the measure they reminded me of the supreme literary form, the fine flower of the human story, the novel: and if I have anywhere said anything else to the contrary, I take it back, at least for the time being.

Only one kind of fiction, apparently, he could not, or would not, read—the detective story; he could even be a little intolerant in his attitude toward it.

O. W. Firkins counted forty-five authors in *My Literary Passions*, of whom eighteen were English, seven American, seven Italian, four Spanish, four German, two French, two Russian, and one Norwegian. But thirty-three of the forty-five are nineteenth-century writers, five eighteenth-century, five sixteenth-century, and two fourteenth-century. The geographical range shown here is remarkable, especially for Howells's time, and this was closely connected with his social convictions. It was his belief that once upon a time nationality had been important in literature, "but in our time this is not possible, and if it were we think it would be a vice. . . . The great and good things in literature nowadays are not the national features, but the universal features." And it seemed to him that foreign authors could perform a very valuable service "in making us intimate with the hearts of men of another faith, race, and condition, and teaching us how like ourselves they are in all that is truest in them."

The chronological range of the Howells list, on the other hand, is not at all remarkable, and in his more iconoclastic moods he could declare bluntly that most classical literature was dead. I can recall only one article in which Howells is even mildly concerned with whether or not the great books of the past are still being read, and even here he adds that "perhaps some modern things are better reading." We shall see this same intense modernism causing some difficulty later in connection with some of Howells's critical evaluations.

CHAPTER ONE

MR. TWELVEMOUGH

I

Howells began writing because he loved it. "To us who have our lives so largely in books," he says, "the material world is always the fable, and the ideal the fact." His brother Joseph wrote of him that "he was an imaginative, sensitive boy, whose head was always full of strange fancies, and after witnessing a play or spending an evening at reading, he would lie awake for hours, unable to set his mind at rest." His family was very dear to him, and even as a boy he was more interested in public affairs than you would believe if you were to take him literally when he describes himself as an exclusively literary character, but somehow or other everything was related to his reading, and, as he says, whenever he admired an author he tried to wirte like him. He imitated *Lallah Rookh;* he found new adventures and modern applications for the comic characters in *Henry V;* at the age of ten he was writing a long story about the last of the Moorish kings. When his social conscience was fully awakened, he felt strongly the need of expressing himself in deeds, not words, but he found no avenue; instead he tried temporarily to change the character of his fiction. Though he became the high priest of American realism, it is in one of his most realistic sketches that he tells us that "nothing real in the world is so affecting as some image of reality." He summed it up accurately in his old age: "Literature and its associations . . . must always be first with me."

The beginning of his serious writing career, as we have seen, was as a poet, and if Fields had been so hospitable to his verses as his predecessor on the *Atlantic*, Lowell, had been, this phase might have continued longer. Fields wanted more like "The Pilot's Story," but he did not care for the lyrics. Browning too admired "The Pilot's Story," as we have seen, and James Woodress admires "Pordenone," an ambitious poem set in sixteenth-century Venice, in spite of its "rather monotonous hexameters." For the hexameters Longfellow may not have been entirely responsible, but he must have had his share in them. Howells wrote or planned an elaborate Civil War poem in *terza rima* in which no editor was ever interested, and he also produced 426 hexameters called *No Love Lost*, involving a Civil War soldier's romance, which was published. Though he ultimately got all his lyrics into print, there was nothing important after he had turned to prose until Harpers brought out *Stops of Various Quills* in 1895. Despite the excellence of some of these sombre poems and of others, I think nobody supposes that Howells could have won as a poet a reputation comparable to that which he holds as a novelist.

"A good many wise critics will tell you that writing is inventing," said Howells; "but I know better than that; it is only remembering . . . the history of your own life." It is clear, however, that he observed others besides himself, and that he read with extreme concentration. When it was necessary to acquire specialized knowledge for a story he never hesitated to do so.

He himself remarks of Verrian in *Fennel and Rue* that "he tacitly noted the face, as the novelist notes whatever happens or appears to him," and in *The Seen and Unseen at Stratford-on-Avon*, he tells Shakespeare that "things that I see are liable to get written of, you know." Joseph Pennell complains that when he traveled with Howells in Italy, the novelist wrote up his notes in the train and then talked to a priest and missed the scenery. I think we may be sure he did not miss anything he wished to see. Of a childhood river trip with his father he reports that "I do not believe that anything which was of use to me was lost upon me," but he did not even look at the industrial plants and processes that his father was interested in. Everybody who met Howells was impressed by his ability to observe and absorb. "His face," says Hamlin Garland, "was impassive but his glance one of the most piercing I had ever encountered." Mark Reardon, meeting him at seventy-seven, was impressed by his humor and kindliness but even more by his ability to fathom unspoken thoughts and questions.

He himself speaks of eavesdropping in public places, and a great deal of what he acquired thus was reported directly in "Easy Chair" papers. Sometimes he deliberately went in search of material, as when, in 1881, he missed a train connection and had to lay over five hours at Xenia, Ohio. Not only did he visit the Eureka Mills, which he had left many years before, and in which he might have been expected to be interested, but also went to "see Soldiers' Home, a most interesting place—a city in itself; a sad metropolis of sickness and suffering." This is one of the many examples available to show that Howells did not always shun the unsmiling aspects of American experience, and it is clear that such alertness often cost him something. In *Their Silver Wedding Journey* he records of his other self Basil March that on the wharf below him he "saw the face of one young girl twisted with weeping" and wished that he had not seen it. But he frequently has such of his characters as are writers taking note of the aesthetic values of even the painful experiences they pass through, and he once told Mark Twain that even when an author makes an ass of himself, the experience is not a total loss, for he can store it up for literature. As he puts it of March: "Like all literary temperaments he was of a certain hardness, in spite of the susceptibilities that could be used to give coloring to his work."

Howells claimed that he never copied any character literally. "What is taken represents a type. . . . Every character created by the author comes from his own individuality. Within every one lies the potentiality of every character known to literature." One man suggested Lindau of *A Hazard of New Fortunes* "but others helped materialize him"; as for Dryfoos in the same novel, Howells could not remember where he came from, "but I suppose

I could think him back to somebody." *The Story of a Play* derived from his own experiences with actors and producers, none literally reproduced, but *The Coast of Bohemia* took its "very first suggestion from . . . a trotting-match at a county fair in northeastern Ohio." The character of the obdurate mother in "A Pair of Patient Lovers" came from a woman Howells disliked, but her asthma was borrowed from another with whom he sympathized. So far as he could remember, on the other hand, "A Circle in the Water" did not begin with any special incident, but was rather "an effect from a smouldering rage of mine against the cruel injustice of things."

Many scenes in Howells's writings are based on places he knew, and many characters derive from incidents in his own life or the lives of his friends. He knew the Negro church described in *An Imperative Duty*, and though the setting of *The Shadow of a Dream* belongs to what Mark Twain called "the composite order of architecture," life itself brought the novelist all the constituent elements. The March wedding journey is the Howells wedding journey,[1] and the March househunting which fills up the first part of *A Hazard of New Fortunes* reflects that of the Howellses when they moved from Boston to New York. Ferris in *A Foregone Conclusion* is Howells as consul at Venice,[2] and Owen Elmore, Percy Ray, Wallace Ardith, Theodore Colville, and others touch him in other aspects.

The story "How I Lost a Wife" in the Ashtabula *Sentinel* in 1854, which is based on Howells's own dog phobia, represents a very early use of personal experience in fiction,[3] and as late as *New Leaf Mills*, Owen Powell leaves his son to struggle with foreign languages quite as Howells himself was left in his youth, while the unlikable miller Overdale is endowed with some of the author's boyish complexes. In *The Vacation of the Kelwyns*, which was based on Howells's own summer experiences of 1876, Parthenope Brook's struggles with German recall his own. Pony Baker frightens and angers his mother by throwing a flower at her from behind when they are out walking in the evening, just as Howells himself had done in his youth. He drew upon his experiences as a visitor for the Boston Associated Charities in *The Minister's Charge*, and *The Albany Depot* seems to have flowered from his own attempt to hire a cook. In *Fennel and Rue*, Verrian is deceived by an impatient reader into revealing in advance what was to happen in a serial story, just as Howells himself had been deceived, and "A Sleep and a Forgetting" was suggested by the tricks which his own memory played on him.[4] Some of the material he used was very fresh. The train wreck in *The Quality of Mercy* was a real wreck of 1887, while *A Masterpiece of Diplomacy* makes use of the New York cholera scare of 1893. Silas Lapham builds a house "on the water side of Beacon Street" at the very time Howells was preparing his residence there, and the streetcar strike in *A Hazard of New Fortunes* took place while the book was being written.

Howells observed his friends closely as sources of material and often used directly what they told him. The adventure of Lily Mayhew in *A Fearful Responsibility* was that of his own sister-in-law, Mary Mead, and Putney was "a brilliant man, very fond of drink, whom I knew on the Western Reserve, when a boy." Thomas Sergeant Perry may well have contributed to Miles Arbuton of *A Chance Acquaintance*,[5] and E. H. Cady has plausibly suggested that Fulkerson of the *Hazard* combined Ralph Keeler and S. S. McClure. One of Howells's finest shorter fictions, *A Parting and a Meeting*, gave the life-experience of an aged Shaker in the settlement at Shirley,[6] and the central action of *The Garroters*, wild as it is, was played out by a friend on Boston Common. Finally, Howells heard of several young ladies who made voyages under conditions similar to those in which Lydia Blood finds herself in *The Lady of the Aroostook*.

Only *The Leatherwood God*, among Howells's novels, has a source, acknowledged in a "Publisher's Note," in the sense in which the term source is used, say, by Chaucer or Shakespeare scholars. "I am almost ashamed," he said, "to think how little *The Leatherwood God* owes to my invention." The book he refers to is R. H. Taneyhill's *The Leatherwood God: An Account of the Appearance and Pretensions of Joseph C. Dylks in Eastern Ohio in 1828* (Cincinnati, Robert Clarke & Co., 1870). Howells reviewed it in the *Atlantic* in 1871 and showed how the history of this frontier Messiah had interested him by the care with which he summarized the facts of the case. He carried it in his mind virtually across his writing lifetime. In 1897 he dealt with it again in *Stories of Ohio*, and in 1907 he wrote his brother Joe that he would like to make the story his "last great novel." The Harper executive F. A. Duneka's conviction that it was "not serializable" seems to have kept him from writing it for about fifteen years. At last it was serialized in the *Century* between April and November, 1916, and The Century Company published the book in the autumn.[7]

This does not mean, however, that *The Leatherwood God* was the only work for which Howells "looked up" material or received impressions from previously published works, Elaine Hedges has reasonably suggested Balzacian influence in *The Rise of Silas Lapham* and perhaps elsewhere,[8] and we have Howells's own word for it that *A Modern Instance* took off from the *Medea* of Euripides. D. G. Cooke thought Alice Pasmer and other girls indebted to Turgenev's Lisa. The drowned girl in *Suburban Sketches* is from life, not literature, but Howells shows how close the two lay together in his mind when he tells Higginson that "she was no worse than Zenobia [in *The Blithedale Romance*]—was Zenobia, in fact, in Putnam Street, Cambridge." *The Shadow of a Dream* certainly reflects his reading of Ribot and William James, and "Editha" may have been related to "fixation of belief," as defined by Charles Sanders Peirce, whom Howells knew.[9]

Before writing *Venetian Life*, Howells read industriously to supplement his own observations. He made a trip to Indiana before writing the divorce court scenes in *A Modern Instance*.[10] Preparing for *The Quality of Mercy*, in which an embezzler flees to Canada, he consulted with the Canadian police, asked Sylvester Baxter to "talk with some skilled reporter, and find how they 'get onto' things," and requested his sister to send him details of life in Montreal. Even when he wrecked a hero on a coral atoll—

perhaps the most fantastic incident in all his novels—he took pains to secure exact information.[11]

He did not enjoy what scholars call research, however, and he never did it except in a desultory fashion. Very early in his career, when Cincinnati was still his idea of a "big bustling city," he wrote his brother that he liked "nothing better than to stroll about the streets alone, and stealthily contemplate the shop windows and orange stands, and speculate on the people I meet." [12] Though he was a "realist," he was also a creative writer, and a creative writer must necessarily prefer what he creates to what he sees. Howells is playful, of course, when, in visiting Petrarch's study, he thinks of the poet as having stepped out for a moment, to return again as soon as his visitor has withdrawn. Playful too are the stories in *A Pair of Patient Lovers* in which a romance begins with the stimulation received by a young man's imagination when he sees a girl's name lettered on a piano crate which is being driven through Boston's Park Square ("The Pursuit of a Piano") and the other in which a man falls in love with a girl through hearing the sound of her voice in the next room ("The Magic of a Voice"). The situation described in "Black Cross Farm" (*A Daughter of the Storage*), in which the writer and his friend go to see the huge black cross nailed on the barn and to mull over its meaning must be typical of many things life brought to Howells and tickled his imagination with, compelling him to interpret their significance in terms of his own aesthetic purposes.

Sources are one thing; influences are another. Critics have sought out many of the latter in Howells. Both *The Story of a Play* and *The Son of Royal Langbrith* have been called Ibsenish. Gibson has plausibly suggested *Pride and Prejudice* in connection with the clash between Kitty Ellison and Miles Arbuton in *A Chance Acquaintance*, and the Kirks see both Björnson (*The Bankrupt*) and Valdés (*Marta y Maria*) in *The Rise of Silas Lapham*. Howells's earliest conditioning was, of course, neo-classical, "reasonable," [13] and the Kirks show quite convincingly that he went back to the eighteenth century as late as the Altrurian romances, for both the *History of Greece* and *The Citizen of the World* appear clearly here. "To turn the leaves of Goldsmith's *History of Greece* is to find oneself in the very atmosphere of Altruria over which played the winds of Attica as well as those of Jerusalem." And it is interesting to note that H. M. Alden's *God in His World* (1895), which Howells admired, was "a Christian interpretation of the glorious period of Hellenic civilization, especially that of the first three centuries."

When everything else has been allowed for, it seems clear, however, that the principal influences were Cervantes, Turgenev, and Tolstoy. The loose, free, simple design of *Don Quixote* turned Howells against the contrived, intricately interwoven plots which the Victorian favored at an early age. From Turgenev he learned, as James did, that a novelist should begin with his characters, not with his plot, and that the latter should develop itself as the natural, unforced expression of their interests and personalities, not something that they were forced into out of consideration for a pre-fabricated design. Moreover, so far as possible, the characters should be permitted to tell the story without interposing comment by the author. As early as 1875, Howells objected to James's story "A Passionate Pilgrim" because the author tended "to expatiate upon his characters too much, and not to trust his reader's perception enough." When he read Tolstoy, he modified this ideal to the extent of giving up the "extreme preference" he had hitherto entertained for "the dramatic conduct of the story," and instead of dealing with five or six characters, involved in a private problem which was being worked out in comparative isolation from society as a whole, he now tended for a time toward the employment of a larger canvas and a more direct portrayal of social forces.

These influences were not all mutually exclusive. Hawthorne had built his novels around a limited group of characters before Turgenev, and he had also used dramatic confrontations freely, though he certainly did not refrain from direct commentary. Flaubert, Björnson, and Auerbach reinforced Turgenevian tendencies. But Turgenev seems to have defined the dramatic method most sharply; he also exercised a moral appeal which Flaubert, for example, could not make. Turgenev looked at human nature "without either false pride or false shame in its nakedness," and he made the whole business of writing—and living—seem "more serious, more awful," more charged with "mystical responsibilities" than it had seemed before. What Tolstoy was to add at a later date was the distinctively religious, distinctively Christian appeal—the challenge of one who believed that Christ meant exactly what he said, even in his "hard sayings," and who had himself set out to follow him. Howells soon discovered, however, as we shall see, that he himself could not be a Tolstoyan literalist, and though he did move toward the Tolstoy kind of novel in such middle works as *Annie Kilburn* and *A Hazard of New Fortunes*, ultimately this type of fiction proved less congenial to his gifts than what he had established before Tolstoy spoke to him. Though Howells finally considered Tolstoy the king of novelists, it might, therefore, be reasonably argued both that Turgenev at least partially anticipated Tolstoy's moral appeal to him, and that he provided a more lasting aesthetic model, and one more congenial to Howells's own gifts and temperament.

II

Howells wrote characteristically in longhand, on half sheets, until, in later years, writer's cramp drove him to the typewriter, and he found that he could write quite as well that way except when the going got rough. On at least three occasions, he speaks of having dictated, but he never took kindly to dictation, as James did. As an *Atlantic* editor, he kept to his work and the *Atlantic* work day and night, but his health gave way under the strain, and as an established writer he did all his writing in the morning. In 1889 he told Walter Brooks that composition was always "slow and laborious for him," and that three or four hours a day of it was all he could stand. Though the routine varied from time to time, he was likely to get up at seven or seven-thirty, breakfast at eight, reach his desk by nine, and stay there until twelve or one. After lunch he would take a brief nap, followed by a brisk walk. He liked to read over what he had written before going to bed and to go over it again next morning before continuing his work.

He told one interviewer that his method of work was "a sort of psychic puzzle" even to himself. "I usually have the last word of my book, the last picture, before I begin." But before he could actually sit down to write, there would be "two or three months of misery getting ready." He told Van Wyck Brooks that he always had his idea in mind but made no scenario. Of *Ragged Lady* he knew only that the story was to come out in a certain way but had no idea how this was to be brought about. He saw a writer's work as "a growth from all his thinking and feeling about it" and did not believe that even Shakespeare could have planned a complete *Hamlet* in advance. The idea for *The Shadow of a Dream* lay "dormant" in his mind for twenty years before he was able to write the novel.

Mrs. Howells thought that her husband wrote novels as other men saw wood, and he himself says, "I sit down at my desk and go to work as regularly as if I were in a mercantile or banking office." It did not always go equally well, however, and his letters are full of complaints as to the difficulty he was having with this story or that. *Private Theatricals* was revised during serialization, and *A Modern Instance* was hard hit by the serious illness Howells suffered after it had begun its serial course but before he had completed his work on it. He had much trouble with both *The Quality of Mercy* and *The Coast of Bohemia*, and he held up *Through the Eye of the Needle* for fifteen years, waiting for the climax, which finally came to him with the idea of taking an American woman to Altruria, after which he finished it in a month. "Her Opinion of His Story" has an amusing commentary on the problems a writer must face in writing a story and the arbitrary decisions he must sometimes make.

His journalistic training taught him how to write anywhere, even in uncongenial surroundings, and though John Langbrith is a rude man who knows nothing of literature, he seems to speak for Howells when he tells his nephew who had gone to Paris to try to become a dramatist that "if you really meant business, you could write plays in Saxmills as well as in Paris. You could get it out of you, anywhere, if you had it in you." But if Howells did not keep in practice as a writer, it might take him many days to get into working trim again. "Shifting about" often troubled him. He found it very hard to work on *A Woman's Reason* in Europe in 1883, and after he had finished it, he devoted himself to non-fiction until after his return to America. He was troubled even more when he had to break in upon his fiction to do his critical articles, which he always disliked. He could be temperamental about names: when he tried calling the Marches Basil and Isabel in *A Hazard of New Fortunes*, as he had called them in *Their Wedding Journey*, they were now too grown up and dignified to respond: he had to call them "Mr. and Mrs. March." His head was full of this novel when Winifred died, but when he tried to write it, he feared his power had gone with her. "For weeks I made start after start, and tore up everything I wrote. I was in perfect despair about it." Ultimately, as with Mark Twain and *Following the Equator* after Susy's death, he found not the comfort he needed but the best remedy available to a man in his circumstances, and "when I had struggled up and found my footing, I believe I went forward with no uncertain tread."

As to the relationship between the creator and his work, Howells took up the same attitude toward writing that Constant Coquelin maintained toward acting. He told Van Wyck Brooks that he never allowed his characters to take control of his story or his own emotions to become entangled.

The essence of achievement is to keep outside, to be entirely dispassionate, as a sculptor must be, moulding his clay. And this is true also, I think, of all good acting. Harrigan, the actor, once told me that the character he was playing was like a mirror held up before him. A good actor never for a moment identifies himself with his part.

In 1892 he told a *Tribune* reporter that whenever he had given way to "inspiration" and worked with "reckless enthusiasm," he had produced "rubbish" which had to be thrown away. Elsewhere he says that the "unbridled" imagination can produce nothing more valuable in waking life than it does in dreams. "It must keep close to truth, and it must be under the law if it would work strongly and sanely." [14]

As to whether he lost or retained his zest for work as he grew older, Howells could speak eloquently on both sides of the question. "I've been working hard, and feel tired of work, almost for the first time in my life." "If I could live without writing, I don't believe I should write any more." "I have come to the time of life when invention does not work readily. This is because the world no longer interests me as it once did." [15] "I don't work much, for me; and I wish I had not to work at all. I am horribly sick of literature, at times, and would be better content if there were some other honest way of earning a living." "I am not writing so much this summer as usual, partly because I don't find my stuff so satisfactory, and partly because I find writing tires me more than it used, just as walking does." And finally, to his sister Aurelia in 1918, "I am conscious that I am wearing out, mind as well as body; my memory fails me distressingly, and I tend to obscurity in my expression. I have two longish stories well started but I cannot force them on. . . . I read my novels of the past aloud to my family, and wonder that I could do them."

Over against these statements, however, we must place others: "My work has always been so 'lief and dear' to me that now in my seventy-third year a proof of the thing I have last written is as wondrously precious as that which I printed from types put together with my childish hands, when I could have been about seven, in an essay on 'Human Life.' " ". . . I hope soon to get at a novel. It is strange how the love of doing it survives. Of course, there is the need, too, but the love seems as great as ever." "I am writing a novel . . . and feeling so much more interest in it than any reader will ever take that it is quite ridiculous. It is a sort of shame to be yarning away at my age, but I might be doing worse things." "I write and find greater happiness in writing than I ever did." And, climactically, to Hamlin Garland, about his last, unfinished novel, "The Home-Towners": "I bring moving-picture folks into it; and you know they abound in St. Augustine, where I have put the scene of the story. It will be quite different from all my other things."

Where, then, lies the truth? In the first set of expressions, I think, and in the second, and also in the No-Man's Land that lies between them. "I am aware of being physically weaker than I once was, and my work, which has always been so dear to me, is not so satisfactory, though it comes easier. I rattle it off at a great rate, but it does not delight me as it used to do, though now and then a little paper seems just as good as anything I ever did." Perhaps he came closest to hitting the bullseye when he wrote his sister Aurelia in 1905: "I am often very weary of writing, but when I take a day off I don't know what to do with it."

III

At an *Atlantic Monthly* dinner at the Parker House in 1874 Howells said that those who had found the magazine dull under his editorship had no idea how much duller he might have made it by printing more of his own stuff in it! Like most authors, he experienced many fluctuations of faith and lack of faith in himself. In 1893 he wrote Mrs. Fields that "I displease myself with everything I write, and upon the whole am in a hopeful state," and while this was clearly the expression of a mood, it recurred from time to time. When he wrote *Their Wedding Journey* he vacillated "between a pyramidal pride in it and a colossal loathing of it." He finished *A Chance Acquaintance*, he told James, "with such triumphal feelings that I would not have exchanged my prospect of immortality through it for the fame of Shakespeare. Now I regard it with cold abhorrence, and work over it, shuddering." He often had a dreadful time choosing a title and was sometimes dissatisfied with the titles he had chosen. In *The World of Chance* he makes Percy Ray full of afterthoughts about his book, wondering whether he should change this or that.[16]

Fortunately he had more general confidence in himself than such utterances, taken by themselves, might indicate. The letters he wrote to his sisters in his early days show a very ambitious young man and a very romantic one too. "I have the assurance that I shall succeed, *but*, O God! sometimes I tremble lest something should happen to destroy my hopes." Visiting Keats's grave in Rome, he fears that his name is destined to be "writ in water." Yet he sends Victoria "a journal which I have been keeping for you this week. I advise you to preserve it. It may one day be useful to my biographers." When he was writing to those who could be counted upon to understand, he was capable of a good deal of the humorous kind of self-vaunting of which Mark Twain did so much; when Charles Frohman asked permission to put on *The Mousetrap*, he wrote in reply that he wished Frohman would put on all his farces every night in the year. He told Theodore Dreiser that he would be ashamed to describe the literary triumphs he achieved in his youthful daydreams, and when Dreiser asked him whether the appreciation of his readers had given him the satisfaction he had hoped for, he replied emphatically in the affirmative. When, in 1902, a New York apartment house was named after Henry James, he was not sure that James would like it, but he knew he would have liked it himself, though he would rather have had it named after one of his books. And I find no lack of self-confidence in his reply to Robert Grant when the latter asked him how sure a grip he had upon his character: "The grip of a bulldog." In his presidential address at the First Public Meeting of the American Academy of Arts and Letters in 1909, Howells admitted the possibility that

by an oversight, which we should all deplore, some artist or author or composer whose work has given him the right to be of us is not of us. It is also possible that time will decide that some of us who are now here were not worthy to be here, and by this decision we must abide. But until it is rendered, we will suffer with what meekness, what magnanimity, we may the impeachments of those contemporaries who may question our right to be here.

I do not sense any overwhelming humility or uncertainty here. And when he received the Gold Medal of the National Institute in 1915, he admitted that, greatly as he felt the honor that had been done to him, he could not pretend that it was altogether unexpected or completely undeserved.

So far as pure criticism has governed your vote, I might say that the novelist whom you have done the greatest honor that the world could do him has striven for excellence in his art with no divided motive, unless the constant endeavor for truth is want of fealty to fiction.

After Howells was an established writer, he would never "submit" his work to an editor. He would describe the idea or send an outline, and acceptance or rejection had to be made upon this basis. Even at the beginning, he had made it clear to Fields that if he was going to write for the *Atlantic*, he would have to write what interested him and not what Fields thought he wanted. When James A. Herne produced *Bride Roses* in 1894, he refused to make the changes Herne wanted, and he refused to alter the dramatization of *Silas Lapham* which he and his kinsman Paul Kester had made to please either Herne or William H. Crane, though he authorized Kester to make them on his own if he chose.[17] In 1919 he wrote his recollections of his visit to the White House in 1880, but neither Hayes's son nor his nephew liked it. Howells wrote the son a very kind letter, but he uncompromisingly refused to revise the article according to directions. Instead he destroyed it. It was understood that he should not campaign against capital punishment in his departments in *Harper's Magazine*, and what he had written was censored only once; this was in 1891, when Alden suppressed an attack on Andrew Lang because the latter had become editor of the English edition of the magazine. To please Osgood he consented to add a kind of epilogue to *A Foregone Conclusion* embracing Don Ippolito's conversion and death and Ferris's service in the Union army and final reunion with Florida Vervain, and when *Silas Lapham* was being serialized in the *Century* he consented to omit Bromfield Corey's suggestion that the poor of Boston might well dynamite the comfortable homes of the well-to-do, left standing empty all summer while their owners were at the seashore. The editor with whom Howells had the worst time was Edward Bok, who paid him $5,000 in advance to serialize *The Coast of Bohemia* in *The Ladies' Home Journal* and then "tampered with" the product. But it is a little surprising to find him saying that he finally stopped using the Marches "because I had come to realize that some of my readers did not share my affection for them." In fact, this sounds a little like Trollope killing Mrs. Proudie after he had heard some men abusing her—and him—at a club.

Howells did not have a high regard for criticism, even when he wrote it himself, feeling that he never achieved more than approximate justice, no matter how hard he tried. "Why do you say that I don't care for criticism?" he asked Higginson. "I hate it abominably." He told young Booth Tarkington that critics would retain their power to hurt him long after they had lost their power to please, and when Aldrich asked him if he had seen a certain unfavorable review, he replied bitterly, "Do you suppose that I have no bosom friends?" His *alter ego* Eugenio felt that he would have liked each book to be reviewed by "some lifelong admirer, some dear and faithful friend, all the better for not being an acquaintance, who had liked him from the beginning and was intimately versed in all his work." This not often being possible, Howells tended to feel that the best criticism was "quotational criticism," which at least allowed the author to speak for himself.

When the author spoke thus—and this is Eugenio again— Howells was sure "that nothing he said or meant, not the slightest intention or airiest intimation in his books, was ever wholly lost." Somewhere, some reader would catch it and respond to it. "If you like it," he wrote his family about one of his articles, "don't be afraid of making me vain by saying so." He confesses that he carried favorable reviews of *Venetian Life* about with him as if they had been love letters. This was when he was young. But it was not very different when he was old. His sensitiveness was personal as well as literary, and when Oxford gave him a degree in 1904, he wrote home proudly that the "great roar of applause" which went up from the undergraduates when his name was called had not been accompanied by "a single jibe."

At the end of 1901, having read a paper about himself by Brander Matthews, Howells wrote:

Your praise seemed the more reasonable because your blame is so just. I know I have those faults which you hint, and if I were not nearly sixty-five years old I should, under the inspiration of your censure, set about correcting them. But as it is I shall have work enough cultivating the merits which you recognize so charmingly that I should love them almost as much as if they were someone else's.

And in 1903, having encountered a letter which Henry James had written in criticism of him years ago, he reacted quite angelically:[18]

. . . I have often thought my intellectual raiment was more than my intellectual body, and that I might finally be convicted, not of having nothing *on*, but of that worse nakedness of having nothing *in*. He speaks of me with my style, and such mean applications as I was making of it, as seeming to him like a poor man with a diamond which he does not know what to do with; and mostly I suppose I *have* cut a rather inferior window glass with it. But I am not sorry for having wrought in common crude material so much; that is the right American stuff; and perhaps hereafter, when my din is done, if any one is curious to know what that noise was, it will be found to have proceeded from a small insect which was scraping about on the surface of our life and trying to get into its meaning for the sake of the other insects larger or smaller.

But of course it was better, even with friends, when they praised. "Your letter gave me so much joy . . ." he wrote William Lyon Phelps after *The Kentons*. "You have touched my heart with your praise of Ellen Kenton; and Boyne *is* good, I won't deny it." Of *New Leaf Mills* he wrote Thomas Sergeant Perry: "What you said of my book went to my heart as well as my head, for one ages into self-doubt, and there are so many to help one doubt one's self." "Your praise is dearer to me in my age than it could have been earlier," he wrote Edith Wyatt in 1912. "When I was young many praised me; then came scornings and buffetings from every side, which now you have turned into sweetness." He was pleased too when Henry Arthur Jones praised his plays:

Your letter gave me the greatest pleasure; thirty, even twenty, years ago, it would have given me courage; but at seventy one does not turn to a new trade. Still, on the impulse you have given me, I am going to show my little pieces to a dramatic agent here, and see what will happen.

But of course the best thing of all was when Tolstoy praised him, and he quoted what had been said in a letter to his son: "Pretty good for a little novelist, what, from the greatest that ever lived?"

He knew that he had "run to quantity" as an author. "And yet the quality is not so bad." When his brother Joe called his attention to a passage in *April Hopes* which he had forgotten, he found that he admired it almost as much as Joe did:

In fact, I am often amazed at the quality as well as the quantity of my stuff, and feel as if it must have been done by a trust named after me. Did you see that the Ohio School Commissioner had sent round to all the school children to know why every American should know my books, and which of them were autobiographical? This is better than having it all on a tombstone.

In 1909 he thought that his "meat" had gone into the books he wrote before 1886, when he moved to Harpers, "and yet there are three or four of the later novels which are as good as any." One of these was apparently *The Son of Royal Langbrith*, of which he says that he did not value it less because it came easily. In 1893 he told H. H. Boyesen that he considered *A Modern Instance* his best novel, adding that *A Hazard of New Fortunes* had sold nearly twice as many copies as any other novel and that *The Rise of Silas*

Lapham was the next most popular. In *The House of Harper* (1912) he chose the *Hazard* as his best book "for breadth and depth," although he denied it the shapeliness of *Silas Lapham* or *Indian Summer* or the intensity of *A Modern Instance*, and in the Preface written for the "Library Edition," this same *Hazard* became "the most vital of my fictions, through my quickened interest in the life about me, at a moment of great psychological import." It was written when

The solution of the riddle of the painful earth through the dreams of Edward Bellamy, through the dreams of all the generous visionaries of the past, seemed not impossibly far off. The shedding of blood which is for the remission of sins had been symbolized by the bombs and scaffolds of Chicago. . . . Opportunely for me there was a great street-car strike in New York, and the story began to find its way to issues nobler and larger than those of the love-affairs common to fiction.

But when William Lyon Phelps praised *Indian Summer* in 1906, he was delighted—"So few people know how good *Indian Summer* is—and in 1911 he was delighted again to have *Silas* used in a freshman English course at Cornell:

I was always fond of Lapham and fonder still of his wife, though I did not realize her so directly from life; he seemed to me of the lasting boyishness which keeps the hearts of Americans sweet. Then, he was finding out, against his selfish ambition and temptations, what a true rise was, and I was following him with pride and joy.[19]

It must not be forgotten that writing was a business as well as an art with Howells, and his attitude toward the financial aspect should be clearly understood. He was a famous man in his time, a "name" known even to those who did not read him, a writer whose opinions were consulted and whose endorsements were sought, and the President of the United States honored him by coming from Washington to New York to attend his seventy-fifth birthday dinner. Yet he was never really a best seller. "The big sales," he told his sister Aurelia, "are for better people," adding that he "tried to keep from feeling greedy and envious of the success of books which I don't respect." *A Hazard of New Fortunes* sold 12,000 copies in advance of publication, but it took *A Modern Instance* ten years to sell 10,000. Harpers sent out 8,500 copies of *The Kentons* during the first three weeks, but in the long run the book did no better than the others he had been bringing out of late. His last years were crowded with honors, but his popularity declined, and the proposed, collected "Library Edition" was given up after six volumes had appeared.[20] "I could not 'serialize' a story of mine now in any American magazine, thousands of them as there are," he wrote James in 1915. And though the *Century* did serialize *The Leatherwood God* the following year, this was the exception, not the rule.

Brought up as he was in poverty, Howells was always careful with his money. There is abundant evidence that he was not mean, but he was economical by nature, and if some of the records he made of how he withheld and reproached himself afterwards, or gave and then felt that he ought not to have given, have a somewhat comical ring, it should be remembered that a less honest man would not have recorded this kind of thing at all. Moreover, the less prosperous members of his own family were a continual drain on him. Theoretically he believed that every man ought to have a guaranteed income for so many hours of work every day and that his art "should be his privilege, when he has proven his fitness to exercise it, and has otherwise earned his daily bread; and its results should be free to all." Theoretically he also disbelieved in tipping ("the practice of beggary without the beggar's excuse of destitution") and in "charity," but he knew that none of this was practicable in the society in which we live. In 1894 he suggested to Clifton Johnson that writers would be better off if they labored physically, as Tolstoy advised, but when Joyce Kilmer advanced the same idea in 1914 he dissented vigorously. Poverty, he argued, is not an incentive for fine art, and if the artist were to serve society, he must have his time at his own disposal. He was sure that his own early work had suffered because he could not devote his full time to it.[21]

Howells did not believe that writers were more commercially minded in his own time than they had previously been. The laborer was worthy of his hire whether he dug ditches or wrote novels, but greed of gold could not inspire good writing. In *A Traveler from Altruria* he makes Mr. Twelvemough argue that, even under capitalism, when an artist "has once fairly passed into his work, he loses himself in it. He does not think whether it will pay or not, but whether he can make it good or not." Asked if the money consideration does not influence choice of subject, he says:

Oddly enough, I don't believe it does. A man makes his choice once for all when he embraces the aesthetic life, or rather it is made for him; no other life seems possible. . . . If he did not love to do the thing he does he could not do it well, no matter how richly it paid.

Nevertheless he used every means in his power to squeeze every possible penny out of his writings. "In the days before my inclusive salary," he told Bliss Perry, "I used to make people pay shocking prices for my things." Howells would have hanged himself before consenting to undertake the salesmanship enterprises in which many modern writers engage. He refused even to give his friends complimentary copies of his first book, *Poems of Two Friends*, lest he should seem to be soliciting their interest, and he was a mature man when he refused to send one of his books to Turgenev on the same grounds. But when it came to negotiating with publishers and having a share in the presentation of his work to the public at every stage and in retaining control of his rights in it, nobody could have been much more canny than he. He was never satisfied with his sales figures,[22] and he worried about copyright limitations and about the losses he suffered through having his books in the public libraries. He contemplated legal action when he was not paid as agreed upon by the Fitchburg Railroad for the pamphlet publication of "Niagara Revisited." [23] He flirted with the idea of subscription publishing and dreamed up endless wild notions of collaboration with Mark Twain on a great variety of impossible enterprises. In 1888 he did collaborate with T. S. Perry on an immense *Library of Universal Adventure by Sea and Land* for Harpers which was going to earn the editors a great deal of money but never did. And the idea of the collaborative *Harper's Bazar* serial, *The Whole Family*, later published in book form, originated with Howells. (He wrote "The Father." Mark Twain refused to produce a chapter written from the point of view of the boy in the family, but Henry James turned out "The Married Son.")

Moreover, Howells always preferred a regular salary to free-lancing, and here too he bargained successfully. He bargained with the *Atlantic* at the very beginning of his career, and though this meant only a weekly increase from $40 to $50, the extra $10 was important at the time. Howells did not accept all the editorial offers that were made to him. In 1890 he turned down what might have been a very advantageous offer from S. S. McClure. But he accepted whatever good offers he thought practicable, though he was always frank to say that he did this out of financial considerations and that he thought he might have written better fiction if he had left journalism quite alone. By 1868 the *Atlantic* was paying him $3,500 a year, but this included his articles. After he left the *Atlantic*, he went on a fixed salary with Osgood, but the details of this arrangement are not clear.

In 1885 he signed a contract with Harpers for $10,000 annually, covering serial publication of a novel and a farce and the "Editor's Study" each month in *Harper's Magazine*. (Book publication of the novels was to yield 12 ½ per cent royalties.) This contract ran out in 1891. If he had continued on Walker's *Cosmopolitan*, he would have been paid $15,000 a year. When Harper and Brothers went bankrupt in 1900, he was very uneasy, but the next year a new $10,000 contract was negotiated with the reorganized firm, now presided over by George Harvey; this involved reviving the "Easy Chair," writing critical articles for *The North American Review*, and, at the beginning, some literary counseling. In 1910 he asked that his payments for the "Easy Chair" articles be increased to $1,000 each, which was granted, but in 1914 he accepted a 10 per cent cut which the firm was making across the board. In 1915 a new arrangement gave him $5,000 a year for the "Easy Chair" alone, with the understanding that the Harpers were to have the first refusal of his other work, but after they had rejected one contribution, he begged off from this feature.[24]

Interestingly enough, the most startling examples of Howells's hardheadedness in financial matters came in connection with two of his closest friends. In 1898, when Frank Bliss wanted him to do an introduction for the new collected edition of Mark Twain, Howells set his price at $1,500, and when Bliss would not pay it, he let the edition appear without it. And after James's death, the plan to write a memorial article for the Harpers was given up because of a disagreement over terms. Howells, old and tired, wrote Harpers's Frank Duneka that he was "truly, almost humbly grateful to you for refusing to give the price I asked for the James paper, because, now I need not lash myself to doing it within a certain time." He did review Percy Lubbock's edition of the *Letters*, however, and he started to write a memoir of James which he never finished.

IV

Disregarding the early experiments—"The Independent Candidate" and "Geoffrey Winter"—Howells's novels may be said to have developed out of his travel narratives; *Their Wedding Journey* was his own honeymoon, and when he had added a plot to the trip and gone over the ground again, he had *A Chance Acquaintance*. For some time after his return to America he literally groped for subjects; surely nothing could have seemed more hopelessly out of his range than a life of Lucrezia Borgia, yet he might well have written it if he had found the necessary material available in the Boston libraries. When it blew up, he was left with the exploitation of such local scenes and incidents as made up *Suburban Sketches*. But when *Their Wedding Journey* at last got under way, the light began to break. Even here, to be sure, his approach is hesitant, and he tells us on the first page that he omitted the antecedent story of the troubled courtship of the Marches because he doubted his "fitness for a sustained or involved narrative." Such doubts did not plague him long. "If I succeed in this," he wrote his father "—and I believe I shall—I see clear before me a path in literature which no one else has tried, and which I believe I can make most distinctly my own."

Of course Howells did not confine himself to travel-novels, but neither did he ever abandon the type. First and last, there is an enormous amount of traveling in his books, and the traveler is often used as the center of perception. He tried the Turgenev-James dramatic novel and the panoramic Tolstoyan, sociological novel. Once he even tried the epistolary novel (*Letters Home*), and handled it well enough, though I think one is always more interested in what is told than in the personalities of the tellers. But with *Their Silver Wedding Journey* he made a late return to the travel-type novel and produced his most elaborate example of it. "You could write an original book of the nicest kind," Mrs. March tells her husband; "mix up travel and fiction; get some love in." He replies: "It wouldn't work. It would be carrying water on both shoulders. The fiction would kill the travel, and the travel would kill the fiction; the love and the humor wouldn't mingle any more than oil and vinegar." But it did work. The travel part worked so well that Howells spent much of the rest of his writing time on travel books. Indeed it may be said that nearly everything he wrote during this final phase was based on either his travels or his memories of his youth.

Temperamentally it was the simple patterns and more modest themes that were most congenial to Howells as fictionist. He once insisted that he was not analytical. "What people cannot see is that I analyze as little as possible, but go on talking about the analytical school—which I am supposed to belong to." What he calls the "historical" form of novel writing (which is what most of us call telling the story from the point of view of the om-niscient author) was always his favorite method, and surely this is the simplest form and the one that has always been favored by nine writers out of every ten who are interested primarily in what they have to say rather than in how they say it. Though Howells insisted on form in poetry, it interested him much less in fiction. Brice Maxwell says in *The Story of a Play*:

"I don't know that you are bound to relate things strictly to each other in art, any more than they are related in life. There are all sorts of incidents and interests playing round every great event that seem to have no more relation to it than the rings of Saturn have to Saturn. They form the atmosphere of it." [25]

He preferred "good natural English" to "good literary English" and liked dialect as a means of making written English freer and more like actual speech; even his enemy H. L. Mencken is forced to praise him on this count.[26] The objectivity of Turgenev, Björnson, Auerbach, and others turned him against auctorial comments in fiction, for which he criticized not only Thackeray, Trollope, and the English novelists generally but even Henry James, whose stories were clearer he thought if one read only what the characters say and not the author's interpretation of it. But he was not always consistent in avoiding this.[27] Carrington counted more than sixty interpretative comments in *The Lady of the Aroostook* and more than one hundred in *The Rise of Silas Lapham*, though he admits that there was a sharp decline thereafter. There is a long passage in *Their Wedding Journey*, Chapter IX ("Do I pitch the pipe too low?") which is not only quite in Thackeray's manner but a direct imitation of him.[28] In *A Foregone Conclusion* he refers to Ferris, amazingly, as "one of my predecessors in office at Venice." In *Private Theatricals* he forecasts quite in the Trollopian manner: "It was not thought from the first that he was in danger, and as it turned out he was not." In *Indian Summer* the author "would not presume to decide" whether Colville and Mrs. Bowen would have married without Effie's intervention. Even in *A Hazard of New Fortunes*, as George Arms has pointed out, though the Marches "dominate as centers of revelation," Howells does not hesitate to go behind the other characters at will. At the end of Part V, Chapter III, where he leaves the strike at a crucial moment and moves to the Dryfoos home, he even uses the old-fashioned method of storytelling which Scott inherited from Leland's *Longsword* and used so characteristically in *Ivanhoe* and elsewhere.

Though Howells himself made something of a point of having avoided "dire calamity" and the "moving accident" in his books, actually he has his reasonable share of both. Never mind for the moment the wrecking of the hero of *A Woman's Reason* on a coral atoll. In *A Hazard of New Fortunes* both old Lindau and Conrad Dryfoos are killed in the strike riot. The flight of the defaulter to Canada in *The Quality of Mercy*, and his return in the middle of the night to see his daughters, is not quite free of Sir Gilbert Parkerism, and nothing could be much more sensational than Denton's suicide in *The World of Chance* after his mad attempt to "sacrifice" his sister-in-law, Peace Hughes. There is a good deal of adventure in *The Undiscovered Country* when Boynton and Egeria get lost in the snow and she is mistaken for a girl who had escaped from the reform school. Richard Kenton horsewhips his sister Ellen's unworthy lover, and Boyne Kenton is arrested when he tries to approach the little Dutch princess he has a "crush" on during a ceremonial procession. In *The Landlord at Lion's Head*, Alan Lynde overtakes Jeff Durgin in his carriage and whips him about the head and face, and later Jeff nearly kills Lynde when he gets him into his power by chance and then lets him go for motives which he never defines to himself. In *The Vacation of the Kelwyns* both a bear-leader and a bear are knocked out by lightning.

In *Indian Summer* a carriage accident brings about the solution of the love problem, and Howells himself describes Effie's role in bringing her mother and Colville together as a *coup de théâtre*. The death of Nevil in a train accident at the close of *The Shadow of a Dream* cuts the Gordian knot of the plot. In *Their Silver Wedding Journey* the meetings between the travelers are freely manipulated for the convenience of the plot, and Howells was well aware of this, for he says that "life likes to do these things handsomely" but that "this is the kind of thing that makes you blush for the author if you find it in a novel."

These are by no means all the examples that might be cited. The burning of Silas Lapham's house, just in time to push him down under his financial burden, and just after the "builder's risk" insurance had expired, is not quite the everyday realism generally identified with Howells, and Mrs. Lapham's "Oh, thank the merciful Lord!" when she hears the news would be more at home in an Owen Davis melodrama. Silas' involvement with Zerilla and her mother is quite natural, but its use, to estrange Silas from his wife, just when they need each other most, which even involves the sending of an anonymous letter to Mrs. Lapham, is contrived, and the long arm of coincidence is stretched again when the letter from the railroad company arrives just when it does.

To be sure, Howells does not use all these things quite as a writer of sword-and-cloak romances would have used them. In *The Lady of the Aroostook*, Staniford demonstrates his manhood by leaping into the sea to save a man who has fallen overboard, but nothing much comes of it, and though Lydia later suffers considerable anguish through the stock device of an accident which causes a delay in the posting of a letter, her romance is not ultimately frustrated by it. Lemuel Barker gets credit for having behaved like a hero in the fire at Mrs. Harmon's hotel in *The Minister's Charge*, but the truth is he was never really in much danger. The storm in *Doctor Breen's Practice* is not very vividly described, and even the coral atoll incident is pretty soberly handled.

In *Letters of an Altrurian Traveler*, the fashionables praise Mr. Twelvemough because you can be sure when you take up one of his books that you have not "got hold of a tract on political economy in disguise." This is usually taken as a "swipe" at popular fiction and fictionists, and up to a point that is what it is. But Howells was of two minds here. Charles Dudley Warner had tried to get him to write panoramic novels, with many characters and presumably involving matters of public concern, as early as the seventies, but Howells had strenuously resisted: "It seems to me that the people of the next age will look with as much amazement upon our big novels as we do upon Richardson's." Warner was not big enough to pull Howells out of his own orbit; that waited for Tolstoy, and though he always recognized the *Hazard* as his biggest achievement, not even Tolstoy could keep him in this field permanently. His final view was that "the phenomena of our enormous enterprise" were not of much use to fiction except in their relationship to the "miracles of the inner world," and in his conversation with T. S. Perry about Russian fiction, he even says of one writer, "I suppose really if he is very much of an artist he has not much philosophy." When, in his old age, he wrote *Years of My Youth*, he harked back to a clerical friend of days gone by who had reproached him for dealing in *A Modern Instance* with questions that had better be left to the church.

I thought he was wrong, but I am not sure that I so strenuously think so now; fiction has to tell a tale as well as evolve a moral, and either the character or the principle must suffer in that adjustment which life alone can effectively manage. I do not say ideally manage, for many of the adjustments of life seem to me cruel and mistaken. If it is in these cases that religion can best intervene, I suppose my old friend was right; at any rate, he knows now better than I, for he is where there is no manner of doubt, and I am still where there is every manner of doubt.

Personally I am far from believing that Howells did not handle the Tolstoyan kind of novel successfully, but in the light of these considerations, we may perhaps conjecture that it was his conscience rather than his own aesthetic temperament which led him to attempt it.[29]

CHAPTER TWO

MR. DEAN

I

Howells's service as "Dean of American Letters" was primarily a matter of his "Editor's Study" years, when he divided literary America into two parties by his championship of realism. And since this influence was exerted primarily as a critic, it may be desirable to begin by looking at him somewhat more closely in this aspect.

This may, however, be a less rewarding enterprise than we might have hoped. As we have already seen, Howells did not care much for criticism, did not believe that he had ever been helped by it or that he had ever greatly helped anybody else, though on the second count there were certainly many who disagreed with him. He believed, also, that criticism should be based on "principles," but he had no very elaborately formulated critical standards, and he had no critical "method" at all. Early in life he read Poe and admired his criticism, but he later called it "bitter, cruel, and narrow-minded." He read Schlegel and the English critical reviews. John P. Pritchard thinks he had surely heard of the *Poetics* and the *Ars Poetica*, but he does not attempt to trace his indebtedness to either Aristotle or Horace, contenting himself instead with pointing out resemblances. Howells does not cite Poe as authority for his view that the imagination cannot create anything—instead he cites Isaac Taylor's *Physical Theory of Another Life*—but the idea recalls Poe nevertheless. Howells also agreed with Poe that the artist is the best possible critic because he alone knows how literature is created, and if he wrote the piece on "Literary Criticism" in *The Round Table* for 1866 (III, 49) which has been assigned to him, then he also at one time believed that the critic's most important function was to point out faults, though the reason he gives for this is that the virtues of the work under consideration will have been sufficiently touted by the publisher, the writer's friends, and careless reviewers, while Poe believed they were self-evident. But this was certainly not Howells's settled view. When he reviewed Thomas Purnell's *Literature and its Professors*, he dissented decidedly from its author's view (which was also Poe's) that the critic should deal "solely with the disposal of the materials, and but incidentally with the quality of the materials themselves," or, in other words, that literature was merely what was written and that the critic's concern was solely with the writing. Howells knew, to the contrary, that "art is not produced for artists, or even for connoisseurs" but for people, and that people "rarely care for their work artistically. They care for it morally, personally, partially." On the validity of the general reader's reaction he vacillates however; sometimes he thinks it infallible in the long run; more often he believes that people have to be taught how to appreciate what is good. The classics, "the best things, the greatest things, the stellar and planetary things" are not kept in remembrance spontaneously but rather by "the zeal of those who love beauty and truth," and the new lights "which swim into our ken from the bounds of mystery where the promise of beauty and truth abides" are still more in need of "a favoring and fostering welcome."

Howells believed further that a work of art should always be judged by itself and not by what the reader knows or thinks he knows about the author personally. Literature makes its appeal through the mind, not the senses, and unless the reader understands what the author is trying to say, then nothing has been said. The critic's prime function is not to "judge" the work at all, but rather to place it "in such a light that the reader shall know its class, its function, its character" and to show that it "springs from the nature of a people, and draws its forces from their life, that its root is in their character, and that it takes form from their will and taste." Beyond this, he felt unable to lay down any critical law which had not been overthrown as often as the French government.

Yet he never feared to take sides in a critical controversy. About the most severe thing he ever wrote about James was said when he criticized him for being so noncommittal in *French Poets and Novelists*, where he betrayed "a certain nervousness that if he curtails his contradictory impressions he may not appear liberal enough." When Howells took charge of the "Study" he warned that he had prejudices, grudges, and opinions to express; later he owned frankly that "one of the evils of having very firm convictions is that you want to deny all merit to people who have different ones." In theory, however, he always recognized that the ideal critic was receptive to every kind of excellence, and he praised Lowell because he thought he had achieved this. Howells warned his readers that a book was not necessarily good because they liked it nor bad because they disliked it. "Remember that you are a consequence, not a cause of literature; seek the author's point of view, and be sure that you understand him before you correct him." Sainte-Beuve, whom Howells admired, once declared that "nothing is more painful to me than to see the disdain with which people treat respectable and distinguished writers of the second order, as if there were no place save for those of the first." Howells was in complete agreement. To him "the worst kind of bore" was the reader "who is always exacting supreme and final beauty in art. There is much beauty on the way to this ultimate sort which affords the right-minded a distinct pleasure."

II

But there is no doubt who the "right-minded" are. As a critic, Howells built everything around the great central obligation of the writer to give a true picture of human life. "Truth and sanity in fiction"—this was his criterion. "Let fiction cease to lie about life; let it portray men and women as they are, actuated by the motives and the passions in the measure we all know."

In addition to being demanded by truth, realistic fiction was demanded by democratic ideals. Howells recognized the historic service of romanticism in overthrowing the classical tradition.[1] But romanticism perished "because it came to look for beauty only" and often refused to face the facts of human nature, because it idealized human beings, fell in love with a dream, and then, disillusioned, rejected the real man or woman who had inspired the dream. In a democratic age, the aristocratic spirit seeks its last refuge in the realm of aesthetics; it must be driven thence. "Men are more like than unlike another; let us make them know one another better, that they may be all humbled and strengthened with a sense of their fraternity."

The fight was a bitter one while it lasted. In 1889 Norton spoke of Howells as suffering from an attack of Russian measles and William Roscoe Thayer wished he might be quarantined while it raged. Aldrich thought his mind unbalanced, and even Henry James declared that he was making Tolstoy himself a bore. In 1892 Horace E. Scudder thought that if Howells recommended a book, he would hereafter avoid reading it.[2] Howells himself wrote in retrospect that he soon had "every lover of romanticism" hating him and attributing much worse to him than anything he had said, "whatever I had thought." He admitted that for a while it was like living in a boiler factory, but when he found that the noise was not going to hurt him, it dwindled to a mere nuisance. In his last "Study" in 1892, he apologized for having opened the gate "with something too much of a bang" and for not achieving the civility of George William Curtis's "Easy Chair." He had tried to persuade readers to think well of "Common Honesty," but he feared she had "rather fewer friends" when he finished than when he had begun. Yet though he was now willing to admit tactical errors and see *Criticism and Fiction*, in which he had reprinted some of his "Studies," as a bottle of gall and wormwood, he did not really take anything back. "You cannot, at this day, be serious about romanticism, it is too much of a joke." While as to the application of his critical principles in his own fiction, even ten years later, when he was disappointed at the reception accorded *The Kentons*, he confessed to Brander Matthews:

I had hoped I was helping my people know themselves in the delicate beauty of their every day lives, and to find cause for pride in the loveliness of an apparently homely average, but they don't want it. They bray at my flowers picked from the fruitful fields of our common life, and turn aside from the thistles with keen appetites for the false and impossible. *Pazienza!*

Yet Howells was not without qualification either a champion of realism or an enemy of romance.[3] He says, "I like the real better than the ideal," and again, "I like a picture of the world more in a hand-glass than in a door-knob, a story better than a fantasy." Character was the element in fiction he loved best, and he thought characterization had a better chance with realism than romance, the realistic hero being an individual where the romantic hero is a type. For all that, he loved stories; despite his tendency to champion the "open ending," he even admits that he liked a "finished story"; it was the "singular shapeliness" of his novels that drew him to Leonard Merrick. He says that "any story that has been lived so transcends every story that has been fancied that but for the difficulty of knowing the stories which have been lived, no stories that have been fancied would be told." He also sometimes champions "books of adventure" as counteracting "the influence of fictitious adventures," which seems to me distinctly a nonaesthetic point of view. But on these occasions I fancy he is trying to be too consistent. He is condescending when he writes that he has "learned to be tolerant of the pleasure which other people find in plots, and tender to the hard necessity of making of them which the novelist is under," and even when he admits that "the picturesque, outlandish material" in Abraham Cahan's *Yekl* is more attractive to the reader than what Stephen Crane was using. But these statements do not stand alone. As a boy Howells was "inwardly all thrones, principalities, and powers, the foe of tyrants, the friend of good emperors, and the intimate of magicians, and magnificently apparalled," and he never quite got over this. "It is not only remarkable for being a good story, he writes of H. H. Boyesen's *Gunnar*, "which is distinction enough." Hamlin Garland's stories prompt the admission: "I like stirring adventure without bloodshed, as I find it in these pages." And though he found much fault with *The Right of Way* by Sir Gilbert Parker, he praised it as indicating "a psychological countercurrent in recent fiction," because Sir Gilbert was not operating

in a world where mere determinism rules, where there is nothing but the happening of things, and where this one or that one is important or unimportant according as things are happening to him or not, but has in himself no claim upon the reader's attention. Once more the novel begins to rise to its higher function, and to teach that men are somehow masters of their fate.

In his most candid moments he could even admit that "I am not sure I am quite logical in not caring for novels of adventure."

He tried to treat the materials of life itself in the same spirit. He tells us that when he went to Venice, he set his face from the first

against that romantic Venice which Byron, and the Byronic poets and novelists, had invented for the easy emotioning of the newcomer. . . . But that to which I was genuinely affectioned was the real life of the place, as I saw it in the present and read of it in the past.

Yet when he encountered Goldoni's plays there, he had to learn to like them.

I was an idealist in those days. . . . I knew the world chiefly through literature. I was all the time trying to see things as others had seen them, and I had a notion that, in literature, persons and things should be nobler and better than they are in the sordid reality; and this romantic glamour veiled the world to me, and kept me from seeing things as they are.

He owns, too, that he sometimes indulged in romancing, spinning fancies out of his own head about Venetian figures concerning whom he knew little, and that when he came to write *Venetian Life*,

it was as hard to speak of any ugliness in her, or of the doom written against her in the hieroglyphic seams and fissures of her crumbling masonry, as if the fault and penalty were mine.

Howells always tried to distinguish between romantic and "romanticistic." The romantic was purely fanciful or ideal.

The romance is of as great purity of intention as the novel, but it deals with life allegorically and not representatively; it employs types rather than characters and studies them in the ideal rather than the real; it handles the passions.

Or, as he puts it when contrasting Salvini and Jefferson as actors: "Realism is giving the thing instead of its symbol." "I do not think fancy a bad thing," he says. And again: "There are two kinds of fiction that I like almost equally well: a real novel and a pure romance." He can speak of "lovers of the supernatural, of which I am the first" or note that "an Italian would rather enjoy a fiction than know a fact—in which preference I am not ready to pronounce him unwise."

The point about romance, of course, is that it does not pretend to be reality, and Howells cultivated his taste for it early under the influence of such pastorals as Guarini's *Il Pastor Fido* and Tasso's *Aminta*. In "Bopeep" he himself wrote a pastoral which winds up at the court of old King Cole. His comic opera libretto, *A Sea Change*, is pure Gilbert and Sullivan, and *Priscilla* is a satisfactory dramatization of *The Courtship of Miles Standish*; though Howells is handicapped by the necessity of preserving Longfellow's measure, all his additions are effective. He did not insist on literal accuracy either in his own work or in that of others.[4] He was wiser and much less pernickety than the Mark Twain who

wrote "Fenimore Cooper's Literary Offences" in granting romantic license to that writer;[5] as a matter of fact, he considered Mark
Twain himself a romancer rather than a novelist, putting *A Connecticut Yankee*, as we have seen, at the top of his bent, and
though he obviously had some trouble with *Joan of Arc*, he was
more intelligent about it than many modern readers have been. He
discerns romanticism in Zola too, and though he obviously thinks
it a weakness here ("his intellectual youth had been nurtured on
the milk of romanticism at the breast of his mother-time"), he
gave him a very generous hearing,[6] Henry James he actually preferred as a romancer, being "sometimes sorry that he declared
even superficially" for realism, for though he thought Milly
Theale too idealized, James's best efforts still seemed to him "those
of romance," and "his best types have an ideal development."

Howells called Edward Bellamy's *Dr. Heidenhoff's Process*
"one of the finest feats in the region of romance which I had
known," though he does fling a sop to Cerberus when he adds that
"it seemed to me all the greater because the author's imagination
wrought in it on the level of average life, and built the fabric of its
dream out of common clay." In reading Edward Everett Hale's
If, Yes, and Perhaps (which includes "The Man without a Country"), he is willing to grant "the author's preposterous premises
almost before he asks you," and though he finds that Frank R.
Stockton's "conclusions . . . are almost invariably reached by impossible means," he still enjoys himself and feels that he has been
treated like a gentleman. Later, H. G. Wells's

fantastic romances have all an air of good faith; the illusion is so art-
fully respected that you are glad to be in it; the people are so much
like your every day acquaintance that you feel the impossibilities in
which they figure to be entirely probable; if things did not happen as
he says, that seems to be a fault in the frame of things, and no mistake
on his part.

And if this seems immensely tolerant, one may well wonder what
to make of his acceptance of such plays as William Gillette's *Secret Service,* which he qualified only on the ground that certain

conditions had to be accepted as "given," and of George M. Cohan's *Seven Keys to Baldpate*, which

brims with the sparkling impossibility which runs over in natural characters and logical situations, and leaves the spectator persuaded that if it did not all happen it ought to have happened, and very probably would, under the circumstances.[7]

What he could not—or would not—tolerate was romance which masqueraded as realism, the kind of romance which treats reality romantically; this is what he calls "romanticistic." "When romance takes an ideal subject and deals with it in a poetical manner, that is all right. But to give false impressions in what purports to be a picture of life is all wrong." This is not only because "half a truth is ever the worst of lies" but, even more, because this kind of fiction unfits its readers for facing life.

Most of the novels now published are absolutely worthless, or worse than worthless; they are not even to be classed with the patent medicines which, if they do not cure, will not kill. They are rather of the quality of those nostrums that dye the hair a beautiful greenish-purple, and leave a twitching palsy as their lasting effect; or of those more darkling drugs which promise a relief from neuralgia and implant a potential insanity.

In *The Minister's Charge* some of the people at Mrs. Harmon's hotel are said to have carried their novels about with them "clasped to their breasts with their fingers in them at the place where they were reading; they did not often speak of them, and apparently took them as people take opium." Howells loved Barrie's *Alice-Sit-by-the-Fire*, which deals with "a wildly romantic girl who has learnt life from the emotional drama," and there are other such characters in his own fictions.[8] For him this was no academic problem of literary criticism; it was a serious life-matter, as we may see by his reference to Napoleon, who, in his view, "lived morally in hallucinations and was full of illusions" but lacked true imagination. "He could not figure to himself any moral fact as it was, but only as he wished it to be. His work, esthetically regarded, was the fiction of a romanticistic novelist."

Even toward "romanticistic" fiction Howells is less intolerant, however, than one might have expected him to be. He knew that human beings have needs which realism will not always satisfy, and the "extremely good likenesses of the defunct cut in bas-relief" on Italian tombs shocked him. "Our simpering angels and marble lambs are better." He will not condemn George Borrow's "romancing" or "lying" in *The Bible in Spain* but prefers to call it "story-telling." As a type of popular fiction, "The Maiden Knight" is discussed far more tolerantly in *Their Silver Wedding Journey* than "Tears, Idle Tears" had been in *The Rise of Silas Lapham*, for though it is an unsatisfactory book, the author has talent, and it is not impossible that he may still do something worth while. "The Critical Bookshop" is a fantasy about a man who establishes a book store on the principle of stocking only the books that he personally thinks good. He nearly kills himself reading, finds only twenty-five current titles that he wishes to handle and stocks 1,000 copies of each, with the result that the customers who cannot find what they wanted go away insulted. He finally concludes that the whole principle upon which he has been operating is wrong.

What is the Republic of Letters, anyway? A vast, benevolent, generous democracy, where one may have what one likes, or a cold oligarchy where he is compelled to take what is good for him? Is it a restricted citizenship, with a minority representation, or is it universal suffrage?

It is on this basis too that Howells replies to William Morris's objection to the cheap holiday junk which men wear out their lives making, selling, and getting the money to buy.

We must allow the children, the old children, as well as the young ones, their pleasure in what is inferior and mediocre. . . . Some of us like to see life in literature as it is; but far more like to see it in circus dress, with spangled tights, riding three barebacked horses at once, hanging by its instep from trapezes and suffering massive paving-stones to be burst asunder on its stomach with sledge-hammers. Again we say, as we have always said, that there is no great harm in that: let the little children have their fairies; let the big children have their heroes.

Not "always," Mr. Howells, but only in your more understanding moods. Then bad taste is bad taste, not bad morals, and you can see that even those who prefer a solid diet on weekdays may relish pastry on Sundays. Howells criticizes Rider Haggard because his novels "make one forget life and all its cares and duties" while great fiction "make[s] you think of these, and shame[s] you into at least wishing to be a helpfuller and wholesomer creature than you are." For all that, the world being what it is, Haggard may well be performing "a work of beneficence" or "at least a work of mercy." Howells thought Balzac a "bit of a quack," but when he finds *Père Goriot* as destitute of repose as the theater, one cannot but remember his own love for the theater and wonder whether it did not satisfy in him a starved hunger for romance. Though I fully share his fondness for *The Old Homestead* of Denman Thompson, I cannot but ask whether he has not succumbed to the sentiment and romance which he elsewhere condemns when he writes:

It is the old homestead in the country which has remained the ideal of a nation tossed in a wider rush of interests and ambitions than ever tempted men before; the heart yearns forward or backward to it, "a home of ancient peace," amidst the turmoil and the strife.

Moreover, Howells can go even farther than this, as when he writes of Thomas Bailey Aldrich's fiction that anyone can learn the novelist's trade "more or less well; but romance requires gift, and he is one of the few who have gift," which seems to me pretty good for a man who elsewhere sees genius differing from talent only in degree.[9]

III

But what, then, of the kind of realism that Howells himself exemplified? The keynote sounds in the oft-quoted words from

Their Wedding Journey—"Ah! poor Real Life, which I love, can I make others share the delight I find in thy foolish and insipid face?"—which inspired William Lyon Phelps to remark that Howells "was a skilful player without any trumps." He himself strikes this note again and again. He once declared that he thought autobiography one of the most interesting types of literature for the astonishing reason that "few lives are in the extreme . . . ; they are only measurably dull or wicked, brilliant or good, and their level is that easy ground which we explore for ourselves in the affairs and characters of our neighbors," to which he adds that "perhaps that which fascinates us most in the self-portraiture of a distinguished man is the strong family likeness between his features and our own."

When, in a famous passage in his book on Hawthorne, James enumerated all the aspects of civilization that were lacking in America, and inquired what, then, was left for the novelist to write about, Howells replied bluntly that "the whole of human life" remained. The trouble with Americans was not lack of material; it was merely that instead of looking at life through their own eyes, they persisted in using "somebody else's literary telescope." Reading George Ade's *Fables in Slang* reinforced his feeling that "our life, our good, kind, droll, ridiculous American life, is really inexhaustible." Of a boyhood companion who served in the Civil War and afterwards had a long career as country editor, valiantly defending the right, he declares that

If his story could be faithfully written out, word for word, deed for deed, it would be far more thrilling than that of Monte Cristo, or any hero of romance; and so would the common story of any common life; but we cannot tell these stories, somehow.

Likewise he writes of Trollope's Lily Dale that

She has never been represented as very beautiful or brilliant, but merely as sweet and good and kind, with an unselfish commonsense which has served her well with every one but the wretch who stole her heart from her.

It is clear that Howells did not need to be kicked in order to be kept awake. Of one of his days of English travel he declares that he found it "full of exciting adventures," and then, perhaps remembering how little had happened, he adds: "But I ask almost as little of life as of literature in the way of incident, and perhaps the reader will not think my visit to Wells especially stirring." Finally he goes so far as to find "every man interesting, whether he thinks or unthinks, whether he is savage or civilized; for this reason we cannot thank the novelist who teaches us not to know, but to unknow our kind." Even nature, when she is at her best, "emulates the best Art and shuns the showiness and noisiness of the second-best." [10]

James described Howells's work in this aspect very vividly when he wrote:

He is animated by a love of the common, the immediate, the familiar and vulgar elements of life, and holds that in proportion as we move into the rare and strange we become vague and arbitrary; that the truth of representation, in a word, can be achieved only so long as it is in our power to test and measure it. He thinks scarcely anything too paltry to be interesting, that the small and vulgar have been terribly neglected, and would rather see an exact account of a sentiment or character he stumbles against every day than a brilliant evocation of a passion or a type he has never seen and does not particularly believe in. He adores the real, the natural, the colloquial, the moderate, the optimistic, the domestic, and the democratic; looking askance at exceptions and perversities and superiorities, at surprising and incongruous phenomena in general.

Nobody has ever doubted that there are limitations to Howells's realism, limitations, on the one hand, from the point of view of those committed, as James was, to "the superior case," and, on the other, to the "perversities" which so many writers of today adore. Mr. Twelvemough tells Mr. Homos that "our cultivated people have so little interest in . . . [working people] that they don't like to meet them, even in fiction; they prefer refined and polished ladies and gentlemen, whom they can have some sympathy with;

and I always go to the upper classes for my types." It must be said again that Mr. Twelvemough is not Howells; in some respects he is rather a caricature of Howells. Nevertheless both Howells and Twelvemough wrote for polite people, and when their characters were not ladies and gentlemen, they *were* presented from the point of view of ladies and gentlemen.

It is not correct to say that, either in theory or in practice, Howells excluded exceptional or unusual personages or events from his fiction. He has often been accused of this; sometimes he has even seemed to accuse himself, but he never really meant it. In 1907 he specifically denied to A. S. Van Westrum that realism meant an exclusive preoccupation with the commonplace.

On the contrary, realism makes all things its province, the uncommon as well as the every-day affairs of human existence, tragedy, disaster and crisis as well as the small round of daily events, but as these predominate, lead up to the climaxes and away from them again, their cause and result, realism holds that they, and not the momentary arrests of life, should be most important in the fiction that aims to reproduce that life with faithfulness.

It was part of the greatness of *War and Peace* itself that it makes "the great assertion of the sufficiency of common man in all crises, and the insufficiency of heroes." [11] Occasionally he himself was tempted to go in for "a supremely tragic outcome, a ruin spreading wide and sinking deep." One such temptation came with *The Son of Royal Langbrith*. But "the tragedy finally seemed too easy, and I shrank from it."

At the beginning of *Their Wedding Journey*, Basil and Isabel March, just married after a troubled courtship, are neither of them very young. "Basil looked at her fondly, as if he did not think her at all too old to be taken for a bride; and for my part I do not object to a woman's being of Isabel's age, if she is of good heart and temper." (You almost expect him to add: and if she has good health, and her teeth are sound.) Their first quarrel is not a serious one, and they are not long estranged because of it. But at the time it seemed that

All was over; the dream was past; the charm was broken. The sweetness of their love was turned to gall; whatever had pleased them in their loving moods was loathsome now, and the things they had praised a moment before were hateful.

When he receives the New York offer in *A Hazard of New Fortunes*, this same Basil March, though not actively unhappy, is professionally speaking, a disappointed man. As a New York editor, he is admirable in many ways, and when he stands up for Lindau to Dryfoos, he even takes on a touch of heroism, yet he never loses a certain ineptness. And Lindau himself, though he voices many of Howells's beliefs, is a combination of saint, fanatic, hero, and "boozer."

All this is characteristic of Howells. In *A Chance Acquaintance* Miles Arbuton is a hero of sorts when saving Kitty from the dog, but the scene is so managed that the girl loses its heroism in its humor. Mrs. Lapham, her husband's conscience through most of the book, fails him when he needs her most, so that he is left to face his greatest ordeal alone. Nobody can say that Dan Mavering does not suffer deeply and sincerely when he believes himself to have lost Alice Pasmer. But he does not lose his appetite, and in three weeks "he had begun to reconcile himself to his fate, as people do in their bereavements by death." He thinks he ought to send the girl's gifts back to her, as lovers always do in novels, but he is frustrated by the fact that he cannot figure out how to wrap them! Even in the short stories this same note is struck. When the hero of "The Magic of a Voice" finally meets the girl whose voice had enchanted him, he finds her "short and of rather a full figure"; though "not plain, she was by no means the sort of beauty who had lived in his fancy for the year past." And Margaret Green of "The Critical Bookstore" has "unfailing grace" but experiences great difficulty in remembering to close her mouth!

For Howells, then, realism was basically a matter of seeing life steadily and seeing it whole, and of keeping things in their proper proportions. He was not concerned to exclude the heroic from fiction, but he was concerned not to allow it to play a more important part than it does in life. And in life he did not believe that human character is most clearly revealed in great crises.

Our common notion of tragedy is that it alters the nature of those involved, as if it were some spiritual chemistry combining the elements of character anew. But it is merely an incident of our being, and, for all we can perceive, is of no more vital effect than many storms in the material world.

Its general tendency, indeed, is to stun the people involved in it, reducing everything to a few fundamental motives in which all men are basically alike. In *Their Wedding Journey* the running down of a canal boat in Chapter III reveals only human fatuity in the passengers. Tragedy can come to the "light and foolish" as well as "the wise and weighty natures," but it does not basically modify either. After Denton's tragic death in *The World of Chance*, the earth closes over "the hapless wretch for whom the dream of duty tormenting us all, more or less, had turned to such a hideous nightmare, and those whom his death threatened even more than his life drew consciously or unconsciously a long breath of freedom." Specifically, Mrs. Denton's fundamentally light, happy nature, which has been unscarred by poverty, undergoes no fundamental change as the result of her husband's madness and suicide or the loss of her children either.

In all this there is of course a certain comfort: nothing is ever quite as bad as it threatened to be, and nothing comes to us that we cannot, in the last analysis, endure. If life "treats the elements of drama" with "a certain caprice," and "mars the finest conditions of tragedy with a touch of farce," if "a headache darkens the universe while it lasts, a cup of tea really lightens the spirit bereft of all reasonable consolations."

The house of mourning is decorously darkened to the world, but within itself it is also the house of laughing. Bursts of gayety, as heartfelt as its grief, relieve the gloom, and the stricken survivors have their jests together, in which the thought of the dead is tenderly involved, and a fond sense, not crazier than many others, of sympathy and enjoyment beyond the silence, justifies the sunnier mood before sorrow rushes back, deploring and despairing, and making it all up again with the conventional fitness of things.

Mrs. Savor serves coffee while Mr. Peck lies dying—"life in its vulgar kindliness touched and made friends with death, claiming it a part of nature too"—and Clem, of *Ragged Lady*, who has no regrets for her marriage with Hinkle, blasted though it was by his early death, and is thankful for the time she had with him, must still admit that "sometimes it doesn't seem as if it had happened." At first she felt that he must be coming back. "But that had to go." And "after a while even the loss of him seemed to go."

But such comfort is bought with a price. "There is no condition of life that is wholly acceptable, and none that is not tolerable when once it establishes itself." This is considerably harder to take than George Eliot's "Life inflicts no injuries that life itself cannot heal." Because joy has been robbed of its power along with pain, both have lost stature. It is terrible when Juliet kills herself with Romeo's dagger, but it would have been terrible too, in a much less meaningful way, if she had gone home and married Paris. When, in *An Imperative Duty*, Olney refuses to be shocked by Rhoda's revelation that she is part Negro, Howells tells us that "as tragedy the whole affair had fallen to ruin." And though Olney defies the ban on miscegenation, he is neither punished nor re-warded for it. He and Rhoda find "the common share of happi-ness" together, neither more nor less, "and when he saw that even his love failed at times to make life happy for his wife, he pitied her, and he did not blame her." All the old heroic passions have been carefully fenced out.

No other single utterance of Howells's has done him so much harm among those who stress the limitations of his realism as his famous statement about "the more smiling aspects of life" being the more American.[12] This has been much discussed of recent years. E. H. Cady has argued that even in "the early summery novels" happiness is likely to be "overcast by social complexities and incompatibility" and that the "important" novels "were mainly pessimistic and critical in tone and intent." [13] Everett Carter shows that the phrase antedates Howells's interest in the Chicago Anarchists.[14] Benjamin Townley Spencer relates the saying to the American tradition and background.[15] Clara M. Kirk points out that the considerations involved take in James as well as Howells.[16] But probably the profoundest commentary is that of Lionel Trilling, who concludes that though the statement may have been ill-advised, "our interpretation of it, the vehemence with which we are likely to press its meaning, tells us . . . more about ourselves than about Howells. It raises the question of why we believe . . . that evil is of the essence of reality." [17]

The discussion was occasioned by Dostoevsky's novel, *Crime and Punishment*, and all Howells actually says, when the unfortunate passage is read in context, is that the American novel is not the Russian novel, that one cannot achieve American realism by imitating Russian realism, that common people are better off in America than they are in Europe, and that in this country there is a "large, cheerful average of health and success and happy life" which is characteristically American, while the "sin and suffering and shame" which we also possess in abundance, relate rather to individuals than to classes. Moreover, he granted that this condition was already changing for the worse, and his subsequent revisions of the passage show that his sense of the change was accelerating. Barring the use of a somewhat unfortunate Pollyanna-like phrase, he was hardly saying more than he had written the year before in *Modern Italian Poets*:

As an average American, I have found myself very greatly embarrassed when required, by Count Alfieri, for example, to hate tyrants. Of course I do hate them in a general sort of way; but never having seen one, how is it possible for me to feel any personal fury toward them? When the later Italian poets ask me to loathe spies and priests I am equally at a loss.

Howells's realism was not always as decorous as many persons believe it to be; neither did it seem as decorous in his time as it now appears to us. If he did not write about nakedness, he did believe that the novelist must always be sensible of the fact that people are naked under their clothes. If it is true that he did not care to spend his life in police courts, it is also true that he never closed his eyes to what went on in police courts and other unpleasant places. In 1882 he visited the Harlot's Market in London, and the Boston jail and flophouse scenes in *The Minister's Charge* were not written by a man who had never viewed these things. Both "Scene" in *Suburban Sketches* and "Police Report" in *Impressions and Experiences* testify further to Howells's observation of the harsher side of metropolitan life.

Certainly Howells's contemporaries in general did not consider him a Pollyanna. O. W. Firkins is misleading when he writes that in the novels

adultery is never pictured; seduction never; divorce once and sparingly (*A Modern Instance*); marriage discordant to the point of cleavage only once and in the same novel with the divorce; crime only once with any fullness (*The Quality of Mercy*); politics never; religion passingly and superficially; science only in crepuscular psychology; mechanics, athletics, bodily exploits and collisions, very rarely.

It seems doubtful that any writer can be adequately described by reference to what he does not do. But let us look at George N. Bennett's positive statement:

He depicts death in many forms including suicide (*The World of Chance*); the frequently terrible stresses of "successful" marriages (*Miss Bellard's Inspiration, The Rise of Silas Lapham*); the tragedy of misunderstanding between parents and children (*A Hazard of New Fortunes, The Landlord at Lion's Head, The Minister's Charge, The Undiscovered Country*); bitter alienation from life (*New Leaf Mills*); acute alcoholism (*The Lady of the Aroostook*); the perversion of maternal love into a calculated appraisal of a daughter's social marketability (*The Landlord at Lion's Head*).

Nor does this by any means exhaust the list.

Even aside from these serious and tragic themes, Howells refers to many matters which must have caused considerable eyebrow-lifting among the genteel readers of his time. His early *New York Times* editorial on "Esthetic Reporting" (September 28, 1865) views both suicide and execution with detachment and without emotion, considering only the skill with which Parisian reporters handle it. Of a cat observed in a Venetian church he remarks coolly that "I do not think this cat has the slightest interest in the lovely Madonna of Bellini which hangs in the sacristy; but I suspect him of dreadful knowledge concerning the tombs in the church." Lottie Kenton notes the generally ignored stench of the Dutch canals. In Boston horsecars "all the breath is in common"; in New York, "pulverized manure . . . is constantly taken into people's stomachs and lungs." And what are we to make of this in *Suburban Sketches* ("A Romance of Real Life"): "When Mrs. Hapford appeared, Julia fell back, and, having deftly caught a fly on the door-post, occupied herself in picking it to pieces, while she listened to the conversation of the others"?

"Do not trouble yourself about standards or ideals"—such was Howells's advice to young writers; "but try to be faithful and natural: remember that there is no greatness, no beauty, which does not come from truth to your own knowledge of things." Certainly he praised many whose realism was starker than his own. It is true that he placed Frank Norris ahead of Stephen Crane because, like Zola, he was poet as well as realist. "Life is squalid and cruel and vile and hateful, but it is noble and tender and pure and lovely too." It is true also that by the time he read *Blood and Sand* he said he was now willing to admit that his "nerves had weakened" since the days when he had thought fidelity to the fact enough in itself. But this did not keep him from praising either Crane or Blasco-Ibáñez. He acknowledged the painful impressions made by both Crane and Abraham Cahan. But

If we have any quarrel with the result, we cannot blame the authors, who have done their duty as artists and for the moment have drawn aside the thick veil of ignorance which parts the comfortable few from the uncomfortable many in this city.

He found beauty in Crane's *Maggie* itself.

This will be foolishness, I know, to the many foolish people who cannot discriminate between the material and the treatment in art, and think that beauty is inseparable from daintiness and prettiness, but I do not speak to them.

Of one of Gorky's books he wrote that it "saturates the soul with despair, and blights it with the negation which seems the only possible truth in the circumstances." In February 1910 he clashed with the dying Mark Twain over the Georgia realist, Will N. Harben: "You seem to require a novelist to be true to the facts and if the facts are not pleasant, to be pleasant himself. That seems rather difficult."

It must also be kept in mind that though Howells always insisted that the moral tendency of a work of art must be sound, he wanted it expressed implicitly, not explicitly. It was his conviction that "fiction, like the other arts, can only do good . . . indirectly; when it becomes hortatory, it is in danger of becoming dull, that is to say, suicidal." To a certain extent, he felt that the great writers of New England's "flowering" had erred on this count, and one of Elizabeth Stuart Phelps's novels inspired him to tell Higginson that while he thought there might "very well be novels of purpose—and sermons," they ought not to read of weekdays. Yet he also told Higginson that "while I despise the *Tendenzromanskt* as much as anybody, I should be ashamed and sorry if my words did not unmistakably teach a lenient, generous, and liberal life: that is, I should feel degraded merely to amuse people." In his very first "Study" he took exception to the view that "art for art's sake" was a "Greek" doctrine, "as if the Greekest of Greek art were not for religion's sake, as the Greeks understood it." If a man had any conscience, being a novelist involved being a moralist. His objections to Scott were entered on moral quite as much as aesthetic grounds—"his mediaeval ideals, his blind Jacobitism, his intense devotion to aristocracy and royalty; his acquiescence into the division of men into noble and ignoble, patrician and plebeian, sovereign and subject, as if it were the law of God." Of Samuel Richardson he declares that

He has all the faults there are, except the prime fault of writing for writing's sake, or contriving a work which shall not live again in conduct. He never even imagined a thing so vain and stupid as that; he was not a man of the sort of imagination which begins and ends in its own foolish toys.

And when he comes to Brieux, who, according to Howells's views might well be judged by severer standards than those applicable to eighteenth- or nineteenth-century writers, he says: "Of course he writes plays with a purpose, as every dramatist has done from the beginning, unless he has the soul of a clown or a mountebank merely." From the beginning perhaps, but even more today. As early as 1888 Howells declared that

Christ and the life of Christ is at the moment inspiring the literature of the world as never before, and raising it up a witness against waste and want and war. It may confess Him, as in Tolstoï's work it does, or it may deny Him, but it cannot exclude Him; and in the degree that it ignores His spirit, modern literature is artistically inferior. In other words, all good literature is now Christmas literature. The old heathenish axiom of art for art's sake is as dead as great Pan himself, and the best art now tends to be art for humanity's sake.

Later, in 1903, he was sure that "we have indeed in our best fiction, gone back to mysticism, if indeed we were not always there in our best fiction, and the riddle of the painful earth is again engaging us with the old fascination."

Howells's theory in this matter seldom gives the impression of having been framed by a logician, and it would be foolish to affirm that he never contradicted himself. Of Maria Edgeworth and her contemporaries he felt that "fiction had not yet conceived of the supreme ethics which consist in portraying life truly and letting the lesson take care of itself." If the writer's evaluation of life was sound, if he had not lost what Dante calls "the good of the understanding," and if he had kept his materials in proper proportions, he could not possibly mislead his readers, for morality "penetrates all things." "Bad art is a vice; untruth to nature is the eighth of the seven deadly sins; a false school of literature is a seminary of crime." How passionately Howells believed this may be seen in the truthful picture he gave of what he and his companions did in *A Boy's Town*, though he was writing for *Harper's Young People*. He knows they were not models, and he apologizes for them when they do wrong, but he cannot misrepresent them. Walter J. Meserve is probably right when he argues that Howells's tendency to identify truth with morality comes ultimately from Swedenborg.[18] Even this will not solve all our difficulties, however, for we still have a Howells capable of telling us both that "if Tolstoy is the greatest imaginative writer who ever lived, it is because, beyond all others, he has written in the spirit of kindness, and not denied his own personal complicity with his art" and that "Jane Austen was the first and the last of the English novelists to treat material with entire truthfulness. Because she did this, she remains the most artistic of the English novelists." Yet Howells must surely have known that being kind or truthful would not in itself suffice to make a writer an artist. I think he is confused too when he calls *Uncle Tom's Cabin* "almost the greatest work of imagination that we have produced in prose," and then turns about to deny that it is a novel because it is fundamentally didactic, as if didacticism and aestheticism were somehow less reconcilable in a novel than in other kinds of literature. But after all, some of these "contradictions" are less contradictions than shifts of emphasis, and with many of these questions it is less a matter of right or wrong than of more or less. Howells *was* consistent (1) in his opposition to overt moralizing, superimposed upon his materials by the author and (2) his conviction that through selection and arrangement the artist must assess the significance of what he describes in its relationship to the total meaning of human life. It is not out of order that Silas Lapham, common man though he is, should ask Bartley Hubbard, come to interview him, "So you want my life, death, and Christian sufferings?" [19]

On the other hand, we have Howells's own word for it that he sometimes failed to distinguish between truth and fact or between life and art.

I have never been able to see much difference between what seemed to me Literature and what seemed to me Life. If I did not find life in what professed to be literature, I disabled its profession, and possibly from this habit, now inveterate with me, I am never quite sure of life unless I find literature in it. Unless the thing seen reveals to me an intrinsic poetry, and puts on phrases that clothe it pleasingly to the imagination, I do not much care for it; but if it will do this, I do not mind how poor or squalid it shows at first glance; it challenges my curiosity and keeps sympathy.

Despite its inexact terminology, this sounds harmless enough in itself. But it did lead Howells (especially in *Criticism and Fiction*, where he seems considerably more dogmatic than in his other writings) to ignoring the importance, and even the existence, of style, ruling the personality of the creator out of his creation, and apparently looking forward to a day when art shall disappear and a scientific, factual report concerning life be enthroned in its place. In such moods he was capable of arguing that because life experience does not arrange itself in terms of plot, novels do not need plots either, and that since life is not symmetrical art does not need to be. There is no more scornful passage in *Criticism and Fiction* than the tirade in Section II against those who prefer a model of a grasshopper to a real grasshopper, but Howells surely knew that insofar as any writer deals with either typical or ideal human behavior, or shapes his materials to what Galsworthy was to call "a spire of meaning," and insofar as he himself preferred Turgenev's selectivity to what he considered the all-inclusiveness of a Whitman, the use of the model grasshopper was quite unavoidable. There is no point then in praising Goethe for allowing characters to appear and disappear in his novels quite as they would in life or in looking forward to the time when Frank Norris, as he grows and develops, shall "achieve something of the impartial fidelity of the photograph."

Howells advised young writers not to think about style either. "If you do your work well, patiently, faithfully, truly," then style, which "has been grossly overvalued" in the hierarchy of literary values, "will infallibly be added unto you." It was one of the glories of Tolstoy that for the English reader at least he had no style, only an "absolute plainness," a "transparency . . . unclouded by any mist of the personality which we mistakenly value in style, and which ought no more to be there than the artist's personality should be in a portrait." But this was not peculiar to Tolstoy; it was also true, in greater or lesser degree, of Turgenev, Zola, de Maupassant, and the Goncourts; once Howells even commits the supreme absurdity of finding it in Dante and Shakespeare! And if you object that he is ruling the literary quality out of literature, he is not disturbed. "I do not know how it is with others to whom these books of Tolstoi's have come, but for my own part I cannot think of them as literary in the artistic sense at all." He can even look forward to the end of art with the complacency of the Ancients in Shaw's *Back to Methuselah*:

It is quite imaginable that when the great mass of readers, now sunk in the foolish joys of mere fable, shall be lifted to an interest in the meaning of things through the faithful portrayal of life in fiction, then fiction the most faithful may be superseded by a still more faithful form of contemporaneous history.

But was not Howells himself a stylist? Of course he was, and he knew it. "Now and then your diction seems to me careless or self-forgetful," he wrote Robert Herrick, "but that does not matter." If we are to take what we have just heard him say at face value, it certainly would not matter—nor be worth pointing out either. But with Hamlin Garland it did matter:

You have got some newspaper diction on your pen point, and you must shake it out. You are so good that you can afford to say things with the distinction they deserve from the best. . . . Be plain as you please; there is nothing better than homespun; but the clothing-store is no place for your thoughts to dress themselves.

And when Albert Bigelow Paine publishes his great biography of Mark Twain, he goes after him in great style:

At times . . . [your book] grovels in newspaper parlance. *How* can you bear to write "as does"? What do you mean by an "ill man"? I suppose, a sick man; but an "ill man" is a bad man. Your book ought to be proof-read for a permanent edition.

But Howells does better than this. He speaks of "the great truth of art, which is above all facts." Even when he affirms that "the moral superiority of good art of any kind is in its truth," he can add that "we can have truth without any art whatever." He praised Pett Ridge because his work "was not merely a transcript, but that sort of truth which fact precipitates after passing through the alembic of a friendly imagination." And when Zola died, Howells showed that his methods did not always reflect his intentions.

He fancied himself working like a scientist who has collected a vast number of specimens, and is deducing principles from them. But the fact is, he was always working like an artist, seizing every suggestion of experience and observation, turning it to the utmost account, piecing it out by his invention, building it up into a structure of fiction where its origin was lost to all but himself, and often even to himself. He supposed that he was recording and classifying, but he was creating and vivifying.

Howells allowed Mr. Homos, inspired by the World's Columbian Exposition and his memories of Altruria, to declare that while nature is irregular and picturesque, the works of man should be symmetrical. He himself declares that "art can never give the thing itself, but only the likeness of the thing." "A touch of truth" is all we need and perhaps all we can endure. "We can stand only a very little radium; the captured sunshine burns with the fires that heat the summers of the farthest planets; and we cannot handle the miraculous substance as if it were mere mineral." In a sense, then, "all portraiture of life on the terms that fiction proposes is impossible," which, whether Howells knew it or not, is precisely what Stevenson said. It is all a matter of accepting conventions and granting a "preposterous premise." If a man's writing does not "express precisely the meaning of the author" and "say *him*," it says nothing and is nothing. "Touch" is what is needed to give delight in any art, and if a writer does not have it, his other gifts are of no avail. Literature cannot use fact as fact but only "as the material of effect."

Sometimes Howells tries to reconcile his contradictory utterances upon this point. Advising the young writer not to concentrate upon style, he qualifies by adding that "he may from time to time advantageously call a halt, and consider whether he is saying the thing clearly and simply." He does not wish him to speak "barely or sparely," and he is sure that "if he has a good ear" he will speak "gracefully and musically." He defends the obscurity of *The Sacred Fount* by Henry James on the ground that we do not understand all we encounter in life either, but he recognizes the weakness of this argument as soon as he has made it, for he adds:

Of course, it can be answered that we are *in* creation like characters in fiction, while we are outside of the imitation and spectators instead of characters. . . . Perhaps, however, I am asking more for Mr. James than he would have me.

He adds that he himself has "mastered the secret" of *The Sacred Fount*, "though, for the present I am not going to divulge it." But that is abdicating the critic's function, as James, if he wrote an incomprehensible book, abdicated the creator's. For if art fails when it does not achieve communication, what of criticism?

I do not believe that all Howells's inconsistencies can be reconciled. He was not a trained logician; he was a practicing writer; with him circumstances modified stresses; and though he sometimes gave theory too much weight, he was generally wiser and more generous as a creative writer than he was when he was giving and taking thwacks in the great war of realism vs. romance. The obviously wrong-headed views he sometimes expressed came off the top of his head; he meant them with that part of him which enjoyed "banging the babes of Romance about," but he could not possibly have meant them as a creator of literature. And it may be that this is one of the reasons why he rated criticism so low in comparison to the writing of fiction itself.

It is quite legitimate to prefer a more romantic type of subject matter than Howells favored in fiction, but it is surely getting everything but the point to suppose that he loved dullness for dullness' sake. "The novelist who could interpret the common feelings of commonplace people," he makes one of his characters say, "would have the answer to 'the riddle of the painful earth' on his tongue." Like Wordsworth, like George Eliot, he believed that the commonplace is meaningful because life itself is meaningful, not only in exceptional persons under exceptional circumstances but in all human beings all the time. And he infuses almost a religious significance into his realistic outlook when he declares that the realist

finds nothing insignificant; all tells for destiny and character; nothing that God has made is contemptible. . . . He cannot look upon human life and declare this or that thing unworthy of notice, any more than the scientist can declare a fact of the material world beneath the dignity of his inquiry.

All in all, it would seem more reasonable to believe that the romantics found life a bore than that Howells thought it so.

IV

One more question must, I think, be asked in closing: Did Howells's critical principles ever cause him to be unfair as a critic?

I am obliged to reply that I think he was unfair to Dickens, Stevenson, and Rostand, and I think he was somewhat unfair to the historical novel as a type.

During his early life, Howells was, without important qualification, an admirer of Dickens. He has a reasonable number of references to and quotations from Dickens in both his early letters and writings, and when he went to England, he looked for Dickensian types and sites there. His early, uncompleted serial, "The Independent Candidate," in the Ashtabula *Sentinel,* has a Thackeray-like digression in which the author explains that he lacks the "high-topping quaintness of Lippard" and other trashy novelists of the day but that he is following, at goodly distance, the less dazzling authors of *Pendennis* and *Bleak House.*

He had tickets for all Dickens's readings in Boston, and he met the novelist at Longfellow's and again at Fields's in 1867, when he wrote his mother that

he was everything in manner that his books would make you wish him to be. . . . His face is very flexible, and he is very genial and easy in talk. . . . But it was hard at the moment to remember that this man so near me was so great and had done so much to please and better the world.

To his sister Victoria he reported of Dickens's reading that "it was the perfection of acting, and as the parts were all well played, it was better than any theatre I ever saw."

By this time Howells had already published the review of *Our Mutual Friend* which was to remain by all means his best piece of Dickensian criticism.[20] At this time he had "slight patience, and less sympathy, with the criticism which accuses Mr. Dickens of exaggeration." He credited Dickens with a Shakespearean universality of art and feeling and insisted that if Wegg and Podsnap were to be condemned, Falstaff and Sancho Panza must fall with them. Though he condemned Boffin's ruse as an insult to the reader, he found Bella Wilfer "delicious" and thought the development of her character well-handled. He also praised the book for "the intimate friendship with the nature of fields and woods and the nature of docks and streets" shown in it, and for the

warm-blooded sympathy with poverty and lowliness; the . . . scorn of solemn and respectable selfishness, and of mean and disreputable cunning; the . . . subtle analysis of the motives and feelings and facts of crime; the . . . exuberant happiness in love and lovers; the . . . comprehensiveness of what Carlyle calls "inarticulate nature"; the . . . gay, fantastic humor; the . . . capricious pathos

that Dickens had displayed. That same year in *The Nation* Howells went after J. G. Holland because he had denied both Dickens and Thackeray the name of Christian.

The rebuke of worldly-mindedness and vanity and uncharitableness which breaks from Thackeray, the unfailing advocacy of the cause of the despised, the poor, and the prisoner in the works of Charles Dickens, prove nothing of their love of Christianity because the name of Christ is not in their works. Does Mr. Holland wear a crucifix about him? Kingsley, though a traitor to the cause of popular reform, and the inventor of the odious muscular piety of second-rate modern fictions, is Christian, because he calls on the name of the Lord; and Ruskin, who has lately discovered the divine beauty of slavery, is likewise a Christian for the like reason.

Nor are these the only kind words young Howells gave the great Victorian. Reviewing Bartlett's *Familiar Quotations* in 1868, he calls Dickens, sparingly represented there, the one who "more than any [other] living author,—perhaps more than Shakespeare himself,—has supplied current phrases and expressions." And ten years later, when Houghton, Osgood brought out an edition of Dickens, he spoke of "the glamour of that great genius."

What, then, caused Howells to change his mind about Dickens? It has been suggested [21] that Lowell was influential here, but the basic cause of the shift would seem to have been his commitment to the twin-cause of realism and modernism in fiction and the notion he developed that the "progress" which had occurred in the art of fiction had somehow resulted in setting all the old masters except Jane Austen aside. "He dreams of an advance in art like what there is in science," observed Stevenson shrewdly in "A Humble Remonstrance"; "he thinks of past things as radically dead; he thinks a form can be outlived; a strange immersion in his own history; a strange forgetfulness of the history of the race!" And nothing that Howells wrote during the days when his critical controversies made him a storm center awakened more antagonism than his attack on Dickens and Thackeray.[22]

It was made quite casually, and apparently without any idea of fluttering the dovecotes, in an article on Henry James in the *Century* for November 1882. Howells evidently regarded what he had to say as axiomatic to such an extent that the reaction took him entirely by surprise. In fact, he could not remember exactly what he had said until a copy of the magazine reached him in Europe. On November 16, Edmund Gosse wrote him from England that he was glad he had been born "in the good old times when . . . [Dickens and Thackeray] were thought good enough for week-day reading." And he added a piece of doggerel:

MOTTO FOR THE AMERICAN CRITIC

Ho! the old school! Thackeray, Dickens!
Throw them out to feed the chickens.
Ho! the new school! James and ————
Lay the flattery on with trowels.

Howells replied that he did not believe he had "arraigned" the Victorians. "I suspect that no Englishman could rate them higher than I do." But three days later he wrote Roswell Smith in New York that whatever he had said, he would stand by it, and "should only wish to amplify and intensify the opinions" that had been objected to. "I knew what I was talking about, and they don't know at all what they are talking about."

Here, then, at last, is the offending passage:

The art of fiction has, in fact, become a finer art in our day than it was with Dickens and Thackeray. We could not suffer the confidential attitude of the latter now, nor the mannerism of the former, any more than we could endure the prolixity of Richardson or the coarseness of Fielding. These great men are of the past—they and their methods and interests; even Trollope and Reade are not of the present. The new school derives from Hawthorne and George Eliot rather than any others; but it studies human nature much more in its wonted aspects, and finds its ethical and dramatic examples in the operation of lighter but not really less vital motives. The moving accident is certainly not its trade; and it prefers to avoid all manner of dire catastrophes. It is largely influenced by French fiction in form; but it is the realism of Daudet rather than the realism of Zola that prevails with it, and it has a soul of its own which is above the business of recording the rather brutish pursuit of a woman by a man, which seems to be the chief end of the French novelist. This school, which is so largely of the future as well as the present, finds its chief exemplar in Mr. James; it is he who is shaping and directing American fiction, at least.

Though only the most hopelessly "up-to-date" critics could be expected to echo these sentiments today, the passage can hardly be described as an "attack" upon either Dickens or Thackeray. What Howells does, rather, is to dismiss both of them with a wave of the hand. As he saw it, they were essentially "untruthful" writers, they and all their colleagues and followers, among whom Howells named, at one time or another, Bulwer, Reade, Dumas, Balzac, Feuillet, Ohnet, Valera, Gogol, and Dostoevsky. When Van Wyck Brooks interviewed Howells he was told that

Dickens was essentially a cold man. He was a born actor and his effects were those of an actor. He was never really touched himself. There is an element of claptrap in many of his highly emotional scenes.

The pathos of the *Christmas Books* was "false and strained; the humor largely horse-play; the characters theatrical; the joviality pumped; the psychology commonplace; the sociology alone funny." When he wrote of the Christmas celebration on Boston's Beacon Hill, Howells even had to drag in Dickens in order to credit him with "repaganizing" Christmas "in a saturnalia of overeating and drinking." He will not even trust Dickens's vernacular, for "he had not a good ear, and he had no scruple in perverting or inventing forms, if it suited his purpose." If he were to be justified it must be as a predecessor of Pett Ridge! In the light of such judgments, it is no wonder that Joseph Pennell exclaims that "when a man incidentally mentions that Dickens' work 'is trash,' I feel like stopping the production of American novels" or that W. C. Cobley should echo "the disgruntled reader who ex-claimed: 'Why Eden Phillpotts is a great writer and Dickens and Thackeray are not' is not a question of literary criticism, it's a conundrum." [23]

Even during the middle period, however, there were more friendly estimates of Dickens. In *My Literary Passions* he was a "mighty magician" (though practicing a "very rough magic") and a "masterful artist."

The base of his work is the whole breadth and depth of humanity itself. It is helplessly elemental, but it is not the less grandly so, and if it deals with the simpler manifestations of character, character affected by the interests and passions rather than the tastes and preferences, it certainly deals with the larger moods through them.

Two years before, in an article on Tolstoy,[24] he had admitted his passionate early affection for Dickens and called him "a great master" still, though he was always sure that he was "making it up." He was a better artist than Thackeray because, though his plots "are not such as come out of his characters," as they should, he does get his plot "to stand upon its legs and walk off," while Thackeray "is always holding his figures up from behind, and commenting upon them, and explaining them." In *Heroines of Fiction*, though dealing mainly with Dickens's female characters, he did not confine himself entirely to them. He now saw Dickens as "a mighty imagination, whose vices grew upon him with his virtues, under the immense favor he almost instantly achieved." But he never gives us "the open air, never the light of day, always the air of the theatre, always the light of the lamps."

In a sense the wheel was coming full circle, The elderly Howells did not take up the same attitude toward Dickens that the youth had staked out but he came much closer to it than the doughty warrior of the "Study" years. *David Copperfield* now ranked with the great novels. In 1902 he praised Dickens because though his characters might be puppets,

he was true to them; but better than this, he was true to certain needs and hopes of human nature. . . . His work made always for equality, for fraternity, and if he sentimentalized the world, he also in equal measure democratized it.

In 1903 he recalled his first reading of *Bleak House* among the enchanted hours of life, and in 1909 he went to the rescue of Dickens against Meredith. In 1911, when *Silas Lapham* was read in a freshman English course at Cornell, along with novels by Scott, Dickens, Thackeray, and George Eliot, he rejoiced in the "high company" it had enjoyed. But the most interesting passage dates from 1918 and relates to *Great Expectations*:

An amazingly meaty book, by far one of Dickens's best. It amazes me by its variety and fulness and makes me ashamed of ever slighting Dickens in my opinions. We ought to have several lives—not so many as a cat, but far more than most men, so as to correct the mistakes of one in another.

With Stevenson I fear Howells's relations were not quite free of personal animus. So far as I know, *Strange Case of Dr. Jekyll and Mr. Hyde* is the only fiction by this "inevitably . . . charming and sympathetic writer" that Howells ever praised, and he commended this for its "lesson." When James, who admired Stevenson, praised him in the *Century* in 1888, Howells called it "really the most remarkable piece of shinning round the question I ever saw. I fancy it was something he was asked to do." In 1910, in a letter to William Lyon Phelps, thanking him for a friendly article, he went out of his way to chide him for having praised Stevensen too. "Stevenson is food for babes—boy babes—in his fiction, though he is a true, rare poet," to which he adds a revealing postscript, obviously written later, "The doctor has just reported my wife a little better. I am sorry I don't, won't or can't praise R.L.S."

Stevenson had admired *The Lady of the Aroostook* and *The Undiscovered Country*. In "A Humble Remonstrance," he had objected, as the leading romanticist of his day, to Howells's adherence to "all the poor little orthodoxies" then current. Howells's own work, he thought, was "of a contrary, I had almost said of a heretical, complexion. A man, as I read him, of an originally strong romantic bent—a certain glow of romance still resides in many of his books, and lends them their distinction." But it was not this that caused the trouble.

After reading *A Modern Instance*, which he interpreted as an anti-divorce novel, Stevenson wrote Howells a letter which was only less outrageous than it was ridiculous, canceling an invitation to a meeting. His wife had "done . . . [him] the honor" to divorce her husband in order to marry him, and he did not wish to meet anybody who considered himself "holier" than his wife. Howells did not reply to this letter, and there was no further communication between the two men until 1893 when Stevenson sent not a "humble remonstrance" but a far more humble apology. Howells replied in warm, kindly, and conciliatory fashion, but he does not seem thereafter to have read Stevenson or in any way to have changed his mind about him as a writer.

Howells's antagonism toward Edmond Rostand was so violent as to suggest a fixation. *Cyrano de Bergerac* was "rubbish" and "tinsel," "false . . . in every movement and motive of the preposterous fable" (when Henry B. Fuller consulted him about the Cyrano libretto he was supposed to do for the Damrosch opera, Howells suggested he burlesque it), but the "falsehood" of *L'Aiglon* was "conscious duplicity" (he praised the Wagram scene but called it lyric rather than dramatic and insisted there was more poetry in Pinero's *The Notorious Mrs. Ebbsmith*). He grants that the theater is "the home of make-believe" and that *Cyrano* is "mechanically very effective," yet he thinks that it "reads less offensively than it plays." This, I should think, would make it better literature than theater, which was about the last thing Howells would have been willing to grant. Surely whatever else may be said of *Cyrano*, it is superb theater, and I think Howells would have had a hard time showing that it was inferior to the plays of Edward Harrigan, William Gillette, and George M. Cohan in which he found so much pleasure. Howells being what he was, one would have thought that Rostand's unexceptionable moral purity—unusual in the French drama of his time—would have been sufficient to endear him to the novelist, but it did not work out that way. His bitterest attack was made in 1903 when he described how the shade of Zola visited him to protest the election to the French Academy of "that *L'Aiglon* juggler, that *Cyrano de Bergerac* conjurer!" who was "factitious from the crown of his head to the sole of his foot, and . . . incapable of even imagining life, let alone portraying it!"

As for the historical novel, Howells seems guilty of elevating his own taste to the level of a universal arbiter when he says:

I think it is asking a good deal of people in these busy, practical times, to go back with you for half a dozen or more generations, and to lose themselves among strange customs and among strange people in a strange land. . . . The real sentiment of today requires that the novelist shall portray a section of real life, that has in it a useful and animating purpose. All the good work of our times is being done on this theory.

He did not even care much for historical fiction in poetry, for he was a condescending reviewer of both Tennyson's *The Last Tournament* and George Eliot's *The Legend of Jubal*, and he thought Madison Cawein's *Myth and Romance* below the level of his best work.

Many would reply, of course, that it is precisely because these are "busy, practical times" that we need to move away from them in our reading, not only for "escape," but, even more importantly, for perspective. There is a suggestion that Howells himself realized this in his review of Bayard Taylor's *The Story of Kennett*, where he comments that through dealing "with the persons, scenes, and actions of a hundred years ago," Taylor "gains that distance so valuable to the novelist."

There was no chauvinism in Howells's preoccupation with his own land and times; he simply sought to confine himself to what he knew best, and he believed that few novelists could ever know the past well enough to be able to write about it in a convincing manner. This, I am sure, is true, but to say that the historical novel, on its highest level, is extremely difficult, is certainly not to say that it is illegitimate.

Here and there Howells exempts one novel or another from his general dislike of historical fiction. The list of favored titles begins of course with *War and Peace*, which he considered the greatest of all historical novels, though I somehow get the impression that it meant less to him than *Anna Karenina*; he adds Gogol's *Taras Bulba*, Stendhal's *Chartreuse de Parme*, Manzoni's *I Promessi Sposi*, "two or three of Scott's," never specified, the Erckmann-Chatrian novels about Napoleon, Mark Twain's *A Connecticut Yankee*, and, among lesser known works, Theodor Mügge's *Afraja*, DeForest's *A Lover's Revolt*, Bellamy's *The Duke of Stockbridge*, and E. P. Tenney's *Constance of Arcadia*. He called Dumas *père* "that saint of romance," whatever that means, and praised Margaret Brandt in Charles Reade's *The Cloister and the Hearth*. *The Scarlet Letter*, which he greatly admired, is not listed because he considered it a romance, not a novel, but why, then, list *A Connecticut Yankee*?

His pet hate seems to have been Hepworth Dixon, whose "Cambyses' vein" in *Her Majesty's Tower* he flayed in the *Atlantic* in 1869. He may have been quite just about this, but one can hardly believe he would have given the space to so unimportant a book if he had not relished the task. When the "Second Series" came out, he went at it again. Two years later, he thought Higginson's *Atlantic Essays* had done the "picturesque historical essay" as well as Dixon did it badly, and he even dragged him in as a bad historical writer in his comprehensive review of "Mr. Parkman's Histories" in 1874. He thought Winston Churchill's *Richard Carvel* far better than most of its competitors, but he could not read *The School for Saints*, despite his admiration for its author, John Oliver Hobbes. His silence about James Branch Cabell and Marjorie Bowen is the more striking because of Mark Twain's admiration for both. Nor does he ever speak of Mary Johnston, though he must have had her in mind while discussing "The New Historical Romances" in *The North American Review* in 1900.[25] Reviewing Charles W. Chesnutt's stories in 1900, he went out of his way to write:

As these stories are of our own time and country, and as there is not a swashbuckler of the seventeenth century, or a sentimentalist of this, or a princess of an imaginary kingdom, in any of them, they will possibly not reach half a million readers in six months.

This, in the very volume of the *Atlantic* in which *To Have and To Hold* finished its serial course!

The article on "The New Historical Romances" is not really intolerant however. Denying that he disliked historical fiction as such, and admitting that he might be viewing the cheaper manifestations of the current vogue somewhat too seriously, Howells gave the new writers credit for good workmanship, decency in sexual matters, and a considerable amount of literary beauty. As a matter of fact, they were *too* literary, and too much removed from life. Their heroines, for the most part, were pert and foolish dolls, and they had invented no memorable personages or actions.

He felt, too, that they had misrepresented the sixteenth, seventeenth, and eighteenth centuries by depicting them as so largely devoted to battle, homicide, and revenge. He was not so foolish as to believe that, having read them, twentieth-century readers would set out to perform deeds of derring-do on their own account, but he did think the ideal that was being set before them uncivilized.

I do not think it by any means a despicable thing to have hit the fancy of our enormous commonplace average. . . . But what is despicable, what is lamentable is to have hit the popular fancy and not have done anything to change it, but everything to fix it; to flatter it with false dreams of splendor in the past, when life was mainly as simple and sad-colored as it is now; to corrupt it to an ignominious discontent with patience and humility, and every-day duty, and peace.

This is not, by any means, altogether wrong, and I must not leave the subject without pointing out that Howells himself was, on occasion, a writer of historical fiction. He once considered writing a novel dealing with Venice in the last days of the Republic, 1794–95. The hero was to be a "commercial" American whom "a splendidly reprehensible illustrima" was to seduce! The story would open and close in Boston, and the interest was to center on the contrast between American and Venetian manners. "I have long wished to touch historical ground in my work," Howells wrote Osgood in 1882, "and here I shall do it." [26]

The subject certainly has fictional possibilities, but I think we may doubt that Howells was quite the man to take advantage of them. He never wrote the book, but he did come at last to *The Leatherwood God*, which several good critics think one of his finest achievements. By some definitions, *New Leaf Mills* might be called an historical novel too, though for Howells it was more strictly speaking a novel of recollection.

Donald Pizer has interestingly suggested that Howells's aggressive contemporaneity may have been importantly connected with his acceptance of the evolutionary philosophy.[27] Wherever it came from, there can be no question of its existence. Once, when he had spoken of the "Walter-Scottismo, not to say the Fenimore-Cooperismo" of ante-bellum Southern writers, he was sternly taken to task by W. P. Trent:

Mr. Howells is too true a man to be arrogant, but sometimes his criticism is so aggressively modern that it falls little short of arrogance. There is surely no need of speaking of the fiction of sixty years ago as one would of a worn-out coat.[28]

There is certainly a suggestion of arrogance too when he writes that taste is now so advanced, and literary skill so diffused . . . that two-thirds of the British Classics in poetry and fiction would be rejected by a conscientious editor . . . because they were wanting in form, or wanting in truth, or wanting in art, or wanting in humanity, or wanting in common decency.

Heroines of fiction, he tells us further, "have constantly grown more interesting as they have grown more modern," and the heroine of a romantic novel does not interest the reader very deeply "for the plain reason that she seldom exists." Though he admits that Archibald Marshall lacks the wide, strong grasp of Trollope, he finds in him "a more delicate and more enlightened sense of his material," and even Shakespeare has been in a sense outmoded by the fact that "questions are questions now which were none in his day." Again, this is not completely wrong, but the attempt to make a creed of it might well have a narrowing effect upon the critic.

CHAPTER THREE

MR. PAPA

I

The title of this chapter exemplifies synecdoche. Howells was very much what Katherine Mansfield called a "Pa-man," and his emotional life may well have culminated in his fatherhood, but this chapter must cover his social and personal relations in general, and before these can be explored, certain aspects of his private personality which we have not yet considered must be defined.

Howells was a short man, never more than five foot four, and in early life he was very slim—"a small, frail, blue-eyed towhead" one of his critics calls him. The frailness soon disappeared, however, and as early as 1871 he was worrying about getting fat. How much he weighed at his peak I cannot say; in 1895 he told Aldrich that he had "faded away to 160 lbs." and that just before election the registrar had startled him by setting down his hair as gray. (His eyes were apparently blue.) In 1896 he weighed 170, but the next year illness had pulled him down to 148. In 1896, too, he was wryly amused by a common man's description of him as "a little old gentleman, in gray clothes, rather chunky." And he adds, "That is what I am, I suppose, to the naked eye." When in 1917 he saw General Joffre, he thought the Frenchman looked so much like himself that he jumped at the resemblance.

The friendliness and gentleness were widely observed—though they evidently coexisted with a quick, keen eye which made some people momentarily uncomfortable. Theodore Dreiser once saw him on Fifth Avenue, a stout, thick-set, middle-aged man trudging solemnly forward. He was enveloped in a great fur ulster, and peered, rather ferociously, upon the odds and ends of street life that passed. He turned out again and again for this person and that, and I wondered why a stout man with so fierce a mien did not proceed resolutely forward, unswerving for the least or the greatest.

But even here the element of gentleness does not disappear.

H. M. Alden, who was so long and so closely associated with Howells on *Harper's Magazine,* found in him "no mark for observation in physiognomy, gait, or gesture," but Lowell thought he looked like the Hoccleve portrait of Chaucer. Julia Ward Howe, at first sight, considered him "odd-looking, but sympathetic and intelligent," and Kipling always remembered "the slow, sideways inclination of the head, and the settling of the chin into the collar that accompanied the even, courteous delivery of the assured words."

He always dressed well, but his daughter Mildred says that one of his few pieces of jewelry was the scarabaeus which Charles Dudley Warner brought him from Egypt. When Myrta Locket Avary met him, she was impressed by his bow being "that of the socialite, which is from the hips." [1] In this connection it is interesting that when Frank Norris and Gelett Burgess went to call on him, they thought evening dress necessary, but Norris's portrait of him as Trevor in "A Lost Story" does not indicate that his behavior was formal in any way. [2]

Perhaps it is William Allen White, who met Howells when the novelist was in his fifties, who gives the most detailed picture of him.

He was heavy-set, with rounding, slightly stooping shoulders, a short neck, a heavy but not paunchy torso, and rather short nimble legs. His voice was low and gentle. I never heard it rise even when he was moved deeply. It was a self-deprecatory voice which did not provoke argument. He was gay, sometimes happily ironic, never pugnacious. He would ward off disagreement with a smile and a patient gesture.

Bret Harte, encountering Howells again, after many years, in 1900, could not see that he looked much older that when he had first met him in Cambridge so many years before. In his old age Howells was annoyed by "this dreamy fumbling about my own identity, in which I detect myself at odd times," but he was also sure that inside he was "as young and stylish and slim" as any young buck of them all; only he didn't look it.

Howells is about the last writer whom a reader who judged him by his books alone would be likely to call "neurotic," but the reality was different from the appearance. His calmness of spirit was a conquest.

Though he records a variety of illnesses from his youth on, his basic constitution seems to have been sound enough. In *Tuscan Cities*, for example, he complains that it is a nuisance to put his glasses on to read the handbooks in the art galleries and then take them off again to look at the pictures. But when he tells us that he has not had his glasses changed for seventeen years, one need not be overly sympathetic on this score. He had a breakdown at Columbus early in 1858 and was very ill until spring or early summer. In the fall of 1881, in the midst of *A Modern Instance*, he was in bed for at least five weeks—"the result of long worry and sleeplessness from overwork," he says—and his wife feared for his life; when he got up again he felt five years older. At first he thought his heart had been affected, but this seems to have passed over. Less than five years later, when he was approaching the end of *Silas Lapham*, he experienced a Jamesian or Swedenborgian "vastation"; his own expression for it, harking back to the canal traffic of his youth, was that "the bottom dropped out." The letters of his later years are full of references to a wide variety of the maladies to which age is subject, of which what he calls a gallstone colic was probably the most serious and painful. Vertigo he had known since nineteen, and sleeplessness often enlisted the aid of veronal or Scotch. And by this time he was complaining of age itself and not merely its maladies. He hated being sixty because it was so close to seventy as to suggest the approaching end of his beloved work, and he would have refused to be eighty if he could have safely done so without dying before he reached it!

The worst of Howells's neuroticism came in his youth; there was one year when, in his own later view, he walked close to the edge of insanity and by which he thought his whole future life had been conditioned. But even in 1862, in Venice, he was so depressed that he thought only God's mercy could save him. "I must learn to fix my mind firmly upon this point: that no great evil has happened to me yet, and that I have either exaggerated or created all the calamities with which I have threatened myself."

I suspect that Howells's record of the many half-real half-imaginative, half-harrowing half-delightful Gothic shivers which he experienced in his youth could be duplicated by a good many of us if we were as honest as he was. Among these I would place his acceptance of all the superstitions of the region in which he grew up, his blind acceptance of signs and omens, his peopling with shapes of horror all the nooks and crannies of his happy home, his dread of graveyards, ghosts (though he never saw one), and of "Centre Claws," a supernatural being "with large talons radiating from the pit of his stomach," his fear of crossing a certain bridge through whose planking the water could be seen, and even his torturing himself insanely over the possibility of having stolen a pencil which a girl at school had mislaid and knowing no peace until she had found it again. He encountered some bona fide horrors as a child, though not so many as gravitated to young Sam Clemens in Hannibal. His earliest memories, one lovely and the other painful, were of peach blossom in bloom and of a one-legged man who drowned trying to step from a yawl to a steamboat in the river. He seems to have been able to watch dead cattle floating down the river in flood time without being sickened or overwhelmed, and he even had some small share in perpetrating horrors upon the hunting expeditions which he shared with the other village boys, though it is clear that he did not achieve this without qualms.

As a youngster Howells was so dependent upon his mother that he could not bear to go away from her even for a night. Once, at least, this involved relinquishing gainful employment, and once, having elected to spend the night with a friend, he had to be taken home at midnight because he remembered his brother had said that the boy he was to sleep with was subject to nightmares and might kill him. One night he woke up in the moonlight with the firm conviction that he would die when he was sixteen and lived with this horror thereafter until this age had been attained, whereupon he mustered the courage to tell his father, who very sensibly explained that it was too late for the premonition to be fulfilled since he was already in his seventeenth year. Because he had heard of a man who died of hydrophobia, this was the death he looked forward to, and the fear was rendered almost insupportable by his having heard the village doctor say that one might be bitten by a dog and have the poison work round in his system for seven years or more, after which it might break out and kill him.

The splash of water anywhere was a sound I had to set my teeth against, lest the dreadful spasms should seize me; my fancy turned the scent of forest fires burning round the village into the subjective odor of smoke which stifles the victim.

He lost his power to work, and when he tried to read there was a "double consciousness in which my fear haunted every line and word without barring the sense of my perception." The climax came one morning when, having awakened in a "sort of crisis," he desperately chanced all by putting his fear "to the test of water suddenly dashed from a doorway beside me." Since the expected convulsion did not occur, he then and there turned the corner which led to recovery. Yet it was years before he could even endure the sight of the word "hydrophobia."

I shut the book or threw from me the paper where I found it in print; and even now, after some sixty years, I cannot bring myself to write it or speak it without some such shutting of the heart as I knew at the sight or sound of it in that dreadful time.

It was very characteristic of him that though this experience caused him greatly to fear dogs, he never disliked them, and that they always gave him what, under the circumstances, was the blessing of a somewhat more than common affection.

Was Howells's neuroticism, then, the result of a gloomy temperament? I do not know of anybody who considers him a "black" writer; the vein of gentle and good-natured humor which runs through his books would alone prevent that. Howells tells us that his father "loved a joke almost as much as he loved a truth," and the same thing was true of his son. Indeed he saw humor as the ally of truth (and of his kind of realism), saw it as inhibiting and preventing the heroics of cheap romanticism, missed it in Tolstoy and felt its lack a shortcoming. From time to time he speculated about its character, its social and moral values or the lack of them. He was not sure that wit was cruel and humor kindly and could "hardly imagine a good joke in heaven." He even thought much of the humor in Shakespeare cruel, and the Englishman whom he found coming closest to Mark Twain as an "entirely humorous humorist" was, of all men, Jonathan Swift! Howells always loved to joke about himself. His wife was "Emmer" and he was "Poppy." He can speak of "the omniscient presence of the Study" or call the Easy Chair "this elderly movable," and he nowhere catches Mark Twain's trick of mock ferocity more successfully than in his expressions of make-believe envy or jealousy, as when he writes George W. Cable after a visit: "You devastated our hearts wherever you went. Those Hartford people made me furious with their praises of you. I hate to see people foolish about a man, even if he *is* a great artist and every way charming." [3]

Yet it is undeniable that many of the more romantically inclined among Howells's contemporaries did think his tone depressing; though he later changed his mind about it, even Theodore Roosevelt spoke at the outset of his "jaundiced view of life." This view might perhaps more reasonably be supported from the poems than from the fiction, and Howells himself says that "any one who can stand up against these gloomy poems of mine must be pretty

robust." Take, for example, this reminiscence of youth in "The
Mulberries":

> We told old stories and made new plans,
>   And felt our hearts gladden within us again,
> For we did not dream that this life of a man's
> Could ever be what we know as men.

Not all the melancholy poems of the early years have an autobiographical basis, however, and some of the more romantic ones
date back to a time when he had not yet sweated the Heine out
of him, as Lowell commanded him to do. Surely he must have
achieved this, however, by the time he wrote *Stops of Various
Quills*, yet the tone here is still very sombre.

> Innocent spirits, bright, immaculate ghosts!
> Why throng your heavenly hosts,
> As eager for their birth
> In this sad home of death, this sorrow-haunted earth?

> Beware! Beware! Content you where you are,
> And shun this evil star,
> Where we who are doomed to die,
> Have our brief being and pass, we know not where or why.

> If He could doubt on His triumphant cross,
> How much more I, in the defeat and loss
> Of seeing all my selfish dreams fulfilled,
> Of having lived the very life I willed,
> Of being all that I desired to be?
> My God, my God! Why hast thou forsaken me?

> Judge me not as I judge myself, O Lord!
>   Show me some mercy or I may not live:
> Let the good in me go without reward;
>   Forgive the evil I must not forgive! [4]

Yet even the *Stops* are thoughtful rather than despairing, suggesting Howells's own statement that he "much preferred speculation to conclusion, which ended the matter, whereas speculation left it always open." Howells did believe that "life is mainly sad everywhere." "I would not live my life over," he says. Looking over old possessions was painful to him, and he thought Christmas Eve a melancholy time for adults. He was often haunted by a sense of insecurity, and he once declared that he had not had much happiness, "though I have had a good deal of fun." In some moods he felt that pessimism had its uses; elsewhere he feels that since neither optimism nor pessimism can be proved, optimism, which is more useful, should be elected. He was never the same after Winifred died, but even then he did not despair, and it was characteristic of his gentle nature that he should feel that "if I could live my life over, it would be to love more, to be gentler and kinder with all. Nothing else is worth while." No matter how discouraged he became, he always retained a certain eighteenth-century faith in man's tendency toward goodness and order. Quakers "would not be hanged in Boston today; the Saviour of mankind would not be burned today even in Spain: so far has His spirit penetrated at last," though Howells granted that grave "anxieties" and "misgivings" would greet Christ's appearance in any center of modern civilization. Though much of the best is rejected, enough establishes itself to give us hope. And, in the last analysis, even evil may make some contribution.

In the moral world as in the material world, Nature takes care of the wrong done; she softly covers it up, transmutes it, turns it even to use and beauty, not for the doer indeed, and usually not for the victim, but for the race. It would not be flattering to our spiritual pride to inquire how much of what we suppose the sum of human good is the far result of human error.

II

Neither Howells's temperament nor his convictions tended to make him friendly toward Society with a capital "S." In 1870 he published in the *Atlantic* a bitterly sarcastic review of *The Bazar Book of Decorum*. He hoped that in the better civilization that was to come "that odious device of society, the polished gentleman, and that invention of the enemy, the accomplished lady, will not exist, and that naturally there will be no books to teach the imitation of their abominable perfection." And twenty-one years later, he was almost equally rough on Ward McAllister's *Society As I Have Found It*.

He did not create society; it created him; and if he is deplorable, society is to blame for him. If society had known how to do something besides dress and dine and dance, we have no doubt he would have . . . written a different book. But you cannot make something out of nothing.

Though in an altogether different field, this is very much the way Mark Twain handled General Funston in his bitter and ironical "Defence."

Howells was never a "come-outer," and it is not surprising that as a famous man, he did not always find it possible to keep out of "society," though he frequently expressed boredom. "For a social animal it is amusing to observe how little man can see of his fellows without becoming demoralized by it." Once he says that if he had plenty of money, he would like to see Newport "thoroughly for one season and then never see it again." Mildred Howells certainly lived an active social life in her youth, and Winifred might well have done the same if illness and death had not intervened, but though her father often went about with Mildred during the years when her mother had become an invalid, he says he wants her "to get her surfeit of society early, so that she will know it means nothing and can come to nothing." One afternoon in 1889 he found himself going to two fashionable teas in the afternoon and a Socialist meeting in the evening! In *Letters Home* the *nouveau riche* Ralsons are shown storming the bastions of New York society, which gives Howells a good chance to portray a variety of social distinctions, but in the ideal civilization of Altruria there is a tendency to avoid large formal assemblies.

Howells told Lowell that he was "sluggish" in company, and especially dull at dinners, and he always had a tendency to worry afterwards over what he might have said and done. I recall only two big "affairs" which the Howellses are recorded as having given—one for Bret Harte and his wife when they came east in 1871 and another for Edmund Gosse when he arrived for his Lowell lectures in 1884. In Cambridge Mrs. Howells had small coffee and card parties on Saturday nights.

It does not appear that his attitude toward these matters ever greatly changed. Thomas Wentworth Higginson thought the best society composed of abolitionists and fugitive slaves, and Howells sees it made up of "our literary men and women, our artists, our actors, our professors, scientists, and ministers, our skilled mechanics and day-laborers." In 1901 the "Easy Chair" mused good-naturedly over why genius is not received in American society, and though there is no animus in the article, there is no admiration for society either. The "wicked grace" of a European aristocracy was impossible for a plutocracy; the best they could manage was always to give the impression of being genteelly bored. Essentially Howells thought the upper crust an anachronism in America, stranded in a world which has no place of dignity for them to occupy. "Like the idle poor, the idle rich suffer because there is nothing for them to do, but the greatest hardship of the idle rich lies in the fact that they do not seem fit to do anything." As late as 1915 he applauds President Wilson for having declared in an address at Berea College that "the world could dispense with high society and never miss it. High society is for those who have stopped working and no longer have anything important to do."

But, as is usual with Howells, this is only part of the story. *The Rise of Silas Lapham* alone would show how well he knew the difference between those who have been bred in society and those who have not, and though he was himself opposed to fences, he always states the case for the socialites fairly. *Out of the Question* attacks social snobbery of the classical Boston pattern and allows the heroine to be united with Blake, who is not, in the conventional sense of the term, a gentleman. But Howells does not

scorn Mrs. Hilary of *The Quality of Mercy*, who finds it easier
to accept Sue Northwick as her son's choice, though her father is
a defaulter, because she belongs to their set, than she does to sympathize with her daughter's love affair with Brice Maxwell, who is
a perfectly respectable newspaper man. Certainly the Howellses
themselves belonged to Boston society to a rather greater extent
than one might have expected of such egalitarians as they were
rapidly becoming. To be sure, there are those who feel that they
were always conscious of not belonging to the inner circle and
that their egalitarianism was not quite unaffected by this. In
"Good Society" (*Stops of Various Quills*) Howells advises

> Yes, I suppose it is well to make some sort of exclusion,
>   Well to put up the bars under whatever pretence;
> Only be careful, be very careful, lest in the confusion
>   You should shut yourself on the wrong side of the fence.

And though he can tell us, in his review of the Valdès novel of
that title that society is the true *Scum*, he was not unaware of the
danger of a kind of inverted snobbery. "We always suppose that
the superiors despise the inferiors," says Kelwyn, "but perhaps it
is really the inferiors that despise the superiors, and it's that which
embitters the classes against one another." This is quite Annie
Kilburn's experience when, after her father's death in Rome, she
comes home to central Massachusetts to try to do some good with
her money and finds it almost impossible to make any vital contact
with her neighbors. When most under the sway of her admiration
for the splendid but uncomfortable clergyman Mr. Peck, who is
so completely the social idealist and reformer that he almost literally forgets the needs and the very existence of his own child,
Annie feels that she should give up everything and go to Fall
River with him to work in the mills. He refuses to accept this, and
his death by accident prevents her from putting her resolution to
the test, but Howells leaves us in no doubt that he did not himself believe that it would do. Even Annie's attempt to sacrifice herself by allowing Idella Peck to go to Mrs. Savor, who has lost her

own child, does not work out, for Idella hates it at the Savors's and runs back to Annie, and it does not seem that Mrs. Savor really wanted her after all.

In a way, to be sure, equality has been achieved in what is called "good society," for once you are "in," you are the equal of everybody else and can be sure of being treated politely and with consideration. "If people in society behaved toward one another from motives of real kindness . . . society would be an image of heaven," but they do not, being only actuated by politeness which, though desirable, is a much less vital and far-reaching thing. People wish to get into society because they think it will make them feel superior to those who are out, but once they are in, "the ideal of their behavior is equality." Though not "quite an image of heaven," good society thus presents "an image of a righteous state on earth," for all it asks is that people shall behave civilly. "It asks of them what Christianity asks of sinners: that they shall cease to do evil, at least for the time being, for that afternoon or evening." In a sense, then, "the new condition, the equality of the future," implies "the enlargement of good society to the whole of humanity." [5] I think there are indications too that, though Howells grew more rather than less radical as he grew older, he also grew more tolerant: "I find myself much abler to mingle with rank and fashion in the past than in the present," he says. And in *Familiar Spanish Travels* he brazenly brings it up to date by speaking of "that love of the fashionable world for which I am always blaming myself."

Social intercourse is, however, a larger thing than "society." In rural Ohio there were "dances at the taverns," "parties at the girls's houses with the games and the frolics, and the going home each with the chosen at midnight and the long lingering at the gate." Though Howells enjoyed it, one gathers that even then he was a little apart, for he was a solitary in the printing office, "not venturing to take part, except once, in their wild hilarity, and scarcely knowing their names." (That "except once" strongly suggests a vivid memory but not a pleasant one.) He afterwards remembered his two "happy winters" in Columbus as "the heyday of life for me," but that was probably because he met Elinor Mead there, for he speaks too of "a youth who danced so reluctantly as I" and tells how he suffered when he was not invited to parties he did not really wish to attend.

In Venice his consulship not only opened doors to him but compelled him to walk through them, and both he and Elinor became devoted "Florianisti," as the Italians called those who frequented the Caffè Florian. When he came to Cambridge there were the Dante evenings at Longfellow's and the other associations with Harvard literati. In 1876 he jokes about being out four nights in one week, and in 1882 Gosse saw him enjoying his literary fame in London, but it is interesting that when he was at Saratoga in 1900 he did not stop at one of the big hotels and spent his mornings writing, though he was "very sociable the rest of the time." In New York he chattered in Italian with the keepers of fruit and vegetable stands along Third Avenue and gave luncheons at Delmonico's for both Stephen Crane and H. G. Wells. In later years he spent much time at the Century Club, and in Boston he was the presiding avuncular genius of the Tavern Club, which he himself described as "made up of all the best and nicest young lawyers, doctors, artists, and litterateurs here." [6]

It may be that Edith Wharton testifies to her own shyness more than his when she speaks of "my timidity and his social aloofness" as getting in the way of the friendship she would have liked to establish with him, but she was not altogether wrong about him. It did not take Howells long to discover that if you are to find the energy you need to swing an important career, you cannot chase round after people you care nothing for and permit them to chase you also. Like the Henry James who wrote *The Tragic Muse*, he knew, as he declares in his essay on Marmontel, that "the world and art are . . . almost as alien as the world and religion," and one of the finest of the *Stops of Various Quills* shows that he knew too what Emerson meant when he said that "we descend to meet."

TWELVE P.M.

To get home from some scene of gayety,
Say a long dinner, and the laugh and joke,
And funny story, and tobacco smoke,
    And all the not unkindly fatuousness
Of fellow-beings not better and not worse
Than others are, but gorged with course on course,
    And drenched with wine: and with one's evening dress
To take off one's perfunctory smile, and be
    Wholly and solely one's sheer self again—
    Is like escaping from some dull, dumb pain;
    And in the luxury of that relief,
    It is, in certain sort and measure, as if
    One had put off the body, and the whole
    Illusion of life, and in one's naked soul
Confronted the eternal Verity.

Gosse, as we have seen, found him eagerly lionizing in London, but Gosse did not know that Howells and his wife cut their stay short because they could not stand any more of it. When Senator Ingalls invited him to Washington to gather material for the Great American Novel, he told him he could not stand the going about in society that would be required to accomplish this. In 1900 both he and Elinor rejoiced that their Annisquam neighbors left them quite alone, "with either a savage indifference, or a strange diffidence, I don't know which," but seven years later, when less considerate acquaintances at Kittery Point intruded upon him and robbed him of his nap, they "turned" him "against all mankind." "No, I do *not* catch on to New York," he had written Aldrich in 1901, "and in my old days I grow very diffident of people. Then, they are not so interesting as they used to be."

He refused George Harvey's offer of a seventieth birthday dinner, but was forced to submit to a seventy-fifth, which he apparently found less painful than he had expected, for he bowed his neck to the yoke of another when he was eighty. There was even a certain hesitation about approaching people whom he admired, though there seems to have been less of this when they were literary or artistic people. When he was doing his campaign biography of Lincoln, he let another do his interviewing for him, and when he encountered the President in a corridor of the White House, after having been appointed consul at Venice, he failed to muster the courage necessary to accost him. But he was famous himself when, a meeting with Harvard's President Lowell in the offing, he asked Bliss Perry to assure him in advance, quite as if he were David Copperfield quizzing Peggotty about her brother, whether Lowell was "a friendly person." But what are we to make of a socialist who will "bribe" the guard on an English train to shut him and his wife into their compartment and admit no one else?

What made our inhuman behavior worse was that we were really . . . professed friends of the common people. The story might show that when it comes to a question of selfishness men are all alike ready to profit by the unjust conditions. However, it must be remembered that those people were only bicyclers. If we could have conceived of them as masses we should have known them for brothers, and let them in, probably.

Friendship was something else again. Howells did not love all his friends equally well. Though he wrote Thomas Bailey Aldrich many warm letters, he was repelled by his capacity for self-appreciation, and after Aldrich had died, Howells wrote Norton that he missed him "out of the world rather than out of my world." It was different when Bret Harte went, for though Howells was aware of all his faults and had been completely honest about them when recommending Harte to President Hayes for a foreign post, yet "he belonged to our youth, which was glad, and knew it, and I find he had a hold upon my heart which I have no logic for." [7]

To be sure, there is a certain reserve even here. Writes Hamlin Garland:

Wholly without pompous egotism he held even intimate friends like Brander Matthews and Charles Dudley Warner at arm's length. He never spoke of any man in terms of a nick-name; he never swore; and yet there was nothing stiff or formal about his speech. He was fun-loving yet never coarse. His dignity arose from something interior, something essentially noble in his thought. He used slang occasionally but always with a smile—with quotation marks.

Nevertheless he loved his friends. "You are the oldest friend I have," he writes J. M. Comly, "and I couldn't bear to think you didn't care for me as much as I did for you." Woodress describes the friends he made in Italy, some of which he kept through life. Sometimes he even reaches out to a stranger, as to T. D. Metcalf, who had written understandingly of the Altrurian:

I wish I might talk with you about all those matters. But life is short, and if we never meet, still I hope you will always think of me as your friend, and not read me as a personal stranger.

Howells can hardly have loved anybody more than he loved Lowell and Charles Eliot Norton, but there was a generation gap that could not but make itself felt. Among his strict contemporaries his great friends were Mark Twain and Henry James. He published them both, and beat the drums for them, and, different as they were, it would be hard to say which he valued more highly. In an advisory capacity he was much more important to Mark Twain, however, than he was to James.

The full, fascinating record of Howells's association with Mark Twain, mirroring the rich give-and-take of their relationship, must be sought in the fascinating pages of the *Mark Twain-Howells Letters*, where everything that is said here and much besides will be found minutely documented. In this light, the once-fashionable idea that Howells emasculated Mark Twain's writings and clamped down an old-maidish censorship upon them is no longer worth discussing. Howells saved Mark Twain from many embarrassing blunders, vetoed many wild and impossible projects (while strangely encouraging certain others), made him distinctly more

publishable under the conditions which existed in his time, and
even improved his taste a little, but in spite of "the Southwestern,
the Lincolnian, the Elizabethan breadth of parlance in his conversation," when it came to literature Mark's taste was often considerably more pernickety than Howells's own. Each told the
other that he himself would be remembered in the future because
he had known his friend, and Howells told Mark that he had no
other pleasure comparable to that of receiving his letters and that
he would rather see him and talk with him than with any other
man in the world outside his own family. In 1906 Mark so much
wanted Howells to live near him at Redding that he offered to
sell him the land for $25, to which Howells, not to be outdone by
the greatest humorist in the world, bluntly replied that $25 was
entirely too much for a ten-acre lot and that he would not be
taken in, and when Mark died, Howells sent Clara Clemens one
of his most beautiful letters.

I found Mr. Paine's telegram when I came in last night; and suddenly your father was set apart from all other men in a strange majesty. Death had touched his familiar image into historic grandeur.
You have lost a father. Shall I dare tell you of the desolation of an
old man who has lost a friend, and finds himself alone in the great
world which has not wholly perished around?
We all join in sending you our helpless love.

Howells advised Mark Twain at every stage of his literary production and read his proofs for him when Mark was too lazy to
read them himself. Being the most modest of men, he was sometimes embarrassed by Mark's theatricalism and unconventionality,
but when Mark visited him and turned his house upside down,
both he and his wife loved it and cried out for more. He timed
his reviews of Mark's books so that they would come out first and
thus "start the sheep jumping in the right places," and on at least
one occasion arranged for another review elsewhere.
Did he, then, contribute more to their relationship than Mark
Twain contributed? Certainly he *did* more for Mark Twain. For
that matter, he did more for James also, and James felt it, for in

the letter read at Howells's seventy-fifth birthday dinner, he lamented that he was never able to reward Howells for all his services by publishing *him* or even reading a manuscript for him. And, though Howells does seem to have given some of his work to Thomas S. Perry to read, generally speaking he never asked anything from anybody. He was more self-sufficient than any of the writers with whom he came into contact, and they were not able to do very much for him because he had no need.

If it be as much a test of character to accept favors in the right spirit as to confer them, then Mark Twain passes the test; for all his being "a man with the bark on," there was a beautiful humility at the heart of him. Not only did he give his friend *carte blanche* to do anything he liked with his stuff, but once, when he had not heard from Howells for some time, he wrote:

Have I offended you in some way? The Lord knows it is my disposition, my infirmity, to do such things; but if I have done it in your case, I can truthfully say that if I had known it at the time, I would not have done it, and if it were to do again I would not do it—and in any case I am sorry.

Howells was well aware of the vagaries of Mark Twain's temperament, but so far as I know he was never victimized by it. He himself showed pique when, on one occasion, Mark Twain had his nephew and businessman, Charles Webster, write to him instead of doing it himself.

If Mr. Clemens is disabled or in trouble, or has some unknown offence with me, I can understand his preferring to write to his friend by the hand of his agent; but not otherwise. I am, of course, always glad to hear from you personally.

This was about the Sellers play on which the two writers were collaborating, which may well have lost its chance of production because Howells finally surrendered confidence in it and withdrew it. Mark stated his position in the matter but with unusual temperateness and self-control for a man of his disposition.

Of course Howells could not help knowing that Mark Twain was more "successful" than he was. "I hate to shiver round in the shadow of your big fame," he told him, and again:

In the notice of the Yale guests, as I noted with my usual grouch where you are concerned, your name came *first*, with some laudatory type round it, and mine followed with the "and others," and nothing attached to it. So I think there is some mistake.

Once he declined an invitation from the Aldriches, giving as his reason that he did not wish to come when Mark Twain was there and play second fiddle to him, and when Mark was out of town at the time of his lunch for George Harvey, he said "it was really better talk without him, for people let him have the talk to himself at such times." He also complains, more seriously and rather pathetically, that "I have a feeling that you don't read me as much as you ought, and I sometimes swear off from you on account of it," and though Mark replied that he did, Howells may have been right, for his type of novel was not precisely Mark Twain's favorite type of reading matter, and in spite of all his expressed enthusiasm for Howells's work,[8] I have often doubted that he would have cared much for it if it had not been written by a friend.

James was a less picturesque, though certainly not a less important (nor, in all respects, even a less eccentric) person than Mark Twain, and not so many details of his relations with Howells call for chronicle. In the early days, when they were both in Cambridge, Howells and James engaged in much more detailed and fruitful discussion of literary principles and problems than Howells ever explored with Clemens, and it may well be that Howells's encouragement was more important to James than that of anybody else during his formative years. In 1911 Howells lent himself to an unfortunately abortive effort to get the Nobel Prize for James. James, in his turn, was appreciative of Howells, though he could be what is generally called "catty" about what he considered his limitations, as his letters to T. S. Perry show. James was less the realist than Howells was (except in such books as *The Son of Royal Langbrith*, where he uses something like the James method), and to confine yourself to what your "fleshly eyes have seen" seemed to him all the more unfortunate if you were going to limit your scrutiny to what he regarded as the sparse, starved American landscape. He also resented Howells's indifference to what he himself regarded as form in fiction, so that he could be comparatively grudging even in his appreciation of so impressive a novel as *A Hazard of New Fortunes*, concerning which he wrote William James:

His abundance and facility are my constant wonder and envy—or rather not perhaps, envy, inasmuch as he has purchased them by throwing the whole question of form, style and composition overboard into the deep sea—from which, on my side, I am perpetually trying to fish them up.

III

Of the recreational activities human beings undertake in association with others, sport is probably the most intense. It was never very important with Howells however. He never cared for fishing at any time in his life, and he hunted only in his youth. In 1878 Charles Dudley Warner's magnificent anti-hunting blast, "A-Hunting of the Deer," roused his enthusiasm, and his daughter says that Easton's opposition to hunting in *Private Theatricals* reflects her father's views. In *A Counterfeit Presentment* he calls hunting "the sneakingest sort of assassination; it's the pleasure of murder without the guilt. If you must kill, you ought to be man enough to kill something that you'll suffer remorse for." One "Easy Chair" essay refers to the " 'prolongation of infancy' into permanent boyhood by sport," with an obvious side-glance toward Theodore Roosevelt. As a boy, Howells seems to have accepted the standards of the group more readily than one would have expected of so humane and literary a youth. He not only hunted but fought, and in *The Flight of Pony Baker* the multilations boys experienced on the "Glorious Fourth" are pretty cavalierly disposed of. I think one may doubt, however, that even then he was much of a hunter or that he found much pleasure in it, for he tells us that the boys would have thought it "sacrilege" to kill a robin or a turtle dove, and though he does say that squirrels were sometimes killed "with what I must now call a sickening ferocity," he adds that he himself killed only one. He also remembered killing only one quail, and when he stepped by accident on a baby snipe and crushed it, he was crushed himself.

There was a certain ambivalence in his attitude toward horses. He thought them a "corrupting" influence among men, and his dislike of the dirt they created in cities helped to reconcile him to the stench which came in with the motor car, though he hated that too. He even speaks of "the innate cruelty of the horse." Yet he loved to see horses groomed, and he enjoyed watching races too, though he never had the slightest interest in who won. He does not seem to have been able to keep to this level where boat races were concerned, and though he considered it completely irrational, he admitted that he had "suffered several defeats of Harvard with a shame and grief which I should not like to have Yale men know." There are some references to going to the Yale-Harvard game and at least one to watching polo. Mildred says that when the Howellses attended the races at Saratoga, they generally went secretly out of consideration for the clergymen among their fellow guests but that when they arrived they generally found these present. In Spain, they planned to attend a bull fight to observe the crowd and the pageantry but to leave before the killing occurred. They also looked in on the gambling rooms at Monte Carlo—and found in them a perfect image of the perpetual dullness of hell.[9]

The Altrurian Mr. Homos regards exercise for exercise' sake as "childish, if not insane or immoral," but he admits that after the day's work is done, young Altrurians "have all sorts of games and sports, and they carry them as late into life as the temperament of each demands." Howells watched Mark Twain at his endless billiards but considered participation in the game quite beyond him, and the only exercises he seems to have pursued anything like systematically are walking, swimming and bathing, and (in early life) skating. When Winny had a baseball craze, he remarked that it amused "me, who never cared a straw for any sort of game, except marbles." In view of the slight interest he himself took in dancing, it is a little surprising that he should have made it "the great national amusement in Altruria, where it has not altogether lost its religious nature." He does not, however, seem ever to have passed up any regulation sight on his travels, however uncomfortable or dangerous it might be, whether it was going over La Cluri Rapids at Montreal, viewing the Blue Grotto at Capri, or sliding down the mountain on a toboggan at Madeira.

Clearly, his attitude toward animals was a factor in all this. Yet, except for cats, his references to animals are not extensive. The only dog described at length is the hyper-sensitive and self-pitying Poppi in *A Little Swiss Sojourn*, who may have been meant for a cat himself since he was on such good terms with them. Going to Italy, Howells was distressed by what he had been told of Italian cruelty to animals, but he observed little to substantiate these charges.

The only animals for which Howells expresses loathing are reptiles—alligators and snakes. In the public market at Venice the writhing eels "set the soul asquirm." In *A Boy's Town* he speaks of having killed snakes, however, and a person with a real snake phobia would never get close enough to one to do that. Originally he despised the pigeons at Venice, but when he returned to the city he joined the other pilgrims in feeding them. Otis Binning, in *Letters Home*, thinks squirrels very stupid little beasts, yet he feeds them and permits them to take liberties with him. So, clearly, did Howells, for he speaks of their climbing up to his knee, and in one of his pieces he discusses them almost as if they were human. At the zoo he did not care much for "the wallowing hippopotamuses, and the lumbering elephants, and the supercilious camels," but he liked "the rugged bison pair," "the beautiful deer," and the sheep.

I do not know whether Howells owned cats (or, rather, per-mitted a cat to own him); though he once speaks of "my black cat," the nomadic habits of the family cannot have been favorable to the keeping of pets. But wherever he goes, he looks for cats and notices them. He is glad he stopped at the Church of St. Magnus, for example, "for there I made the acquaintance of three of the most admirable cats in London." There is a good, though brief, portrait of a cat at the end of "'Staccato Notes of a Vanished Summer" in *Literature and Life* and a much more detailed account of a New York cat encountered on a Sunday morning walk in one of the periodical essays:

I encountered a Maltese cat crossing the walk under one of the trees and made some half-hearted advances toward her acquaintance, but she mewed impatiently, as if she asked why I could not see that she was after the sparrows on the grass just beyond; and she passed among them with a demure pretence of unconsciousness, which may or may not have deceived them. A little later, when I came back that way after making a circuit of it, the cat was occupying one of the empty benches with her paws gathered under her, and her eyes closed. The sparrows were gone, and I could not tell whether she was inviting the quiet favorable to digestion or was massed there in the mute apathy of despair. Another cat, a black one, was by this time making across the grass towards a workmanlike-looking man who was sitting in Sunday indolence on another bench, with his newspaper across his knees. They were apparently friends, or if not that, affinities; for the cat at once went up to him and rubbed against his leg, while he smoked and scratched her neck.[10]

Beaton in *A Hazard of New Fortunes* has a pistol loaded, ready to fire at cats, but he is a nasty person anyway. In *The World of Chance*, Mrs. Denton is forever stroking her cat—a kind of Dickensian tag-action—and at one point she is accused of showing more affection to her cat than to her children. Idella's fondness for her cat plays its part in *Annie Kilburn*, and in *The Seen and Unseen at Stratford-on-Avon*, Shakespeare is made to stroke one tenderly, though there is no evidence in his plays that he cared for cats.

But if Howells was moderate about sports, no American of his time seems to have been more badly bitten by the travel bug. As Van Wyck Brooks remarks, "one gathered from his novels that Americans were always moving." He always was. As he summed it up in *Familiar Spanish Travels*: "I had lived five or six years in Italy; I had been several months in Germany; and a fortnight in Holland; I had sojourned often in Paris; I had come and gone a dozen times in England and lingered long each time."

There are obvious limitations and omissions here. Howells never went to the Orient, despite his relish for books of Oriental travel, nor yet to the American West. Nor were his travels evenly distributed over his life. After his mid-forties he did not go abroad again for a dozen years, but between 1894 and the summer of 1913 he went eight times. During the last seven years he went to Florida and the Bahamas, and in 1903 he said he would like to spend the rest of his winters at Florence or Rome.[11] Once he remarked of Rome, "I indeed recognized certain difficulties in living there the year round; but who lives anywhere the year round if he can help it?" Like everybody else in their America who had a nickel, all the characters in the Howells novels rush to "the country" as soon as summer begins, at first so that they may live under the most uncomfortable possible conditions in farm boarding houses or shacks called "cottages," later to try to bore themselves to death in the huge summer hotels whose decaying hulks now dot the Eastern American landscape waiting for fire to come along and make an end of them. There are suggestions that, like most men of imagination, Howells sometimes enjoyed his travels more in retrospect, as when he recalls Florence, its people and its smells: "I am happy,—happier than I should probably be if I were actually there." But on the whole he enjoyed himself; at least he was never sufficiently disturbed by the discomforts involved to relinquish his traveling habits. "As in every other time," he wrote his brother Joe from Paris in 1908, "I am saying to myself 'Never again, never again!' But there is really no telling, and while there is life there is despair—despair of staying put." [12]

Was Howells, then, a great lover of nature? His father loved her, we are told, and taught his children to love her too, often taking them out into the woods and fields and under the open skies. There is more natural beauty in Howells's books than he is often given credit for. O. W. Firkins wrote that "if Mr. Howells were cast upon a desert island, a hackman would meet him on the edge of the surf, and a waiter would offer him a menu on the first available grass-plot in the primeval forest," and Delmar G. Cooke adds that he cannot "keep the human element out of the landscape for even a paragraph of moderate length."

Since he was a novelist and not a nature-writer, it would have been rather odd if Howells had been able to do this last. He was no nineteenth-century pantheist at any time, and he knew with Mr. Squeers that nature is a "rum 'un" when she is not in an amiable mood. Yet he realizes frontier Ohio in *New Leaf Mills*, *The Leatherwood God*, and the unpublished "Luke Beazeley," the Mississippi River in "The Pilot's Story," the lushness of the deep South in "The Home Towners," the New England country-side in *The Undiscovered Country* and many other stories, the Saratoga area in *An Open-Eyed Conspiracy*, Campobello in *April Hopes*, and rural Canada in *The Quality of Mercy*. And when he needs a tropical isle in *A Woman's Reason* he is quite capable of describing that too.

In all these cases and in many others, however, he gives only what he needs and keeps it strictly subordinate to the needs of the story. This, from *Private Theatricals*, is about as specific as he gets:

The summer was past, but the pageant of autumn was yet un-dimmed. In the wet meadows of the lowlands, even in the last days of August, before the goldenrod was in its glory, the young maples lit their torches; and what might have seemed their drooping fires crept from sumac to sumac, by the vines in the grass and over the walls till all the trees, kindling day by day, stood at last a flame of red and gold against the sky. The jay scolded among the luminous boughs; across the pale heaven the far-voiced crows swam in the mellow sun-shine. The pastures took on again the green of May; the patches of corn near the farmhouses rustled dry in the soft wind; between the ranks of the stalks lolled the rounded pumpkins.

Trees and birds were, as will be seen, important elements, flowers somewhat less important. Peach blossoms, as I have already pointed out, constituted his earliest vision of beauty; he lovingly describes the laurel near Fitchburg, Massachusetts—"a snow of blossom flushed with a mist of pink"; and he uses only authentic names for the flowers employed in his play, *Bride Roses*. He was devoted to gardening, but he seems to have been more interested in raising vegetables than flowers, though he did not always get what he had tried for, and Mildred says that his cantaloupes "seldom ripened in the New England climate" and that "even his optimism was dashed one year when his carefully tended melons lengthened unmistakably into infant cucumbers." There are many letters about his gardening; once he tells Aurelia about going out to work at six and getting in two hours before breakfast, and once he told James Parton that he was looking forward to an old age occupied with "poultry and English violets, perhaps varied with a pig or two." In 1903, too, he reported having planted nearly 150 trees and shrubs.

It always helped nature with Howells when she could muster literary associations; thus a forest of yews recalled the yew in Gray's "Elegy," and the place had "a rich, Thomas Hardyish flavor." But he loved trees, associations or no. "The olive is the tree which, of all others, is the friend of civilized man; it is older and kinder even than the apple, which is its next rival in beneficence." He loved New England's elms also, and he was charmed by the rich human note in the German forests, where he found "nothing of the accident of an American wood." Having been "watched and weeded by man ever since they burst the soil," they were "nurseries," retaining "the charm which no human care can alienate."

In Charleston, Howells thought that "the mocking-bird does not compare in its 'melodious bursts' with our bobolink or oriole, or catbird, and might well be silent in the presence of our hermit-thrush." But this sounds more knowledgeable than most of his references to birds or "other small deer." Of one bird, heard each morning in Rome, he says, "I do not know what make or manner of bird it was . . . but it had a note of liquid gold." Once he speaks of "the singing of larks, or the singing of robins, Heaven knows what, but always angelically sweet"! He can be equally vague about trees: "I, for my part, made the dizzying circuit of the brief drive on foot in the dark shadows of the roofing ilexes (if they are ilexes). . . ." At one point in *Italian Journeys,* he even advises the reader to turn to Manzoni's novel, *The Betrothed,* if he would know "how all the lovely Como country looks at that hour."

What Howells is always clear and sure about is the effect that nature has on him. We are told that Isabel's heart "beat with a child-like exultation" when she confronted Niagara, and Howells carefully adds that the same must be true of anybody who is worthy to behold the Falls. Isabel also preferred fresh water to salt water, and Howells seems to have agreed with her, for Buffalo "had all the picturesqueness of a sea-port, without the ugliness that attends the rising and falling tides," and though the "delicate blue of the lake" lacked "the depth of the sea-blue," it was "infinitely softer and lovelier." Speaking more generally, he can declare:

I always count it a year lost out of my life when I do not see the spring coming over the fields and through the woods; and I feel that if I had my rights I should see some twenty or thirty more Mays than I am likely to see.

When he was young, autumn filled his heart "with a passionate pain that is sweeter in its sourness than pleasure," and he seems always to have felt that only a very happy person could confront a summer evening without melancholy. When the Erlcorts stay too late in the autumn in their country cottage, they are over-whelmed by loneliness.[13]

Howells carefully avoids all the easy antitheses between city and country. He tended to believe, against general, unverified assumptions, that, morally speaking, "the average of men are rather better in the city than in the country."

But the average boy or girl nurtured in the country seems of greater force than the city born and bred average of their kind. It might be fancied that there was some mystic property of the mother-earth infusing itself into her children and strengthening them through contact with her breast, which does not reach their souls where she is battened down with asphalt.

On the other hand, when he visited Shirley, he did not think the Shakers looked very healthy for all their living close to nature and abstaining from alcohol and tobacco.

Is it possibly true that our climate is healthful only in proportion as it is shut out by brick walls and plateglass, and battened down under cobble and flag stones; that the less fresh air we have the better, and that Nature here is at best only a step-mother to our race?

Even when it came to beauty there was no clear-cut antithesis to be set up between city and country, and the Marches are often much struck by the picturesqueness of New York and feel sure that artists would admire it more if it were less familiar to them.

IV

The reading of William Dean Howells has already been described in considerable detail in these pages. But while literature was for him the art of arts, it was by no means the only art which interested and influenced him, and since the other arts are generally considered more "social" than literature, they fall for consideration here. Architecture is first and foremost a matter of public buildings. Painting and sculpture are enjoyed mainly in museums and in the company of others. In our own period the phonograph, the film projector, and the television set have helped music and theater to move at least part of the way out of assembly halls and into our homes, but this was not true in his time.

That architecture expresses the spirit of a people Howells learned first from Ruskin. He never prided himself on his "architectural terminology," and he had little faith in the power of literature to convey the sense of any work of art, but many of his judgments are as clear-cut (and quite as moralistic) as Ruskin's own. Rome, whether republican or imperial, was not a state for which Howells felt any genuine reverence; it is not surprising, then, that he should have been sure that the Forum in its glory was ugly and crowded, an example of "the pride of the eyes and all ruthless vainglory" vaunting itself in unseemly fashion, and only tolerable now through the picturesqueness which the barbarians gave it by tumbling it into ruins. Moorish architecture was monotonous compared to the Gothic and undignified in comparison with the Greek. The Escorial, dedicated to death, pride, and gloom, can speak only of death, and the Duomo at Florence too is "a temple to damp the spirit," while the Casino at Monte Carlo suggests only the art of the pastry cook. On the other hand, the Cathedral, the Leaning Tower, the Baptistery, and the Campo Santa at Pisa made up a group which could not be matched upon earth, and he remembered Saint Mark's

with no less love than veneration. This church indeed has a beauty which touches and wins the heart, while it appeals profoundly to the religious sentiment. It is as if there were a sheltering friendliness in its low-hovering domes and arches; as if here, where the meek soul feels welcome and protection, the spirits oppressed with sin might creep nearest to forgiveness, in the temple's ominous recesses, faintly starred with mosaic, and twilighted by twinkling altar-lamps.

As long as he lived, I am sure Howells continued to think of the Gothic as "that architecture which Heaven seems truly to have put into the thoughts of man together with the Christian faith" and as that which "more mystically lifts the soul" than any other. One night he went to see the Cathedral of Siena by moonlight.

The moon was not so prompt as we, and at first we only had it in the baptistery and the campanile,—a campanile to make one almost forget the Tower of Giotto. But before we came away one corner of the edifice had caught the light, and hung richly bathed, tenderly etherealized in it. What was gold, what was marble before, seemed transmuted to the luminous substance of the moonlight itself, and rested there like some translucent cloud that "stooped from heaven and took the shape" of clustered arch and finial.

But in England you did not need moonlight to glorify the cathedrals for they were beautiful enough to break the heart by day, and when you could stand no more of their loveliness you had to turn away.

Some cathedrals, like that of Wells, makes you think of gardens; but York Minster will not be satisfied with less than an autumnal woodland, where the trees stand in clumps with grassy levels about them, and with spacious openings to the sky, that let in the colored evening light.

He loved Tudor houses too and would have been glad to live in any of them. He saw the Houses of Parliament as springing "from the riverside as if they grew from the ground there far into the gray sky to which their architecture is native." St. George's Hall, Liverpool, was not Gothic, but he thought its "coal-smoked Greek arch" had "a singularly noble presence." But St. Paul's Cathedral he did not like at all, for its classicistic arch was wholly "alien to the English sky and alien to the English faith."

By the time he wrote the Preface to the 1907 edition of *Venetian Life* Howells was not ready to abandon Gothicism, but he did admit that he had been "the helpless slave" of Ruskin's "overethicized criticism" when he wrote the book.

I doubt now whether the baroque churches offended my taste so deeply as I pretended; I suspect that they more amused me, and that I would not have turned them Byzantine or Gothic if I could.

In *Roman Holidays* he could still describe St. Peter's as "not so badly baroque as the Church of the Jesuits either in Rome or in Venice, or as their Cathedral at Würzburg; but still it is badly baroque." But Mrs. March feels—and I think it clear that Howells feels with her—that "at Nuremberg I wanted all the Gothic I could get, and in Würzburg I want all the baroque I can get."

Of America not much more need be said than that Howells kept his eyes open and was always intelligent, though quite un-tutored, in his architectural judgments. There is much to be learned about both Boston architecture and décor from *The Rise of Silas Lapham*, especially in connection with the building of Lapham's house "on the water side of Beacon Street," and there are those who view the novel as a profoundly educative force. In *Annie Kilburn* he comments on the Richardson-designed railroad stations. Though he disliked skyscrapers, he found beautiful things to admire even in New York, among them Stanford White's old Madison Square Garden, which, even after visiting the Giralda at Seville, he thought "no servile copy," finding in "its frank imitation a grace and beauty which achieves originality." The basic trouble with New York was the architectural hodgepodge created by the absence of all planning and by unchecked industrial individualism. Whether Howells was right or wrong, he never admired anything because he was told that it was the thing to do. Take the old Medical College in Columbus, with its queer blend of Tudor and Gothic.

It was the distinction of people who wished to be known for a correct taste to laugh at the architecture of the College, and perhaps they do so still, but I was never of these. For me it had, and it has, a charm which I think must have come from something like genius, if not quite genius, in the architect.

While Howells was still in Dayton, he saw a then famous picture of Adam and Eve by Dubufe, but his scrutiny of it was not wholly aesthetic:

This had the double attraction of a religious interest and the awful novelty of the nude . . . ; the large canvas was lighted so as to throw the life-size figures into strong relief, and the spectator strickenly studied them through a sort of pasteboard binocle supplied for the purpose. If that was the way our first parents looked before the Fall, and the Bible said it was, there was nothing to be urged against it; but many people must have suffered secret misgivings at a sight from which a boy might well shrink ashamed, with a feeling that the taste of Eden was improved by the Fall.

Howells seems to have believed that both painting and sculpture were less intimate than writing and that the artist was "more exterior" to his work and "less personally in it." In a sense he believed that all the arts were one, and he admired the work of Bessie Potter Vonnoh because he thought she had got into sculpture "the things I am always trying to get into fiction." When he thanked Howard Pyle for the gift of some pictures, he carefully spelled out the grounds of his appreciation: "My wife and daughter were most incredulous of our good fortune, because they best know how great it was. I can only feel the literary quality of pictures, but as yours are full of this, the drawings were precious to me too." And he takes up exactly the same attitude when he writes a sketch of the life of his Belmont neighbor, George Fuller: "Of his work I think myself unqualified to speak, except on its literary side, which, however, was full." [14]

There is genuine modesty here, but since Howells seems also to have believed that literature was "the only art that fully satisfies," the rest being "clever makeshifts," it is not all modesty. Nothing could sound more modest than his comments on the spring shows of the National Academy in 1896; only one cannot be quite sure that he is not "kidding." He had no use for the "critical jargon, a sort of chinook or pigeon" which had attached itself to art criticism, and he believed that art, like literature, should address itself to "the average man." ("He is a terrible fellow . . . but there are a great many of him, and it is worth while trying to find out his secret if he has one.") In *Tuscan Cities* he urged the Florentine visitor to view Botticelli's "Primavera" and the "exquisitely refined Mino da Fiesole sculptures" precisely because they may be enjoyed "without technique, and simply upon condition of his being a tolerably genuine human creature." He believed that

Certain of us have got a franchise from the government of the universe to take delight in lovely things, and we have no more merit in it than if we were so many traction companies or gas trusts in a usufruct of the streets from the city council.

Certainly he must have known that he was one of these persons. Being what he was, he must often apply the criterion of social usefulness too, as when he valued the "awful canvases" of Vereshchagin "for what they showed of the cruel and hideous disaster of war."

Howells's opportunities for developing standards of aesthetic judgment were superior to those of many of us. His wife had aesthetic capacity; one of her brothers was a sculptor and another belonged to the most distinguished American firm of architects— McKim, Mead, and White. When Howells was in Venice, art study became one of his leading interests; much later, at Chicago, he was tremendously stimulated by the World's Columbian Exposition; through his membership in the Century Club and other groups, he came in contact with Abbey, Sargent (of whom he once remarked that if he didn't find a bad conscience in a sitter, he put it there), Whistler, Beardsley, Pennell, Shinn, Sloan, and many, many more.

I shall not try to catalogue here the paintings and statues which Howells admired. He has been studied extensively in this aspect by Clara Marburg Kirk (*W. D. Howells and Art in His Time*), and I shall only try to note tastes and trends which illuminate his character and personality. In his international novels he sometimes uses great paintings for background. In *Indian Summer* Colville tells Imogene of his "boisterous joy" in Giotto and how difficult it is to keep from laughing at some of the Cimabues, while praising "the great Cimabue" at Santa Maria Novella and the Ghirlandajo frescoes there. Titian's "Assumption" is referred to briefly in *A Foregone Conclusion*, and in *The Lady of the Aroostook*, Lydia and Staniford are married in Venice "under Titian's beautiful picture of Christ breaking bread." In his own person Howells speaks of "the imagination and the power of Tintoretto, . . . the serene beauty, the gracious luxury of Titian, the opulence, the worldly magnificence of Paolo Veronese," whose canvases "glowed from the walls." But he is never afraid to write such a paragraph as this in *Venetian Life*, and never mind if it does not quite jibe with everything that he says elsewhere:

I have looked again and again at nearly every painting of note in Venice . . . but at last I must say, that, while I wondered at the greatness of some, and tried to wonder at the greatness of others, the only paintings which gave me genuine and hearty pleasure were those of Bellini, Carpaccio, and a few others of that school and time.

He often found himself "unequal to the ecstasies which the frescoes of Raphael and his school demanded," and he objected that Michelangelo did not often "condescend" in sculpture to "a colloquial and natural pitch," which is, of course, the same complaint that he makes against various romanticists in literature. "Moses" is "improbable" and therefore "unimpressive." He "never lived." "Day" is "too muscularly awakening" and "Night" "too anatomically sleeping for the spectator's perfect loss of himself in the sculptor's thought." He was inclined to prefer Canova, who, with all his tameness, "more than any other" stayed sculpture "in the mad career on which Michelangelo . . . had started it." He praises the Andrea del Sartos at Pisa regardless of what Browning had said of them, and when he thought the "Farragut" in Madison Square and the "Logan" on Chicago's Lake Front superior to any London statues, he said so frankly. Moreover, when he finds himself admiring John Gibson's tinted creations he says that too. "They do not impress one at all as waxwork, and there is great wrong in saying that their tinted nakedness suggests impurity any more than the white nakedness of other statues."

On his first trip to Europe, on the other hand, Howells complained of the "sensual nudes" at Würtemberg. Much German art failed to please him. In decoration the Nuremberg style was "at best quaint, and at the worst puerile." He hated the monuments glorifying German victory in the Franco-Prussian War; here is the criterion of social usefulness again, and here, too, he ties up art with literature, for he says that this stuff bears the same relationship to "the old German romantic spirit" that "modern romanticism in literature bears to romance." He liked Overbeck ("I perceived in his work the enthusiasm which led many Protestant German painters and poets of the romantic school back into the twilight of the Romish faith, in the hope that they might thus realize to themselves something of the earnestness which animated the elder Christian artists"), but he found the pictures unreal in expressing "the sentiment of no time" and thus standing "without relation to any world men ever lived in." Cranach, however, was another story. He "had sincerity enough . . . to atone for all the swelling German sculptures in the world" and was, indeed, "the only German worth looking at when there were any Dutch or Italian pictures near."

Spain was in another class, if only for Velásquez. "In the Prado there is no one else present when he is by," and it is well that his pictures should have a room to themselves,

not only that the spectator may realize at once the rich variety and abundance of the master, but that such lesser lights as Rubens, Titian, Correggio, Giorgione, Tintoretto, Veronese, Rembrandt, Zurbaran, El Greco, Murillo, may not be needlessly dimmed by his surpassing splendor. I leave to those who know painting from the painter's art to appreciate the technical perfection of Velasquez; I take my stand outside of that, and acclaim its supremacy in virtue of that reality which all Spanish art has seemed always to strive for and which in Velasquez it incomparably attains. This is the literary quality which the most untechnical may feel, and which is not clearer to the connoisseur than to the most unlearned.

In 1904, in London, he learned the glories of the National Gallery ("it is in these rooms that the grandeur of England, historically, resides"), but it was not only her own painters that she had to show,[15] for there were Veroneses and Peruginos and Botticellis and Titians and Rubenses and Rembrandts and Hobbemas there too.

Since Howells sooner or later refers somewhere to everything that belonged to American civilization in his time, it is not surprising that in *The Vacation of the Kelwyns* he should speak of the aesthetic craze of the early 'seventies, when young ladies "abandoned themselves to decoration of interiors; their storks stood about on one leg on stone bottles, flower-pots, and chairbacks everywhere; their lilies and rushes bent and bristled on the panels of all the doors." In *A Modern Instance* he seems to think the Victorian décor of the Halleck house hideous, but since it expresses the character of the people who live there, he gives them credit for good sense in not trying to change it. And certainly his commentary, in *A Little Girl among the Old Masters*, on the pictures his daughter Mildred (later a very competent artist) made after having been exposed at ten to the Italian masters, show that he was no more scornful of humble, sincere effort in art than in literature. Some of these comments may suggest Mark Twain's upon his own aesthetic creations, but though Howells was fully aware of the humorous aspects involved, his mood was far from that of burlesque. Though Mildred did not of course have the gifts of the artists who had inspired her, she had caught their way with symbols, and her father's comments on her pictures show that he was fully aware of this. Of her pictures in general he says that "they are simply the reflection, in a child's soul, of the sweetness and loveliness of early Italian art."

In Ohio "nearly everybody played or sang, and in the summer nights the young people went about serenading one another's houses, under the moon which was then always full." But it was not only under the moon that they sang; there was even singing at the compositors' cases in the printing office. Howells claimed connoisseurship in music even less than in art however, for though one of his diaries records eight "music lessons" in 1857, he also

said that the typewriter was the only instrument that ever responded to his touch. Music with meals, on boats, forms a point
of departure for an "Easy Chair" in 1909, but the writer's main
interest is, as always, with the persons he observes. In the remarkable "Closing of the Hotel" in *Impressions and Experiences*, he
tells us how he waited each day and night listening to the band
playing on the veranda

till it came to that dissolute, melancholy melody to which the Eastern
girls danced their wicked dance at the World's Fair; not because I like
dissolute and melancholy things, but because I was then able to make
sure what tune the band was playing.

The Boston novels contain references to Symphony concerts
and other Boston musical events, and one of Howells's less successful innovations as editor of the *Atlantic* was printing a piece
of music in each issue. Two of his poems—"Folk Song" and "The
Sea"—were set to music by Edward MacDowell, and Howells
was charmed with the results, as he ought to have been. There are
a number of references to Negro spirituals, and one story[16] contains an appreciative account of the Easter morning singing by
the Moravians at Bethlehem, Pennsylvania. At a Baptist chapel in
Wales, Howells once heard "a company of Welsh miners" sing
"like a company of Welsh angels," but he did not attend a music
festival in Wales, "not being good for a week's music without
intermission." Besides Caruso, I have found mention of only
three celebrity artists—Ole Bull ("the fiddle did everything but
walk round the room") and two singers: Patti and Euphrosyne
Parepa-Rosa, who quite enraptured him when she sang at the
Boston Peace Jubilee in 1872. Yet even here he must add:

I knew by my programme that I was enjoying an unprecedented quantity of Haydn or Handel or Meyerbeer or Rossini or Mozart, afforded
with an unquestionable precision and promptness; but I own that I
liked better to stroll about the three-acre house, and that for me the
music was, at best, only one of the joys of the festival.

Opera was a special case. In his Ohio days he thought it a "stumbling-block and a foolishness, though I liked dramatic singing, and indeed singing of all kinds," and in 1906 he wrote Mrs. George Harvey that

opera is terrible to me . . . . it is perhaps because of the light gossamer which now alone protects my scalp that music seems to get in its merciless work, and makes an evening at the Metropolitan like a sojourn in a boiler factory.

How seriously we are to take this I am not sure. During his Italian years, Italian opera was "that divinely impossible thing which defies nature and triumphs over prostrate probability." He wrote of hearing *I Puritani* and differentiated between the tawdriness of a production of *Nabucco* and what he calls the sublimity of Verdi's music. Boston's Wagner fever is referred to in *A Hazard of New Fortunes*, though Basil March himself is a Verdi man. In *Letters Home* the Ralsons hear *Tristan und Isolde* at the Metropolitan, and in *Their Silver Wedding Journey*, *Hänsel und Gretel* is mistakenly spoken of as an "operetta." He enjoyed Caruso especially in *L'Elisir d'Amore* and praised the Metropolitan for having offered it to "an over-Wagnerized public." The Gilbert and Sullivan comic operas were "the most charming things in the world," and Howells shows their influence in *A Sea Change*, for which George Henschel composed the music and which missed production only through the accidental death of the producer who had taken it on. Many years later it was heard over the B.B.C.[17]

While still in Hamilton, Howells saw the Batemans in such plays as *The Beacon of Death*, *Bombastes Furioso*, and *Black-Eyed Susan*; during his first summer in Dayton, he witnessed among other plays *Richard III*, *The Stranger* (Kotzebue), *The Wife* (Sheridan Knowles), and *A Glance at New York* (Benjamin A. Baker), which last seemed to him excessively vulgar in retrospect but at the time it made him wish to appear on the boards himself, preferably as a villain.[18] His brother said that by the time he was thirteen Howells had written five plays. Walter Meserve's definitive collection of his dramatic works embraces thirty-six titles (which is really crowding Shakespeare!), mostly one-act farces, but including also dramatizations of his own novels and of *The Courtship of Miles Standish*, translations of serious plays from Italian and Spanish (two in verse), and even, as I have just stated, a comic opera. Tomasso Salvini acted in *Sansone* and Lawrence Barrett in both *A Counterfeit Presentment* and *Yorick's Love*. The farces must be unique in the American theater for the number of amateur productions they have had (they were also avidly read in the *Atlantic* and the Harper periodicals and in book form), and at least two of them were put on by professionals in London, where they pleased such good judges as William Archer and Bernard Shaw.

It has been said of Howells as of Henry James that he loved the drama but hated the theater. Once at least he comes pretty close to saying this himself, and once he calls the theater "that arch-enemy of the drama." But whoever makes it, the statement is a monstrous oversimplification. Few literary men who have wooed the theater have been consistent in their attitude toward that skittish dame, and Howells was no exception. Nevertheless he was stage-struck all his life. Once he tells us that he "would ten times rather write plays than anything else"; again he says that one gets "closer to nature" and finds "ampler room for the imagination" in prose fiction. Sometimes plays are like bad fiction, and again he identifies showy culture with "the culture, say, of plays and operas rather than books." [19] Yet he loved going behind the scenes, took Winifred there, and found that being able to see the machinery increased his pleasure in the performance. In *The Vacation of the Kelwyns*, Emmerance shocks Parthenope by wavering between the pulpit and the stage, and Elder Nathaniel's son has left the Shakers to become press agent for a popular actress. His father is not shocked, for in his eyes the theater is no worse than the rest of the world. When "Friend Mabel" played in Boston he went to see her but thought her play silly: "it pretended that when the young folks who had got foolish about each other were married they were going to be happy because they were married." But he thinks that "any piece that shows the life of the world-outside as it really is would teach a good lesson." Howells must have agreed with this, for he established a theater in Altruria, where the actors improvise their material in the manner of the *commedia dell' arte*, and in *The Seen and Unseen at Stratford-on-Avon* we are even told that there is theater in heaven. "Eternity gets a bit long," says Shakespeare, "now and then, and a vivid representation of some sort makes it go again."

To be sure, Howells finds much that is wrong in the theater. He disliked its being left to irresponsible speculators, and, like so many others, begged for an endowment. Apparently he did not feel that the "crickets," as Edwin Booth called them, helped much, for he never says a good word for them. In the 'nineties, when the best seats went to $2.00, he began complaining that only the well-to-do could now afford to attend and that probably they could not do it long; the price, he thought, should not be higher than seventy-five cents. It seems odd that he sometimes argues that one does not need to go to the theater; one had better stay at home and read the play. But this was "at the time of life when one hates to go out after dinner," and when one would not go to the theater at all unless he could sit somewhere in the first eight rows orchestra center.[20]

He was so convinced that actors are nearly always better than their plays that at least once he argued in favor of their improvising. Among those mentioned, some repeatedly, are Modjeska, Mrs. Mowatt, Mrs. Fiske, Mrs. Campbell ("a great creature, as good as Duse . . . and with more theatre about her"), Fechter ("I am wholly his, as far as Hamlet goes"), Mansfield, John Drew, Maude Adams, George Arliss, and Irving and Terry (he thought *her* unpleasantly self-conscious). In *The World of Chance*, Coquelin comes to New York—and occasions a bit of literary work for the hero.[21] Older mimes like Clairon, Fanny Kemble, Charlotte Cushman, and Edwin Forrest are sometimes referred to. There is a veiled reference to Mary Anderson in *The Seen and Unseen*, and when Sada Yacco's Japanese company came to New York, they got into one of his novels too.

As early as 1865 Howells wrote his wife that Edwin Booth had "one of the most beautiful faces I ever saw; it is so finely cut, so sensitive and full of character." On the evening of their reception for the Gosses, the Howellses took their visitors to see Booth in *The Merchant of Venice*, and the actor appears in the autobiographical story, "The Pearl," published as late as 1916.[22] Howells thought the haste with which James disposed of Sarah Bernhardt in *French Poets and Dramatists* outrageous, though he himself considered her Hamlet "an offence against public morals." But Bernhardt's performance in *L'Étrangère* must have made a strong impression on him, for he refers to it in both the *Hazard* and *Their Silver Wedding Journey*. And when Colville meets Mrs. Bowen again at the beginning of *Indian Summer*, he notes "a graceful lilt of the head and a very erect carriage, almost Bernhardtesque in the backward fling of her shoulders and the strict compression of her elbows to her side."

In 1895 Howells called Sir Herbert Tree's production of *An Enemy of the People* "the very greatest theatrical event" he ever knew. But the player and the performance upon which he comments in the greatest detail is Julia Marlowe as Juliet. He saw her first in 1896 and found her much more faithful to Shakespeare than Duse as Pamela was to Goldoni. Howells followed Julia Marlowe as breathlessly as if he had never seen *Romeo and Juliet* before, and found her giving a true impression of both Juliet's youth and her development into womanhood. "I could not see where at any time she failed, where her art fell short of her ideal; and as her ideal was so beautiful, I do not know that I could say more than this in her praise." She was always free of the inferior artist's desire to shine at the expense of the play.[23] On the other hand, he seems inclined to place Margaret Mather's Juliet higher than theater historians in general do. When scenes from *Romeo and Juliet* are given for Hatboro's Social Union in *Annie Kilburn*, Mr. Brandreth refers to the Mather production, and though, in

The World of Chance, Brandreth tells Ray that if he has not seen Marlowe, he has not seen the play at all, he adds, "I used to think Margaret Mather was about the loveliest Juliet, and in fact she has a great deal of passion."

Actors fascinated Howells off the stage also, and though he thought of them as a race apart, he never slandered them. "To us of the hither side of the foot-lights, there is always something fascinating in the life of the strange beings who dwell beyond them, and who are never so unreal as in their own characters." He was fascinated by novels of the theater, and in *The Seen and Unseen* he makes Shakespeare rejoice in the actresses the theater has acquired since his time.

His most elaborate treatment of the actor's personality is in *The Story of a Play*. Here the star actor, Godolphin, who gives Brice Maxwell such a hard time in connection with the production of his play, represents a race whose "obligations are chains of flowers," but he is not unsympathetically portrayed, and when *A Counterfeit Presentment* was in rehearsal, Howells was primarily impressed by the seriousness and difficulty of the actor's life. Not only does Godolphin not smoke, he does not even drink tea or coffee, and in his mercurial way he is devoted to the drama as well as to his own career. The closest Howells comes to exploiting theatrical scandal in this novel is in connection with the actress Yolanda Havisham, the woman with the "smouldering" eyes, but we really learn nothing to her discredit except that she is rather "catty" to Maxwell's wife, and since Mrs. Maxwell detests her, and she knows it, the score is about even here. It is true that Grayson, who represents the better type of theatrical manager, tells Maxwell that she has been "marrying and divorcing," but it turns out that she has only been widowed.

Howells's affection for the lighter forms of theatrical entertainment would alone suffice to show his feeling for the theater. His love for circuses and parades dates back to his childhood, and though in later years he sometimes indicates that the charm had faded, it is clear that it lasted long. In Italy he loved Goldoni, the Stenterello plays which had preceded Goldoni, and the marionettes, to say nothing of the procession of Corpus Christi! When he got to English resorts, he developed a "passion for Pierrots." If not all these blessings were available in America, we did have Negro minstrelsy, which he sometimes called "our one original contribution to histrionic art," and vaudeville and the dime museum. One interviewer says that in Howells's last years vaudeville became a passion, sometimes taking up two or three afternoons a week. In *Letters Home*, Wallace Ardith takes Essie to Keith's, and a typical performance is described. When, in the early years of the twentieth century, Howells stopped off in Boston on his way to Kittery Point, he would always take T. S. Perry to a vaudeville show.

He took Perry to the "movies" too, not thus contributing much, one gathers, to that gentleman's enjoyment. There are various references to the "cinematograph" in the travel books: the Marches see it in Germany, and Howells seems to have gone to the movies even in Stratford, where he represents the ghosts of Shakespeare and Bacon as being interested in it. As early as 1912 he was defending it against its enemies. The film was "far more innocently tedious as well as innocently entertaining than the ordinary musical comedy or the problem play of commerce." It had "come to stay," and, as it had already been shown capable of good things, "we may fitly ask ourselves not only what it esthetically is, but what it ethically may be." He found the actors "more rather than less skilled than the average," and "the pantomime has its fine moments, when one quite loses one's self in the artistic pleasure of the drama." Two years later he was sufficiently addicted to the films so that he could write that "there was a sudden flick in our experiences, as at the moving-picture shows, when a new film has been substituted," or, with reference to Kathleen Norris, "I who have always loved the films and their measureless possibility for good will not be thought to underpraise her work when I call it a moving-picture show." [24]

With all this interest in the movies, it seems odd that Howells never refers to any particular film or player. Surely he must have seen Chaplin, and surely he must have seen the great Griffith spectacles, *The Birth of a Nation* (1915) and *Intolerance* (1916), but I have found no references to them. By 1916 he seems indeed somewhat less sympathetic toward the cinema than before, for he now fears that the stage (including vaudeville) may be threatened with extinction by it. "It does all that money can do, but its limit seems strictly financial, and within its bounds are not the things which money cannot buy: as inspiration, as the personal equation, as the illusion of the first time." That same year Howells found movie-makers active in St. Augustine, but though the films being exhibited there were nearly all bad, he here speaks one of his few kind words for "romanticistic" material: "They were less offensive as they were more romantic; when they tried to be realistic they illustrated the life of crime in the East, and of violence in the East." He put the movie-makers into the last novel he ever started, "The Home-Towners" ("it will be quite different from all my other things"), but the story did not get far enough to show us what he intended to do with them. In 1918 he wrote Mildred, "I wish I were with you and Evelyn at the movies this afternoon."

V

The closeness of Howells's attachment to his mother has been discussed elsewhere in this book. He was still dreaming of her when she had been dead forty years and seeing her "as alive and contemporary with the living people of this day." As a small child he was also so attached to his Welsh grandmother, Anne Thomas, that he regretted he himself must become an old man and not an old lady.

Of his father Howells wrote that he was "not a very good draughtsman, not a very good poet, not a very good farmer, not a very good printer, not a very good editor . . . but he was the very best *man* I have ever known." Late in life he admitted to his brother Joseph that father was "trying" and "what God made him," but since he simultaneously affirms that mother was not equipped to do justice to his "limitations," this is not really derogatory to him. In 1905, however, he wrote his sister Aurelia that he never knew how much he loved his father until after his mother had gone, as she had almost absorbed his youthful affection. During the last month of his father's life, he stayed by his side and felt afterwards that his passing had marked an epoch. "I can go back with him to my childhood no more. It has aged me as nothing else could have done. I am now of the generation next to death." And when his own son grew up and went away from home—"homes, strangely enough, are founded to furnish the materials of other homes by their overthrow"—he relived the past with new understanding.

John's short vacation is over, and he leaves for New York this afternoon. I hate to have him go, and now I understand father's pain at parting with me, as I once could not. What a pity that we learn everything in life too late! All the time I remind myself of father, in some way or other, especially when I unexpectedly catch sight of myself in the glass. I have lived a very intensely personal life, but now I seem more ancestral than individual.

There were eight children in the Howells family, and the novelist was close to them all. Aurelia and Annie had literary aspirations, and Howells, who thought Annie's conversation better than the best of his own books, did everything possible to encourage both sisters. If any one sibling was dearest, it must have been John, the second youngest; Howells wept when he said good-bye to him upon leaving home, and later, when John died at school, he wrote the "Elegy on John Butler Howells" which is one of his most ambitious though not perhaps most successful poems. In 1859 he wrote Joe,

As boys, and members of the great evil brotherhood of boys, we had many fights and quarrels; the first are now become impossible, and the latter I hope we have left behind us forever. It seems a foolish superfluity to write this, but I have never yet told my brother in words how dear he was to me.

The last sentence is characteristic of Howells's reserve, but the "great evil brotherhood of boys" is interesting because it shows how far he was from Wordsworth's idealization of childhood. "I wish I had been on that island," he wrote Mark Twain after reading *Tom Sawyer*, but he never made childhood the lost Eden of innocence that Mark did.[25]

Sam and Henry were perpetual drains, Sam because he seems to have been inept financially, if not lazy, and Henry because, probably as the result of an injury suffered in childhood, he became both epileptic and feeble-minded. Since he lived until 1908, he was a dreadful burden to his father and sisters. In the 'eighties Howells was having a recurrent dream about Henry attacking him in an "odious way." In 1886 he did attack his father, causing Howells to warn him that unless Henry were locked up, "he will cause your death." Fortunately he was not always violent, and his famous brother never forgets to remember him in his letters home nor to send him gifts, though he does not seem to have been sentimental about him except perhaps after his death, when he spoke of him as "our poor beautiful brother" and expressed the opinion that if he had not been afflicted, he would have been the most gifted of the family. The drain on Howells's bounty was not, however, confined to Henry and Sam, for he was by all means the most prosperous member of the family and he was not often permitted to forget it. Like most such persons, he never hesitated to give advice on all subjects from grammar to haircutting. When the family fails to tell him whether or not some smoked tongue has been received, despite his repeated inquiries, he thinks the tongues themselves might well have answered by this time. And though he realizes that Joe may well resent advice on economy from one who himself lives wastefully, he adds bluntly that he has the money to waste and Joe doesn't and that this makes a difference.

The sexual love that has created the family in which a boy grows up is pretty far in the background so far as he is concerned; it is different with the family he establishes. For all the prudery with which Howells has been (sometimes unjustly) reproached, it must not be forgotten that he was a country boy. In his youth, manners were freer in the country than among equally respectable people in the city, and his innocence cannot long have remained ignorance. When Jeff Durgin and Cynthia are engaged in *The Landlord at Lion's Head*, Howells tells us that "it was not the first kiss by any means; in the country kisses are not counted very serious, or at all binding, and Cynthia was a country girl." Lemuel Barker of *The Minister's Charge* is shocked by the courting he observes at country school, but it does not take him long to learn how to kiss Statira Dudley in Boston.[26]

Howells has a surprisingly large number of references to public love-making. It was his considered view that love is a passion that enthralls the possessed but bores the observer, yet he seems to have spent a good deal of time watching it. He found it more frankly displayed in England than in America, yet it is observed on Boston Common on the very first page of *A Woman's Reason*, and the Marches are driven home from Washington Square when the lovers take over in the spring. But his favorite ground of observation for "Public Billing and Cooing" was clearly Central Park, and he is honest enough to recognize this as the inevitable "baleful blossom of our overgrown and overcrowded urban life" and even to suggest the possible advisability of "bowers built for two" to afford privacy![27]

Howells discovered the complexity of human motives early, and even in his early novels, his people do not behave quite so properly or conventionally as those who have not read them imagine. By implication *A Foregone Conclusion* attacks clerical celibacy,[28] and in the early verse narrative, *No Love Lost*, the lovers are approved of for following the dictates of their hearts instead of clinging to an Evangeline-like fixation-loyalty. In *A Modern Instance* Hannah Morrison becomes a prostitute. In *A Woman's Reason*, Helen Harkness, though a very different sort of girl from Marcia Gaylord,[29] is quite as passionate in her love for Robert and quite as frankly unhappy when she believes herself to have lost him. There is one passionate love scene in *The Shadow of a Dream*, and the evangelist Dylks in *The Leather-*

wood God is a frontier Elmer Gantry, no less honestly observed for not being caricatured.[30]

Howells was brought up on the sexual ethic of Swedenborg, which does not read morality and legality as synonyms and rejects only the "casual fruition" which Milton associated with harlots. But his own behavior must always have been extremely discreet, and though the bitter "Thistles" in *Poems of Two Friends* suggests that he may have experienced rejection, we have no evidence to confirm this. We know the names of two girls who attracted him in Jefferson—Mary Ellen McAdams and Julia Van Hook—but he tells us he was so in awe of Julia that he wanted to run away from her, and in his old age he could not remember that she had ever spoken to him. One Easter Sunday, in Columbus, he fell in love with "*A Being*" whom he saw at the Catholic church, and in 1860 "a white-faced being in a blue dress" caused him to die "three several divine deaths," but, alas, when he encountered her in a low-necked dress at a party, his passion "dashed itself to death against a sharp and poignant shoulder blade." In Venice, before Elinor Mead came out to marry him, he missed the girls he had known in Columbus; there is even a diary reference to "KJ my first love," though he adds that he could not fall in love with her now.

The most shocking example of prudery in Howells's life came very early. He set down the terrible story in *Years of My Youth*, and it must have taken much more courage to do so than it takes to confess the kind of faults that are so much more popular in autobiographies nowadays.

There was a poor girl, whose misfortune was known to a number of families where she was employed as a seamstress, and the more carefully treated because of her misfortune. Among others my mother was glad to give her work; and she lived with us like one of ourselves, of course sitting at table with us and sharing in such family pleasures as we knew. She was the more to be pitied because her betrayer was a prominent man who bore none of the blame for their sin; but when her shame became known to me I began a persecution of the poor creature in the cause of social purity. I would not take a dish from her at table, or hand her one; I would not speak to her, if I could help it, or look at her; I left the room when she came into it; and I expressed by every cruelty short of words my righteous condemnation. I was, in fact, society incarnate in the attitude society takes toward such as she. Heaven knows how I came by such a devilish idea of propriety, and I cannot remember how the matter quite ended, but I seem to remember a crisis, in which she begged my mother with tears to tell her why I treated her so; and I was put to bitter shame for it. It could not be explained to me how tragical her case was; I must have been thought too young for the explanation; but I doubt if any boy of twelve is too young for the right knowledge of such things; he already has the wrong.

Of course the mature Howells would have been quite incapable of such cruelty as this, but he still expresses many opinions and reactions which a great many would now call prudish. He would not vote for Cleveland with "that harlot and her bastard" in the background, and though he tended to feel that newspapers had no right to suppress anything but the "very loathsome" and "unnatural" happenings,[31] he more than once indicated approval of bowdlerizing the classics, and indeed of extending bowdlerization from the realm of morals into that of taste. "Bowdler went only half far enough. He left the lewdness out of Shakespeare, but he didn't leave out the dullness. I want an edition of the English poets with both left out." He refused to write an introduction to a collection of de Maupassant's tales for Harpers unless they were willing to allow him to free his mind "about *one* master who was also a blackguard," and he refused to accompany Mark Twain when he called on Elinor Glyn! Though he died too soon to learn how wrong he was in assuming that readers in general are necessarily revolted by the immorality they find in books (if this were true, corruption could not exist) and that it would be impossible for a vicious work to be successful in modern times, he was still aware that the younger writers were doing and saying things that would not have been tolerated in his time. "I like you, my dear young brother," he wrote Joyce Kilmer, "not only because you love beauty, but love decency also. There are so many of our brood I could willingly take out and step on." And he was never more winningly innocent than in the letter he wrote Robert Herrick after having read *Together* but before reviewing it, in which he requested to be informed whether the author had intended the book as an impartial picture or "as a polemic for wider freedom in the sexual relations that the accepted ethics now grant." From the beginning his own longing was for the "cleanly respectabilities," and he never forgot the advice of an early editor: "Never, *never* write anything you would be ashamed to read to a woman." After his children came, "palpitating divans" were ruled out of his stories by the embarrassment he would suffer if his children read his books. He even objected to one of Augustus Hoppin's illustrations for *Their Wedding Journey* because it showed Isabel undressed in the sleeping car.[32]

This was less prudery, however, than fine sensibility. Hoppin's picture presented Isabel in an undignified aspect, and Howells felt obliged to be courteous even toward the characters he had created, though in this case he was probably not wholly uninfluenced by the fact that the character had in a measure been modeled upon his wife. Howells did defend Zola, regarding indecency itself as a necessary condition of the important work he was trying to do. He carried the torch for James A. Herne's *Margaret Fleming*, which caused many people to stalk out of the theater when Margaret nursed her husband's bastard on the stage. And he championed James's later novels, though admitting that they were not "quite jeune fille" in their implications, because he thought that "maturity has its modest claims." In 1902 he published in *Harper's Bazar*[33] a remarkable article called "What Should Girls Read?" His answer was that "if the proper study of mankind is man, and if self-knowledge is the sum of wisdom, there would seem to be no reason why girls should not read everything." Citing the frankness of the great literature of the world, including the Bible, he even ventures the bold opinion that innocence will not be corrupted even by that which is truly corrupt.

Howells accepted sex as the basic postulate of human life. He saw celibacy as the fatal flaw in Shakerism[34] and would not even grant that it was the "logic" of *The Kreutzer Sonata* that marriage was wrong, though he admitted that Tolstoy pushed on to this conclusion. Viewing Tolstoy generally, Howells found him telling the truth about passion as no other writer has ever told it, but he is clear that Tolstoy's own commentary on the *Sonata* was his great mistake.

Though Howells was distressed over the increasing prevalence of free love and easy divorce in America, he saw both George Eliot's Dorothea Brooke and Henry James's Isabel Archer as "sublimely true to a mistaken ideal in their marriages." In 1895 he gave divorce problems pretty sophisticated consideration in a review of a group of English social comedies, and in 1916 he gave a favorable review to Jesse Lynch Williams's comedy, *Remating Time*, in which these matters are viewed anything but solemnly.[35] In 1897 he frivolously declared "that I like heroes and heroines to be born in wedlock when they conveniently can, and keep true to it; but if an author wishes to suppose them otherwise I cannot proscribe them except for subsequent misbehavior at his hands." And in 1916 the "higher journalist" had an interview with a divorced man who wished to marry a divorced woman and had been turned down by four Protestant clergymen.[36]

He also faced the basic facts of human psychology and allowed for the effect of historical conditions upon it. The license of the Restoration period disgusted him, but he knew that it was an inevitable reaction against the preceding Puritan repressions. In 1915 he saw signs that another age of license was beginning, but he was not shrill about it. Knowing that it is possible for a man to "love and wholly cease to love, not once merely, but several times," he thought it time to abandon the "superstition" that the same thing was not true of women.[37] When Gorky aborted the success of his revolutionary mission in New York by coming there with a woman who was not his wife, Howells recognized the inevitability of the uproar which ensued but he did not rejoice in it. "He is wrong, but I feel sorry for him; he has suffered enough in his own country." As for his partner, she did not look at all like what she was supposed to be, though Howells admitted he was "not versed in those aspects of human nature."

In 1917 Howells reviewed William McFee's *Casuals of the Sea,* which has a heroine who stoops to folly and does not regret it.

It will be very shocking, if you look at the affair in the old-fashioned way; but the modern-minded reader may ask why you need look at it in that way. If you do, you will be apt to say that her story is very immoral, more immoral than the stories of the French realists when they were at their worst, but were perhaps indecent rather than immoral.

It seems a pity that H. L. Mencken did not encounter this before writing his monstrously ill-informed article about Howells.[38] For it does not stand alone nor represent a point of view elsewhere unexpressed. Reviewing Pinero's play, *The Notorious Mrs. Ebb-smith*, Howells had written, "It is the bare, cold, ugly truth from beginning to end, without a cut-flower to cover its nakedness," but he had immediately added that "there is not a trace . . . of the slobber of *Camille*." Howells did not *enjoy* sexual corruption under any circumstances. But so far as his critical convictions concerning its use in art were concerned, he could face whatever needed to be faced if the motive was right. Wallowing in corruption for the love of it was something else again.[39]

VI

Howells knew that woman's basic appeal to man is sexual and that marriage is primarily a sexual relationship; in *Heroines of Fiction* he declares that "women exist in the past, present, or future tenses, the infinite, the potential, or imperative moods of love-making; otherwise they do not exist at all." But he knew too that the sexual relationship is not all there is to it and that it is entirely possible for a marriage to succeed on the sexual level and yet come at last utterly to grief.

Theoretically Howells was willing to grant that no man can know much about women. In *Fennel and Rue*, the mother of Philip Verrian the novelist tells him that "you can paint the character of women, and you do it wonderfully—but, after all, you can't know them as a woman does." In practice, however, he seems to have thought he knew women very well (since he tells us that novelists are to be judged primarily by reference to their portraits of women, he could hardly have undertaken the writing of fiction on any other basis), and he once playfully told Charles Dudley Warner that he had acquired his knowledge early, being the Serpent who tempted Eve.

Many of Howells's contemporaries thought he had slandered women, and once when he was asked, "Why don't you give us a grand, noble, perfect woman?" he replied that he was waiting for the Almighty to set him the example. He speaks of "women in their endearing inconsistencies, incoherencies, and illogicalities" (from the masculine point of view, that is to say, for he always makes it clear that the intuitive feminine way works pretty well for women), and his farces are full of scatterbrain, charming, utterly unreasonable creatures. But such women appear in the novels also, and one might cite among many others, Mrs. Ellison in *Their Wedding Journey* and *A Chance Acquaintance*, Mrs. Elmore in *A Fearful Responsibility*, Mrs. Langbrith in *The Son of Royal Langbrith*, Louise Hilary Maxwell in *The Story of a Play*, and both Miss Bellard and Mrs. Crombie in *Miss Bellard's Inspiration*. But perhaps the best example is the woman of whom we see most in Howells's novels, Isabel March. Isabel is certainly not expected to forfeit our sympathy, but though she is never again quite so unreasonable as she is on her honeymoon, when, terrified of crossing a bridge in the Goat Island area, she announces that she will not cross it again to go back, remaining deaf to all her husband's pleading, and then jumping up and recrossing without a tremor when embarrassed by the approach of strangers, she remains a wilful creature nevertheless and often takes up an attitude of maddening superiority toward her husband. When she reaches a decision, she treats his "consent as a matter of course, not because she did not regard him, but because as a woman she could not conceive of the steps of her conclusion as unknown to him and always treated her own decisions as the product of their common reasoning."

Howells believed too that women always take a personal view of everything, and that when anything goes wrong, "a woman always wants some one punished; some woman first, and then some other woman's men kindred." This is partly because they are ignorant: personality is the only thing they know. In *A Modern Instance* Marcia enters into her husband's affairs "with the keen half-intelligence which characterizes a woman's participation in business," and if we are to judge by *Doctor Breen's Practice*, which is full of idiotic women but which makes out a poor case for this or any other thesis, Howells took a rather dim view of woman's future in the professions; as Grace herself tells Libby, "a woman isn't something else first, and a woman afterwards." But though Howells may have agreed with one of his characters that women "do their thinking in their nerves rather than their brains," he generally attributes their ignorance to their defective training. He once told an interviewer that girls were too much restrained and that their emotionalism and childishness were the results of faulty upbringing. On this occasion at least, he doubted any fundamental differences in character between men and women. But I must repeat that in his eyes the feminine mystique works pretty well for women. In love a woman is always more than a match for a man, and Van Wyck Brooks was right when he observed that Howells saw woman as the pursuer and man as the pursued long before Shaw. Women are unscrupulous in love too, for selfish and unselfish reasons alike. They do not necessarily mean "no" because they say it, yet they are capable of a directness in love-making which must frequently dismay their lovers.

Howells praises both Brieux and Tolstoy for what he regards as their generous attitude toward women, and he sometimes affirms "woman's primacy in things of the heart and soul." Like all sensitive men, he was impressed by what women go through to bring men into the world, and he wished to amend the so-called "double standard" not by lowering woman to man's standard but by raising man to hers. Though he was at times cool toward woman suffrage, he devoted many "Easy Chairs" to it and never opposed it; when he was seventy-five he marched up Fifth Avenue in a suffrage parade. He once argued that since politics is a matter of conduct, woman, who is primarily "a moral being," was better qualified for it than man, who is primarily intellectual. Mr. Homos thinks women better Altrurians than men because they are less competitive, and Basil March does not even believe that beauties are always vain. Even woman's penchant for husband-managing is often for the man's good, and Howells makes Shakespeare defend Anne Hathaway against the ungenerous speculations the world has entered into with regard to her.[40]

Howells is nowhere more like Trollope than in his portraits of admirable, thoroughly believable girls. The daughter of the convict Tedman in "A Circle in the Water" (*A Pair of Patient Lovers*) is not portrayed full length, but her attitude toward her father and her power of forgiveness certainly testify to a generous reading of feminine character on Howells's part. Peace Hughes in *The World of Chance* is very neatly a saint, and the more complex Margaret Vance in *A Hazard of New Fortunes* is a cross between saint and society girl. In *The Son of Royal Langbrith*, Hope Hawberk heroically faces her father's drug addiction and cares for him tenderly, though her gayety of spirit seems hardly credible. But perhaps the most impressive girl of all is the proud, incorruptible Suzette Northwick of *The Quality of Mercy*. Though we are told that she has faults, her behavior seems wholly admirable—her willingness to give up the money upon which her father's creditors have no legal claim, her generosity toward him, and not least the frankness with which she meets and accepts Matthew Hilary's love.

Kitty Ellison of *A Chance Acquaintance* has plenty of girlish weakness, but she also has excellent good sense, reasonable pride, and the courage to make a difficult decision and hold to it in spite of her own inclinations. (Howells must have liked her, for he gave her a taste for his kind of fiction!) Helen Harkness of *A*

Woman's Reason is one of the most charming girls he ever
created when we first meet her; when she is thrown upon her own
resources, she turns out a dreadful little goose, but she never
ceases to manifest both honor and stamina. In *A Modern Instance*,
the passionate, undisciplined Marcia Gaylord falls in love with
Bartley Hubbard before he has shown any interest in her, loses her
pride altogether when she thinks she has lost him, and takes a
bold, desperate initiative to win him back. But with all her faults,
Howells permits Marcia more integrity than her husband, and the
collapse of their marriage is due more to him than to her.

Florida Vervain of *A Foregone Conclusion* is a "superb creature, so proud, so helpless; so much a woman, so much a child,"
with a "passionate nature" and a "proud, helpless femininity." "In
the attitude of shy hauteur into which she constantly fell, there
was a touch of defiant awkwardness which had a certain fascination." Yet I think Ferris and (by implication) Howells are a little
hard on her for her outburst to Don Ippolito: "You are not asked
to comment on my behavior to my mother; you are not invited to
speak of my conduct at all!" Don Ippolito was out of order, and
the girl is very young; especially in view of her quick repentance,
Ferris's judgment that she is "a perfect brute" seems ill-advised. In
The Lady of the Aroostook, Lydia Blood says some sharp things
to Staniford, with much less provocation, and is not judged nearly
so harshly for it.[41] But if Howells is unfair to Florida here, he
makes it up to her in the end. Her attempt to comfort Don Ippolito, when she learns that he is hopelessly in love with her, is not,
as most novelists would have made it, a mere theatrical trick,
which gives Ferris, who observes it unseen, a misapprehension
concerning her, but a manifestation of true womanly compassion
—as Don Ippolito himself says, "not a woman's love, but an
angel's heavenly purity."

Lower-class women are less frequently encountered in Howells's novels, but when he does introduce them, his humanity does
not falter. David Gillespie's sister in *The Leatherwood God* is a
good example, or even the slatternly Mrs. Kite in *The Vacation of
the Kelwyns*, who cannot learn to cook a decent meal but has

pleasant manners and is free of malice. In *The Minister's Charge*
Howells's portraits of the ignorant, brainless, and in a sense man-
crazy Statira Dudley and her friend 'Manda Grier are merciless,
but he does not malign them. One is touched by Statira's illness
and by her affection for and loyalty to Lemuel, even though one
knows she would be bad for him, and the loyalty of the tart,
"smarty" 'Manda toward her is, in its way, admirable also.[42]

In *A Fearful Responsibility* the conflict between a man's and a
woman's approach to the business of mating is very skilfully portrayed, and much too subtly to be summed up in a phrase. Readers
of *Indian Summer* have always been aware of the unwisdom
shown by both Colville and Imogene Graham in permitting themselves to be drawn into an unsuitable love affair, but it seems to
me that Mrs. Bowen has generally been regarded as considerably
more blameless than she is, and I confess that when, at the end, she
and Colville get together, I feel much as I do when Henry Esmond, having lost Beatrix, settles for her mother. Mrs. Graham
shows considerable sexual jealousy toward Imogene, and she must
bear her share of the responsibility for the situation which develops. Howells must have been aware of this also, for he tells us
that a girl Imogene's age has no settled character but is all potential.[43] He develops the incompatibility which appears between
Colville and Imogene quite convincingly. He also convinces the
reader that Imogene does not really love Colville, though she is
quite sincere in supposing that she does. But, for that very reason,
generalizations cannot be erected on the basis of their failure.
True love *can* exist under the circumstances postulated, and had it
done so in this case, a wholly different development might have
ensued.

This is perhaps another example of Howells's refusal to idealize
even good women, and it is not the only one. The case of Mrs.
Lapham has already been examined. Both the Lapham girls are
lovesick. Penelope keeps her feelings to herself out of consideration for Irene until Tom himself upsets the applecart, whereupon
what Ellen Glasgow would have called Irene's "vein of iron"
comes heroically (and quite convincingly) to the surface, while

Pen not only quixotically refuses to accept Tom's love but makes herself a burden to everyone around her until at last her mother's harsh, salutary words, when Silas's ordeal comes to a head, causes her to get her mind off herself and snap out of it.

As to "bad" women, Howells can be surprisingly clear-sighted for so chivalrous a man. Thus he thought George Eliot's Rosamond Vincy a great achievement ("such women literally kill men, and the more generous the men the more easily they fall the prey of such women"), and when he reviewed Robert Grant's *Unleavened Bread*, which has a bitch-heroine, he spoke of "the sort of insensible selfishness which appears oftener and more notably in women than in men, and renders them the monsters they can never see themselves." Henry Arthur Jones's play, *Mrs. Dane's Defense*, caused him to declare that "a certain kind of evil is done only by a certain kind of woman, and that she is never a good woman, no matter how much she is sinned against." He refused to believe that all unfaithful wives have been "seduced." Many of them, he thought, were seducers.

Bessie Lynde of *The Landlord at Lion's Head* is probably Howells's most unworthy young girl; she enjoys playing with fire and displays considerable malice toward Jeff even when she is attracted to him, being completely capable of sincerity, it seems, only toward her alcoholic brother. The invalid Mrs. Mavering of *April Hopes* is charming at her best, but under physical suffering she turns into an ingenious tormentor of her family, and Christine Dryfoos of *A Hazard of New Fortunes* almost matches some of Charles Reade's viragoes. In *Ragged Lady*, the society woman Mrs. Milray is jealous and spiteful toward Clem while posing as her benefactor, and nothing could be too harsh to say of the gross, ignorant hypochondriac, Mrs. Landers, who virtually adopts Clem with the idea of leaving her money to her and fails through pure inadvertence, having eaten herself to death. ("I don't think she was herself some of the time," says the girl charitably, to which the vice-consul replies, "Well, if she'd been somebody else *most* of the time it would have been an improvement.") But perhaps the worst women in the novels are Bittridge's mother in *The*

Kentons, who is as nasty as Mrs. Heep in *David Copperfield*, and Mrs. Mervison of *Miss Bellard's Inspiration*, who is a cross between a lunatic and a fiend. She aborted her husband's career as a painter, preferring to have him live on her money rather than to have any interest apart from her, and she spends her life tormenting him and asking for a separation, so that when he finally agrees she may make up with him again and rivet the chains more firmly than ever.

Some Howells women require further consideration. One is the "manoeuvring, humbugging mother" of Alice Pasmer in *April Hopes*, who "lived a thousand little lies every day" and was yet "a better woman, a kinder woman" than her idealistic daughter. Alice is no such monster as Editha in the short story of that title (*Between the Dark and the Daylight*), who sends her conscientious-objector lover to be killed in the Spanish-American War so that she may enjoy an emotional jag, but she comes close enough to her so that the marriage at the end of the novel is the unhappiest happy ending that could have been conceived. Alice is religious, high-minded, and idealistic, but she is so ignorant, and her idealisms are so ill-directed, that she becomes a self-tormentor and a burden to others. Thus, though her mother is hardly an authority on high spiritual matters, she is quite right when she tells her that "your Church makes allowance for human nature, but you make none," and it is not surprising to find Dan turning for comfort to Mrs. Pasmer even before the wedding. The elder Mavering sums it all up when he says:

Some of the best people I've ever known were what were called worldly people. They are apt to be sincere, and they have none of the spiritual pride, the conceit of self-righteousness, which often comes to people who are shut up by conscience or circumstances to the study of their own motives or actions.

Another, more complicated woman is the central character in the novel which was called "Private Theatricals" when it was serialized in the *Atlantic* during the seventies and rechristened by her name, *Mrs. Farrell*, when it appeared in book form after

Howells's death. "Your Mrs. Farrell is terrific," wrote Fanny Kemble to the author. "Do for pity's sake give her the Small Pox —she deserves it." Mrs. Farrell lives in a world of perpetually dramatized emotions; she has a passion for situations, and since she is a woman, these generally take the form of involving some man emotionally. For all that, I should hesitate to call her an evil woman, and I think Rachel may be assumed to speak for her creator when at the close she says of her, "She did more than she meant, and I don't know as we ought to be made to answer for more harm than we mean." All in all, I should say Howells's best summary of his ideas about women was probably achieved in his essay on the fiction of W. Pett Ridge,[44] whom he praised for his knowledge of the sex, and where he spoke of

their nobility of character, their courage, their goodness in circumstances which would turn men cruel, their superiority to origin and environment, their gracious mindedness, their maidenly, wifely, motherly devotion to all types, good, bad and indifferent, of the other sex, as well as their lightness, weakness, narrowness; their often vulgarity, whether in high life or low; their readiness to flirt and make fools of themselves as well as of men; their deceit and insincerity, their suspicion and jealousy, and the other ugly traits that deform their character, and are at least as much a part of their natures as the corresponding defects of their qualities are in men.

Howells was far too sensitive to human experience to take up a dogmatic attitude toward love; here, as in other areas of experience, he realizes that there are many more questions in the world than answers. In *The Rise of Silas Lapham* he speaks of love as "the most tremendous of human dramas, the drama that allies human nature with the creative, the divine and the immortal, on one side, the bestial and the perishable on the other," and the Saratoga clergyman of *The Day of Their Wedding* is quite as serious and even more idealistic when he speaks of it as "the very symbol of eternity in human life" and "the giving up of self." Yet Howells also tells us that "love is always an illusion," "the most selfish and fatuous of the passions," and "the most decrepit of human interests," and Fairford of *An Indian Giver* tells a woman that she attracts him because she attracts him and not because he admires her character. "You might at least say," she pouts, "you believe I could *become* your ideal," but he replies that he does not believe this at all. "I don't trust you in the least, and I care all the world for you." When Don Ippolito of *A Foregone Conclusion*, desperately in love with Florida Vervain, asks Ferris, "Can there be any higher thing in heaven and on earth, than love for such a woman?" Ferris replies, "Yes; both in heaven and on earth." Howells's Swedenborgian training had taught him that there is such a thing as mating for eternity, but Swedenborg did not believe that such unions always begin here. In the vast majority of cases, human love is "a plain, earthly affair, for this life, for this trip and train only." [45]

But perhaps these commonsensical views did not completely satisfy Howells any more than they have satisfied other men. Love-making may have bored him as a man, but no novelist ever used it more. He often comments approvingly on "the wild, sweet liberty which once made American girlhood a long rapture." In *Indian Summer* Mrs. Bowen looks back upon such a girlhood with pleasure, though she cannot, and will not, give her daughter the same kind of thing in Europe. And though Howells never goes quite so far as Mark Twain went when he declared that sexual delinquency was not even thought of in Hannibal, he always takes it for granted that this freedom will not be abused, though he must certainly have known that in some cases it was.

Courtship is the "prettiest" phase in the history of love.

All is yet in solution; nothing has been precipitated in word or fact. The parties to it even reserve a final construction of what they themselves say or do; they will not own to their hearts that they mean exactly this or that.

When in *Private Theatricals* Mrs. Gilbert describes courtship as "woman's reign" ("her lover is never truly subject to her again"), she comes considerably closer to court-of-love notions than she (or possibly even Howells) realized. In *April Hopes*, the only novel he ever devoted wholly to a courtship, he suggests that it is "only the man-soul which finds itself" even then. "The woman-soul has always something else to think of." And in *The Story of a Play* he adds: "It is the convention to regard those days as very joyous, but probably no woman who was honest about the fact would say that they were so from her own experience."

For all that, Howells can be quite romantic enough. Ellen Kenton suffers as much from love-sickness as anybody in mediaeval literature, yet for all the trouble she makes, we are supposed to sympathize with her and admire her, and to hope for the best when, as soon as she comes to herself again, she prepares to plunge into a fresh shipboard romance with Breckon. Indeed, for all Howells's convictions as to the need for caution in marriage, his lovers often plunge recklessly ahead, the man proposing when he hardly knows the girl. When Matt Hilary chooses the daughter of the defaulter Northwick in *The Quality of Mercy*, he knows how "grievous" his choice must be to his father and mother, "how disappointing, how really in some sort disastrous; and yet he felt that if there was anything more sacred than another in the world for him, it was that love." Howells himself was scornful of Gibbon's "I yielded to my fate; I sighed as a lover; I obeyed as a son" as a justification for giving up Mlle. Curchod, who became the wife of Necker and the mother of Mme. de Staël, and when, in the Gallery of Fine Arts at Liverpool, he found young people frankly looking at each other instead of the pictures, he did not blame them: they could come and see the pictures when they were old "but now they had one another in a moment of half-holiday which could not last forever." Perhaps the most sentimental character in Howells is Owen Elmore of *A Fearful Responsibility*, who moons for years over the possibility of having "spoiled two lives" by spiking Lily Mayhew's romance with Captain Ehrhardt even at her own request. But it may be that we come closer to what he really felt in the Shaker stories. *The Day of Their Wedding*, in which the Shaker lovers leave the Family and come to Saratoga of all places, where they are married but fail to consummate their marriage and return to the Family instead, is tenderly, humorously, and non-committally presented. In *A Parting and A Meeting*, too, Howells is noncommittal, for the woman who chose love and the world and the man who sought the heavenly life among the Shakers are equally disappointed. But in his account of the real Shaker at Shirley who obviously suggested this story, Howells opts for love: "But perhaps in an affair like that, a girl's heart had supreme claims. Perhaps there are some things that one ought not to do even with the hope of winning heaven." What champion of "all for love and the world well lost" ever went further than that? In another passage Howells says: "The sum of Shaker asceticism is this: they neither marry nor give in marriage; but this is a good deal." In *The Undiscovered Country*, where Ford and Egeria carry on their courtship under the very noses of the Shakers, who cannot openly sympathize with them, yet cannot bring themselves to condemn, we have a beautiful example of the classical comedy situation of the gap between human aspirations and the realities of human nature. And the Shaker Elihu tells Ford that "there is no need of a reason for love. I learned that before I was gathered in." And he adds: "We say nothing against marriage in its place. A true marriage is the best thing in the earthly order. But it *is* of the earthly order." And with this too Howells seems to have agreed.

The institution of marriage, then, was inescapable. "The only question with the philosophic mind is how to make it tolerable when it cannot be made happy." Reasonableness in choosing life partners is supremely desirable, but it is also extremely unlikely. Children of twenty or twenty-three, whose judgment we would not trust in any other matter, are simply not qualified to choose a life partner intelligently. Young people marry as if their marriage concerned themselves alone. Actually it involves both the families represented—that was what Howells wanted said in the composite novel, *The Whole Family*—and if it fails it may affect "the peace and comfort of the whole community." Sometimes he wished that society would take the kind of interest in a marriage that is shown by the Quakers and the Mennonites, making divorce more difficult by making marriage more difficult, but he must have known that the chances of that were pretty remote. "A broken engagement," says Mr. Waters of *Indian Summer*, "*may* be a bad thing in some cases, but I am inclined to think that it is the very best thing that could happen in most cases where it happens." Is it really a bad thing that the marriage plans of "A Pair of Patient Lovers" should be frustrated? "What if they should gradually grow apart, and end in rejoicing that they had never been allowed to join their lives? Wouldn't that be rather Hawthornesque?" Dr. Anther is somewhat surprised, after Mrs. Langbrith has finally refused to marry him, to find that he does not suffer as he had supposed he would; the time comes indeed when he wonders "whether he had ever really felt a passion for her, such as even in middle life a man may feel for a woman." And even Isabel March knows that if she had never had her children, she would not have missed them, and that if Basil had died just before their marriage, she would have got over it. All this is no solution, however, and Howells must have known it. Breaking an engagement is no insurance against becoming engaged again, quite as unwisely, and bachelorhood creates as many problems as it solves.[46]

Howells did, however, hope that people might help to solve the marital problem by training themselves not to expect too much of marriage. The one thing you can be sure of, if you are a man, is that your wife will run you,[47] but this is no guarantee of a meeting of minds.

Ah, you cannot befriend me, with all your love's tender persistence!
  In your arms' pitying clasp sole and remote I remain,
Rapt as far from help as the last star's measureless distance,
  Under the spell of our life's innermost mystery, Pain.[48]

Moreover a good deal of the pain will proceed from the unkind things which even husbands and wives who care for each other will say and do. When Maxwell and Louise Hilary (*The Story of a Play*) have been married only six months, he is obliged to admit to himself "that, though they loved each other so truly, and he had known moments of exquisite, of incredible rapture, he had been as little happy as in any half-year he had lived." Silas Lapham and his wife say terrible things to each other, such as would end any other relationship for good and all. And the Reverend Mr. Sewell in *The Minister's Charge* finds that it is much easier to "make one's peace with one's God than with one's wife."

In *A Foregone Conclusion* Howells tells us that Ferris and Florida Vervain were not able to sustain the "operatic pitch" of their betrothal after marriage. The circumstances of their coming together were far more romantic than those which prevail with most Howells matings; so too were those which involved Rhoda and Dr. Olney in *An Imperative Duty*. Yet neither couple is deliriously happy; what they find they have on their hands finally is a good, sensible, tolerable, every-day match.

There are times when Howells seems to be somewhat overplaying his conception of the inevitable disappointments of marriage. In the addendum, twelve years after, to *Their Wedding Journey*, Basil tells Isabel that she is "certainly a little wrinkled," and she tells him that he is "very fat." At the ages indicated this seems a little like blowing out the gas to see how dark it is. I think he forces the note, too, at the end of his "Idyl of Saratoga," *An Open-Eyed Conspiracy*, where the Marches dismiss the Gage-Kendricks romance with these terrible words:

"She is very beautiful, and now he is in love with her beautiful girlhood. But after a while the girlhood will go."
"And the girl will remain."

This seems to me bad art, not because it is untrue, but because it has not been prepared for; it is like Poe's abruptly calling the dead girl "poor child of sin" at the end of "The Sleeper." On the other hand, the hopeless ending of *April Hopes* is quite perfect because here we have been convinced both of Alice Pasmer's hopelessly idealistic unreasonableness and of her husband's fatal disinclination to face any issue he can possibly evade:

> If he had been different she would not have asked him to be frank and open; if she had been different he might have been frank and open. This was the beginning of their married life.[49]

VII

The marriage of William Dean Howells and Elinor Mead seems to have been quite as happy as that of Samuel L. Clemens and Olivia Langdon, and Elinor was quite as important to her husband, both as a writer and as a man, as Livy was to Mark Twain. We know much less about her, however, though no doubt we may infer something from Isabel March and the other Howells women who resemble Isabel. At the party which the Howellses gave for the Bret Hartes at Cambridge in 1871, John Fiske thought Elinor "very pretty and charming; vivacious and amusing as always." She had designed the house on Concord Avenue without the help of an architect, and Fiske considered her to have done a remarkable job.[50] Brand Whitlock, who saw her in 1909, after she had been many years an invalid, got a very different impression. Sahe came "fluttering in," he tells us, "a thin, nervous, little woman, all in black, with an effect in dress . . . that reminded one of the 'seventies. She poured tea for us . . . talking rapidly and nervously," and he goes on to record that she spoke of the money value of some paintings that were leaning against the wall and adds that he was glad Howells did not hear this, for it would have embarrassed him.[51] Howells himself tells us that Elinor wouldn't meet guests in later years but "took it out in eavesdropping and spying round." But he also says that on an ocean crossing of 1908 she was "the belle of the ship. She talked with everybody, and ran to and fro like a girl of 17 instead of 70."

In the early days Mrs. Howells called her husband "Pokey," and in her Venetian diary she chose Hawthorne as "the author whom I most admire" and called the Pope a murderer for allowing men to risk their lives to illuminate the dome of St. Peter's. Her husband thought she never got over regarding their son as a small boy, and he told Mildred both that she praised her letters more warmly than she ever praised her to her face, and that, since she herself knew much more about art than she did about poetry, she was more in awe of Mildred's literary than her artistic achievements. She was taking enough iron "to run a machine shop" as early as 1871, and since she seemed to have no positive disorder, her husband could not understand her continued feebleness. She seems to have suffered a miscarriage in 1869, and four years later Howells says she weighed only seventy-eight pounds. Her handwriting was handsome, strong, and bold, a refreshing contrast to her husband's.

Howells wrote little about her directly, because, as he says, what he felt was quite inexpressible. There is practically nothing in *Venetian Life*, though their marriage occurred during the period covered by the book, and when, after her death, he wrote *Years of My Youth*, their meeting and their marriage and their married life get only a paragraph. At the very end of his paper on "The Closing of the Hotel" he says, "We are the last guests in the house," but there has been no mention of his wife in the entire essay and no previous suggestion that he was not there alone.

Fortunately what he did write leaves no doubt how he felt about her. At the very beginning there was some sort of misunderstanding between them, but this was removed by an unexpected letter he received from her in Venice on January 6, 1862. It turned the world into heaven for him, and by June, when a letter was late, he stopped work to worry about whether she was "dying, or dead, or indifferent or anything of that sort." Early in their married life he wrote her, "I *hope* you are coming down here next week. When I think of seeing you possibly on Monday, I'm almost crazy." It was strong language for him, but he meant it. She was never well again after Winifred's death, and he always looked after her devotedly. When, in 1909, she had to undergo a serious operation, she managed to do it when both he and Mildred were away, so that they knew nothing about it until it was all over. The next Christmas he was reading *The Tragic Muse* to her and trying to lengthen it out because she said there were not many things she cared for any more, and when he asked her what they were, she replied, "Well, James, and his way of doing things—and you."

The next year she died,[52] and her husband began waking up every morning at two or three and descending "into hell, with blank despair." He would go to vaudeville shows to try to forget and find himself sitting there blindly staring, or start to tell her something and then stop. Two years later he was writing his brother that Kittery Point was "terribly strange" without her. "I miss her more and more as time passes, and *realize* that I shall never see her again unless I somehow, somewhere go to her. She will not return to me. Death, which parted us, can alone unite us." Two more years and he was telling W. B. Dean that he was "only half in this world since my wife left it. I work still, but life is like a dream, and flows away shadowily." In 1915, nearly five years after her death, he was still dreaming of her nearly every night, "and sometimes glad dreams." And in 1918, when she had been gone eight years, and he had only two years left himself, he dreamed that he had to arrange a second marriage between Elinor and himself. "The only second marriage," he calls it, "I could imagine for myself." Even, it seems, in a dream! And this was the man who had insisted in his fiction that marriage was "a plain, earthly affair, for this trip and train only"!

Elinor Mead Howells was a lifelong Unitarian and, I should guess, less imaginative or spiritually-minded than her husband. She did not believe in immortality, and this can hardly have helped him in his struggle to believe. He could tease her over such a remark as she made when Winifred was born—that she wasn't "an intellectual-looking child"—but I have found only two remarks of his about her that seem in any way disrespectful. One is in a 1909 letter to Mark Twain—"I can't leave the old lady alone"—and the other dates back to 1863, when he wrote his father from Venice that he had made her his amanuensis: "As I always have a great deal to say without much disposition to say it, and as Elinor never has anything to say with the greatest possible desire to talk continually, I think you will be perfectly satisfied with the result of our arrangement." She seems to have failed him only once—over the Spanish-American War—and in 1898 he wrote Mark Twain,

Everything literary here is filled with the din of arms, but Providence, which has turned our war for humanity into a war for coaling-stations, seems to have peace in charge and to be bringing it about. I hope so; for then Mrs. Howells and I will stop fighting, she being a Jingo.

She supported him in his brave attempt to help the Chicago Anarchists, though they both believed he was jeopardizing his position with the Harpers, and when we remember that until her health broke, he read her every word he wrote and discussed it with her before printing it, and then remind ourselves how clear-sighted much of what he wrote about women was, we get some idea of how tolerant and open-minded she must have been.

In *A Fearful Responsibility*, Owen Elmore, writing the history of Venice that Howells so long planned to write, "made a point of admitting his wife as much as possible into his intellectual life; he read her his notes as fast as he made them, and he consulted her upon the management of his theme." Howells himself did exactly this. Once, in an "Easy Chair," he declared that critics were of no use to an author; the book must be helped while it was being formed or else it could not be helped at all. Instead of the critic, therefore, "it was some unknown friend who came to the author's help, his wife, or his brother or sister, and saved him from such folly and shame as he escapes." With him it was his wife who "became with her unerring artistic taste and conscience my constant impulse toward reality and sincerity in my work." He told Abraham Cahan that she was his "severest critic" and that "if something doesn't please her, she rips it to shreds mercilessly" and Charles Hanson Towne that "she often points out the way to me." [53] She read his proofs too, and once when Horace E.

Scudder took over during Howells's illness, the novelist thanked him for saving him "from the merciless excisions of Mrs. Howells!" Apparently she did not like all his work equally well, and apparently, too, he himself was always the final judge. In 1888 he wrote Higginson that she thought one of his books too grim. Later he reports to Henry B. Fuller that she had found an error in a review: "she will not suffer me to use *brute* as an adjective, and I do not know what I shall do about it, adjectives are so scarce." But in the same letter he speaks of the "brute pen" he is using; "Mrs. Howells is not by." Like most authors' wives, she took considerable interest in her husband's earnings, and in 1892 she thought $500 too much for one of his pieces and then decided it was not enough. "Such is the effect of prosperity on the female mind." The only literary secret I know of his ever keeping from her was the $500 he lost on the Sellers play he wrote with Mark Twain. As for her pride in his work and the charmingly feminine way in which it extended to his person, I do not know any more touching bit of testimony to this than the fact that when Henry Rood came to see him on business, she fondly made him put on the Oxford gown he had just worn for a photographer.[54]

Howells had the normal man's love of children, but I should not say that he was sentimental about them. Mildred Howells said in 1906 that when, as a child, she would come to her father when he was working and ask him if she could do something, he would reply, "Yes, but go away." Commenting on the son of the Marches in the addendum to *Their Wedding Journey*, he declares bluntly that "in his actuality a boy has very little to commend him to the toleration of other human beings." On the other hand, there is a very early letter to his brother Joseph in which he congratulates him on the birth of a son and adds, "Girls are not the thing until they get to be about seventeen or eighteen years old." [55] He was still a young man when he felt that trying to talk to children was a "sad business," though he was inclined to blame himself for this rather than them. When he was left alone with his own son, he admitted that his questions tired him.

In the introduction to the anthology of stories about children called *The Heart of Childhood*, Howells cites Dickens, Thackeray, Barrie, and Aldrich as having pioneered in writing stories about children for their elders to read. In *Christmas Every Day and Other Stories Told for Children*, the "Papa" who tells the stories is mercilessly pummeled by his children whenever he tries to tease them or fails to give satisfaction. It is interesting too that the title-story has the little girl coming "into her papa's study, as she always did Saturday morning before breakfast," and asking him for a story.

Then he saw that he would have to mind, for they were awfully severe with him, and always made him do exactly what they told him; it was the way they had brought him up.[56]

"The Amigo" in the story of that name (*The Daughter of the Storage*) is a non-malicious, Buster Brown-kind of boy on shipboard. Rose Adding in *Their Silver Wedding Journey* is an appealing portrait of a sensitive, delicate, idealistic boy. Boyne Kenton is fine too, and the scene in Chapter XXI of *The Kentons*, in which, troubled over his infatuation for the Princess, he steals into his sister Ellen's bedroom in search of comfort, is perhaps the tenderest thing Howells ever wrote. DeForest thought Effie Brown of *Indian Summer* "simply a wonder—the most perfectly painted child in fiction—at least so far as I know." This tribute is deserved, I think, so far as the narrative is concerned, but Effie ceases to be at all childlike when Howells makes her talk.

As we have seen in connection with his wife, it was not Howells's way to expand in public concerning his own emotions, but there can be no doubt as to his love for his children and later grandchildren. In 1870 he wrote Higginson of his son, "He's something to eat up—something between peach and olive, with such a smooth, solid surface. Well, children *are* nice—one's own especially." In 1909 he sat up until midnight writing a valentine to one of his grandsons, and that same year he wrote one of them, William White Howells:

It is very sweet of you to send that birthday card, where we are walking toward the sunset together. It is a lovely sunset, but sad, and the
night is beyond it. Hold fast to my hand, dear little boy, and keep me
with you as long as you can. Some day, I hope not too late, you will
know how I love you.[57]

All three of Howells's children were gifted. The son, John
Mead Howells, became a ranking architect, best known to literary
folk because he designed Mark Twain's "Stormfield" at Redding,
Connecticut. Mildred, her father's closest companion and comfort
after the death of his wife, had gifts both as artist and writer.
Once he went to see her off for Bermuda for her health, "and
then from pure homesickness could not let her go." And in 1902
he had "a great talk" with her in the woods which left him feeling
that she was his equal, but, he adds, she may not think that is
much. Yet one gathers that it was his first-born, Winifred, who
was closest to him and upon whom he had built the most, and
her death, in 1889, when she was not quite twenty-five, was to
him much the same tragedy as that of Susy Clemens was to be to
her father Mark Twain.

Winifred was born in Venice, December 17, 1863, and her
father thought she looked "ridiculously" like him. (Her mother's
unpublished journal records her first days in charming detail.) By
her second birthday Howells was writing his father that he was
already thinking as much about her as he did about her mother.
When she was a little child, he had to "come down the parlor
chimney, 'with a bound,' " for her, "the idea being represented by
rattling on the screen and then jumping out into the middle of the
floor. Then I am Winifred Howells, and lie asleep on the sofa
while she brings me a Christmas Tree." In retrospect it seemed to
him that her early maturity ought to have warned him of her fate;
there was one party at which she enjoyed herself greatly because
a charming young man talked to her about John Stuart Mill!

Winifred was the high-minded, talented (she wrote poetry),
idealistic nineteenth-century girl who has been preserved for us at

her best in the fiction of Henry James. Her health began to fail as early as 1880, but the acute stage did not set in until 1885. Her malady, never diagnosed in her lifetime, was so capricious and subject to fluctuations that both she and her parents were kept on a perpetual seesaw of hope and despair. Up to the very end, they were speaking of her "stubbornness" and her "hypochondriacal illusions," and she was gaining weight under the forced feeding and other agonies to which she was subjected, when suddenly, on March 3, 1889, she confounded all the diagnoses of the wise men by suddenly dying. Then Dr. S. Weir Mitchell ran an autopsy and found that she had been suffering from an organic disease.

Mrs. Howells was permanently crushed, and though Winny's father went on with his work, he hardly suffered less. One day he stretched himself out beside his daughter's grave in the Cambridge Cemetery and "experienced what anguish a man can live through." He could not feel her nearness there, but at a hundred other places in Cambridge, she was still the little child who used to cling to his hand. In one of the Prefaces for the abandoned "Library Edition" he spoke of her death as "the bereavement which left life in the shadow not to be lifted on earth." "I wonder how we live," he wrote James; "it seems monstrous." And to his sister: "I suppose I shall grow to bear it better but I cry every day, and more bitterly than at first." In 1890, in one of the wildest of his many wild dreams, he dreamed that he was going to be hanged and had a chance to escape but refused to take it: "No, I am tired of living; and it's only a momentary wrench, and then I shall be with her."

Since he was a writer, of course he had to write about her. What he wrote did not please him, for when he matched it with "the truth in her," it had "a false ring. But it seems the best I could do; and it will only be one more blunder for her wisdom and goodness to forgive. That will be easy for her." And the one source of comfort that not even death could take away was the knowledge of what she had been:

I can only try to give some notion of her character in saying that as I look back upon it, I can see nothing to blame in her. "To be young and gentle and do no harm, and to pay for it as if it were a crime"— that was her part "in the great play of destiny," as she called this phantasmagory. She was, if I may so express it, an unconscious conscience; every impulse in her was wise and good; she seemed no more to think or feel evil than to do evil. She had the will to yield, not to withstand; she could not comprehend ugliness, it puzzled and dismayed her. She had an angelic dignity that never failed her in any squalor or sickness; she was on the earth, but she went through the world aloof in spirit, with a kind of surprise. She was of so divine a truthfulness that in her presence I felt the shame of insincerity as in no other.

Her voice was gentle and soft, and her utterance somewhat hesitating and low. She was slender and rather tall, with a quick, undulating walk. Her face was of the mediaeval type; the outline was oval, but the chin was heavier than that of the classic mould; her hair, dense and almost black, grew low upon her forehead, which was of a perfect loveliness above her level eyebrows; she was dark rather than fair, yet with a warm color in her cheeks and lips, and she had eyes of a strange, starry, wondering purity. Mr. Lowell once wrote us, after meeting her, "All New England looks from her beautiful eyes." [58]

When Susy Clemens died in 1896, Howells wrote Charles Dudley Warner that Winny had died again in her. And he wrote her mother a letter of consolation which she kept in her New Testament until she died.

The only really surprising thing about the domestic arrangements of the Howellses was their everlasting moving. Once they even set up their household goods at Lee's Hotel in Auburndale, Massachusetts, and though they lived "off and on" for many years in an apartment house on West Fifty-ninth Street, they moved in and out of it a number of times. In the perpetual shiftings of Mr. and Mrs. Landers in *Ragged Lady* Howells shows his awareness of the disadvantages of not having a settled home, but he never really did anything about it. Once he declares that he couldn't write "while shifting about so much," but this was obviously not true. If it had been, he would never have written anything.

"Redtop," the beautiful house in Belmont, Massachusetts, designed by McKim, Mead, and White, was supposed to be permanent; so was the Beacon Street house in Boston. Neither turned
out that way. He bought a summer place at Far Rockaway, Long
Island, but traded it for a house on West Eighty-second Street.
In March, 1901 he bought a house at 38 East Seventy-third Street,
which gave him something more like a library than anything he
had had since Beacon Street days. But by July, the Howellses
were moving into an apartment again, Elinor being incapable of
looking after the house and the location being noisy. Many of
these changes were made on account of Mrs. Howells's health
and some because of Winny's health. Sometimes financial considerations were involved. But it is hard to believe there was no
underlying restlessness—the great American disease of moving
about. "I have long looked forward to settling for life," Howells
wrote his father in 1893. "Now at times I have to recognize that
there is very little of this life to be settled for [as it turned out
there were to be twenty-seven years], and that I ought to be
settling myself for the next, if I wish to be settled at all."

CHAPTER FOUR

MR. AMERICAN

I

In *Years of My Youth* Howells wrote that his father "took a personal interest in conventions and nominations" but that he himself "took no interest whatever in them; their realities did not concern me as much as the least unrealities of fiction." He adds:

I was never at a meeting, a rally, or a convention; I have never yet heard a political speech to the end. For a future novelist, a realist, that was a pity, I think, but so it was.

This was something of an exaggeration however. Howells was not a "party man" nor a "joiner," and except for theater-going, he seems to have been disinclined to take any of his pleasures in crowds. He never cared much for sermons either, though he liked them better than political speeches or lectures. But he was not altogether innocent of political conviction. He himself admits it in *A Boy's Town*, when, recording his father's desertion of the Whigs when they nominated Taylor, he says, "My boy [that is, himself] then joined a Free-Soil club, and sang songs in support of Van Buren and Adams." His writings of 1857 ff. in the Cincinnati *Gazette* and elsewhere deal largely with the doings of the legislature, and though they are not the work of a dedicated politician, they are not that of a political ignoramus either.[1]

Howells was less shrill in his denunciation of monarchy than Mark Twain was, but the feeling was there just the same. He speaks of "the dreadful Philip II" (who seemed humanized a little only when a Spanish guide referred to him as "Philly") and of "that merciless miscreant," Queen Christina of Sweden. He did not admire either Mary Queen of Scots or Queen Elizabeth—"the poor, brilliant, baddish Scottish queen" and "her brilliant, baddish English cousin." He calls Charles I "my enemy," which would certainly seem to be overpersonalizing the matter, and Charles II "a godless blackguard." In 1903 he even regarded the adultery of the Crown Princess of Saxony with uncommon toleration for him because it contributed to show up the "putrescence" of regal splendor.[2] In his early novels at least, as Fryckstedt has pointed out, Howells shows a certain tendency to regard Europeans as "only children as yet," who have not grown into "the manhood of freedom," and to play down the cultural advantages for which Americans are inclined to envy their cousins. He was pleased when he thought Matthew Arnold was at last "beginning to understand, that the secret of our political success is in the easy and natural fit of our political government, the looseness of our social organization," and when Parkman finished his great history, he hailed it as showing "that spiritual and political despotism is so bad for man that no zeal, or self-devotion, or heroism can overcome its evil effects" and "that the state which persistently meddles with the religious, domestic, and commercial affairs of its people, dooms itself to extinction."

The glory which Lincoln shed over the Republican Party lasted quite some time for Howells, though by 1892 he was sure the reactionaries were in control. He could not believe Greeley actuated by the evil motives his enemies ascribed to him, but he supported Grant in both 1868 and 1872. Though he did not admire Blaine, whom he regarded first as an ass and then as a rogue, he supported him against Cleveland. It has been said that in 1896 he voted for Bryan, but what he wrote his father in November was that he *would* vote for Bryan if it were not for the free silver heresy, and he had already told his sister in June that he expected to vote for McKinley for President and then support the state Socialist ticket.[3] As for Theodore Roosevelt, Howells appreciated both his abilities and his character, and responded to his charm and vigor (though he admits he found him wearing), but at the outset he thought him rash and impulsive, as many people did, and he found it hard to forgive him his part in bringing on the Spanish-American War. Later the two men were on very good terms personally. Roosevelt read everything Howells published, as he apparently read everything else, and the President and the novelist agreed on a number of issues ranging all the way from simplified spelling to a tax on incomes and inheritances. Roosevelt also appointed Howells's brother, Joe, American consul at Turks Island. Yet as late as 1906, Howells thought him "a strange man" and believed that nobody had yet "plucked out the heart of his mystery."

The two presidents with whom Howells had close personal ties were Hayes and Garfield. Hayes was Mrs. Howells's cousin once removed, and Garfield knew the Howellses well from Ohio days; it was he who got from Grant the appointment of Howells's father as United States consul first at Quebec, then at Toronto. During the Hayes administration, the Howellses were welcome at the White House and Howells could have had an ambassadorship if he had wanted it.[4] He would not have been himself if he had not used his influence with the President with the greatest modesty and restraint.[5]

II

Though the Man in the Street still thinks of Henry James as having deliberately chosen Europe while Howells preferred America, the antithesis is not quite that simple. Howells defended James against his critics when, during his last year on earth, he became a British subject, though he added that "I myself could not bow the knee to any crowned head, even poor George V," and in 1919 he refused a decoration from Albert, King of the Belgians. He resented Lowell's calling America the "Land of Broken Promise"—"I don't believe you believe it"—and thought it "a dull, sad fate" for an American to go to live and die in a foreign land, "for somehow we seem born in a certain country in order to die in it." When James published *The American*, Howells found the fact that he "could write likingly of such a fellow-countryman as Newman . . . the most hopeful thing in his literary history since *Gabrielle de Bergerac*." [6] Much later he called *The Bostonians* "one of the masterpieces of all fiction" and pleaded that it should not be omitted from the "New York Edition," which it was. Yet he told Thomas R. Lousbury that he himself had enjoyed doing *Indian Summer*, whose scene is laid in Florence, better than anything he had written since another international novel, *A Foregone Conclusion*, because it gave him a chance "to segregate characters and study them at leisure." But his American readers did not want Howells novels laid on foreign soil, and "I shall hardly venture abroad again in fiction."

Like most cultured Americans in his time, Howells was inclined to be of two minds toward Europe. During his Venetian years in the 'sixties he was much in the position of a man who finds himself falling in love with a woman of whom he cannot quite approve. Even the great monuments of the past tended to lose their charm when he reflected upon "what the past really was . . . how stupid, how cruel, how miserable!" As for the present, he does not seem to be sure whether he is more repelled by discomfort and high expense in Italy or by what he regards as the social rottenness and "filthy frankness" of the Germans. Once he wrote his father that when he got home, he planned to go to Oregon "and live as far as possible from the influence of European civilization," but when he feared family affairs might necessitate his return to Ohio, he was very unhappy about it, and in 1864 he wrote Lowell that he must go home soon, because "I am too fond of Italy already, and in a year or two more of lotus-eating, I shouldn't want to go home at all." Rome was "hideous," "the least interesting town in Italy," with "hopelessly ugly" architecture, and primarily distinguished by its "noisome smell," and when Howells was there again in 1883, "the idea of the Colosseum" made him sick. Yet as late as *Roman Holidays*, he finds in the city "a pull with Occidental civilization" which no other city can rival, and when he compares her with New York, he is not far from James's conviction of the essential provincialism of things American. It was not until late in 1905 that Howells wrote Mark Twain that he had forever given up all idea of living in Italy again.

Howells's America, to be sure, was a limited America. He never saw the Far West, and though in youth he considered himself influenced by the proximity of Kentucky and Virginia, anti-slavery considerations caused him to regard the civilization of the South as "spurious" and "semi-barbaric." [7] To all intents and purposes, his America was New York and New England plus the frontier Ohio into which he was born.

His attitude toward Ohio was as ambivalent as Willa Cather's toward Nebraska. When he lived there, hot on the trail of aestheticism, he could not wait to get away, yet Ohio gave him a good deal of his best material for literature. He lived more and more in his early memories as he grew older,[8] and in *Stories of Ohio* he calls himself a Buckeye and takes pride in the state's achievements. Moreover, some of Howells's most advanced social ideals rest directly upon a mid-Western foundation, and Daniel Aaron is right when he says that "Altruria is the neighborly village on a grand scale." To make it quite perfect one only had to impose upon it the culture of Cambridge, Massachusetts in the age of Longfellow.

His first contacts with New Englanders were made in Ohio, and he thought them "cold and blunt," though he never had any doubts about their virtue. In his book about Hayes he wrote:

Work, faith, duty, self-sacrifice, continual self-abasement in the presence of the Divine perfection are the . . . old New England ideal. It was a stern and unlovely thing often in its realization; it must have made gloomy weeks and terrible Sabbaths; but out of the true stuff it shaped character of insurpassable uprightness and strength.

Boston, of course, was a special case. After his first visit there, Howells wrote Fields:

Better "fifty years of Boston than a cycle of New York" . . . . The truth is, that there is no place quite so good as Boston—God bless it! and I look forward to living there some day—being possibly the linchpin in the hub.

But this was written when he was trying to get a berth on the *Atlantic*, and it might be well to discount it a little. When he reviewed Samuel Longfellow's life of his brother in 1886, Howells spoke bluntly of Boston respectability, "its culture, its barbarism, its refinement, its meanness, its servility, its arrogance." Later he thought of Boston faces as "good, just, pure, but set and severe, with their look of challenge, of interrogation, almost of reproof." When you looked at them, you felt like searching your conscience "for any sins you may have committed . . . and make ready to do penance for them." He toned down his satire of Boston while revising *Their Wedding Journey*,[9] but Bromfield Corey, in *The Rise of Silas Lapham* and elsewhere, almost duplicates the legendary Boston lady who asked, "Why should I travel when I'm already here?"[10] Though there is a warm tribute to Boston in *A Modern Instance* (Chapter XX), there is no denying that in the lives of Bartley and Marcia Hubbard, it is an influence which makes for corruption. Even when Howells seems most friendly, his tribute takes a form which one can hardly expect the old-time Bostonian to accept quite without wincing, as when he speculates upon the improvement to be expected when the Irish and the Italians, "two gifted races, with their divinely implanted sense of art, shall join forces with the deeply conscienced taste of the Puritans."

Perhaps Howells's fullest consideration of the Proper Bostonian was made in connection with Kitty Ellison's encounter with Miles Arbuton in *A Chance Acquaintance*. She

was oppressed by the coldness that seemed perpetually to hover in Mr. Arbuton's atmosphere, while she was interested by his fastidious good looks and his blameless manners and his air of a world different from any she had hitherto known.

For all his "weakness and disagreeabilities," she feels that there is "something really *high* about him," and she is quite right about this. Arbuton has so many virtues that it would be reasonable to argue that his rudeness is not quite credible when, at the end, he fails to introduce Kitty to the two Boston ladies he has encountered (thus making her aware of the gulf between them and causing her to break off their engagement). But it is clear too that though he is fully aware of Kitty's inferiority to Arbuton in manners and in style, Howells still prefers her rearing by an abolitionist uncle in Eriecreek, New York, to what Arbuton has had, and that she speaks for her creator as well as herself when she says, "He's a very elaborated person. But I don't think it would make much difference to him what our opinion was. His own good opinion would be quite enough." And again, when she remarks of his superior air, "I can't help feeling that it's a little— vulgar." For Arbuton himself is made to perceive, when it is too late, that throughout the unpleasant scene which terminated their connection, "she has been the gentle person and he the vulgar one." Then he knew at last that "the young girl whom he had been meaning to lift to a higher level than her own at his side had somehow suddenly grown beyond him; and his heart sank."

Perhaps the clue here is to be found in the fact that, even more than Thomas Bailey Aldrich, Howells was never really genuine Boston but only "Boston-plated." He himself says that he "always knew himself alien and exterior to the city that suffered him." The greatest writers of the region laid apostolic hands upon him on his first visit there, and later, when he was editing the *Atlantic*, they even suffered him, in a way, to sit in judgment upon them. But there are still indications that there was uneasiness on both sides. Robert Grant felt that Howells's sympathies were all with the newcomers, his knowledge of such as the Coreys being skin-deep,[11] and Howells himself admitted to Lawrence Barrett that he did not understand Yankee character. Longfellow was not a snob, and he would not have known how to be rude even to a yellow dog, yet though Howells almost worshipped him, he says, "I claim in no wise to have been his intimate." Holmes he knew much better, but Holmes always kept him waiting in the study until a servant had announced his name. ("In the things of this world," wrote Howells, "he had fences, and looked at some people through palings and even over the broken bottles on the tops of walls; and I think he was the loser by this, as well as they.") Beyond all the others, Lowell was his friend, and he was happy to have his correspondence with Lowell deposited in the Harvard Library, when Charles Eliot Norton asked for it, as proof that they had cared for each other. But though it was Howells who got Lowell his appointment as Minister to Spain, there were gaps of years and taste and class and even conviction between them, of which both were conscious, and it was Lowell who said of Howells that he always wrote about Bostonians "as if some swell had failed to bow to him on Beacon Street." There is no sense in blaming the Boston aristocrats for failing to span this gulf; Howells did not accomplish it any more successfully, for all his membership in St. Botolph's, the Tavern Club, and the Saturday Club, which last he did not get into until after he had been blackballed twice.

Toward the very different phenomenon known as New York, Howells took up, at one time or another, almost every conceivable attitude. In *Letters Home*, Wallace Ardith is enraptured by it, but Otis Binning says, "If you wish to lose yourself, this is the shop; if you wish to find yourself go somewhere else." Howells can hardly be said to have found himself there. He did not care for "primordial, abnormal" skyscrapers; "there is a point beyond which sublimity cannot go; and that is about the fifteenth story." In 1888 he liked it at the bottom of his "wicked heart" and hoped to get some of its "vast, gay, shapeless life" into his fiction. In 1891 he declares both that he prefers it to Boston because it is less "dour" and has more to teach him but that if it were not for John he would prefer to live in Cambridge. In 1897 New York "is so ugly that it *hurts*." In 1902 he thought the Boston of days gone by had spoiled him for the New York of today. In 1912 he told a *Sun* interviewer that New York was the most interesting place in America and perhaps in the world, but that it still lacked symmetry and beauty and that he was too old for it. In 1915 he writes, "New York is dreadful and as yet without the charm I used to feel in it."

He resisted moving from Boston to New York so long that one wonders why he ever did, especially since he never saw New York as the capital of literature but only as its mart. Even after he had moved there he summered in New England. During later years he found Cambridge full of ghosts, and once he tried to establish a home at Long Beach. "But whenever I go back to New England I find that so much lovelier that my gorge rises at this region." At York Harbor, in the summer of 1898, he found New England

more amazing than ever, coming from slipshod New York. It is really another nation, and you don't get the full force of it till you reach Massachusetts; Connecticut fringes upon Philistia.

In 1900 he tried to sum it all up in a letter to James:

I can understand your hunger for New England, in these later years. I feel it myself in New York, even, though it is not my country. It has a sort of strong, feminine fascination. It is like a girl, sometimes a young girl, and sometimes an old girl, but wild and shy and womanly sweet, always with a sort of unitarian optimism in its air.

After he died in New York, his ashes were returned to Boston, where they rest not in fashionable Mount Auburn but across the road in the Cambridge Cemetery, near the edge of a ridge overlooking the Charles, not far from James's own.

III

So far in this chapter we have been thinking mainly of Howells's relationship to other Americans. But Howells was no chauvinist, and he thought of people first of all as human beings. He can speak severely of "dogs and pigs of people" and find the face of the average passenger in a horsecar giving the lie to the

notion that nature abhors a vacuum, yet though William Lyon
Phelps tells us that Howells

disliked any person or any book that did not ring true; he hated snobs
and snobbery because they illustrated the vice of affectation, and in
talking about such things he was as violent as he knew how to be,

only Robert L. Hough seems to think that he was "a good hater."
He did praise William J. Stillman's "mediaeval," Benvenuto Cel-
lini-like rancor toward dead men in his autobiography, but that
was a literary judgment. He also says that George William Curtis
is "a man of wholly different make from me; he does good because
he loves; I because I hate," but this refers not to people but to
evil conditions. In one of the *Imaginary Interviews* he asks why
any human being should be called upon to respect another, "seeing what human beings generally are?" But even here he adds,
"We may love one another, but *respect!*"

Here again it must be admitted that Howells was helped by
not setting his sights too high; even in Altruria human nature is
not quite perfect. He sometimes found himself liking James's
anti-heroines better than the heroines, "because I always find
larger play for my sympathies in the character which needs the
reader's help than in that which is so perfect as to get on without
it." He writes of Grace Breen that "she had a child's severe morality, and she had hardly learned to understand that there is much
evil in the world that does not characterize the perpetrators."
Even the people in the London gin palaces "did not look very
bad; bad people never do look as bad as they are, and perhaps
they are sometimes not so bad as they look." He feels the same
way about the criminals he observes in the police courts, even
when what they are involved in is so unsavory that it cannot be
reported for decency's sake: "they seemed rather subjects for
pity than abhorrence." Perhaps the truth is that "humanity adjusts
itself to all conditions, and doubtless God forsakes it in none, but
still shapes it to some semblance of health in its sickness, of order
in its disorder, of righteousness in its sin." March is well aware

of the weaknesses of the ex-convict Tedham in "A Circle in the Water" (*A Pair of Patient Lovers*). He does not "like" him either, yet "his punishment, like all other punishments that I have witnessed in life, seemed to me wholly out of proportion to the offence; it seemed monstrous, atrocious." Even to "forgive" is humiliating and may well embarrass him who forgives more than him who is forgiven. So Howells says, not quite frivolously, that he is "a disbeliever in punishments of all sorts. I am always glad to have sinners get off, for I like to get off from my own sins; and I have a bad moment from my sense of them whenever another's have found him out." He praised President Hayes for having helped to establish the principle "that an insane person is not morally responsible for a criminal act, although entirely sensible of the difference between right and wrong," as in the Nancy Farrer case. And even when Garfield was shot, Howells refused to surrender to blood lust, his sole concern with Guiteau being that he should "receive neither more nor less than justice." Actually, Howells believed human beings incapable of achieving justice: they simply do not know enough. There is justice only with God. For us the choice lies between mercy and cruelty. And in *The Son of Royal Langbrith* the long discussion as to whether or not the sins of a dead rascal who has long masqueraded as a saint should be unveiled or not eventuates in this:

I have never seen any instance of justice in the world. I have seen many instances of mercy. I should say we have a duty to mercy. We are warned more than once to make sure first of our own sinlessness before we offer to judge the sins of others.

It was Howells's own opinion that during the years he led the "realism war" in the "Editor's Study" he had practised "the invariable courtesy toward persons which is possible with those who treat of methods and principles" and that he himself had "every month been assailed with personal offense from the whole cry of anonymous criticism." Generally speaking, I think this true. Some people find it difficult to keep their friends; Howells found it hard to keep his enemies. He was always scrupulously honest, even when reviewing books written by those he loved, and while it would be too much to say that he was never influenced by his friendship, he was careful to enter qualifications and exceptions even when he was reviewing people he liked as well as James and Valdés and Hardy. In the early days he very occasionally carried over the sharpness of his youthful political despatches. He later regretted his attacks on Dr. J. G. Holland, though I am not sure he ever believed he had been unjust, and the two ultimately became friendly. After many years, he apologized to Barrett Wendell for the "abominable spirit" he had shown in a review of his *Literary History of America*, and Wendell replied in the same generous spirit; it would be hard to say which man showed up more attractively. But for sustained and violent invective his review of Max Nordau's "senseless and worthless book," *Degeneration*[12] is unique in the Howells canon. Nordau is "very impudent, or very ignorant," dishonest or at least "shuffling," a dealer in "cheap legerdemain." "Besides, he is offensive in manner, and writes in a vulgar, noisy style; he stamps about, and shouts, and calls names; so that when you dismiss the notion of the amusing madman, you are not sure that Dr. Nordau is altogether sober." But if this is violent attack, it is also impassioned defense of the fine writers and artists whom Nordau had maligned. As we have seen, Howells was considerate even in his judgments of characters of fiction. He has been criticized for not giving Bartley Hubbard any great vices, not making it inevitable, we are told, that he should fall. These critics do not realize that they are paying the novelist the greatest possible compliment: he knew, if they do not, that petty faults can be no less destructive of character than great sins or crimes. Bartley's moral weaknesses are made clear to us from the beginning of the book, and the novelist's achievement is all the greater because there are no melodramatic climaxes. It is effective irony, too, that he should have been innocent of the charge Marcia brings against him to precipitate the final break, and that it should be an accident which prevents his returning to her. What Howells is saying is that with men like Bartley Hubbard everything goes, as it were, by default.

Good people are not all good in Howells, and few of the bad are all bad. There are not many saints like young Conrad Dryfoos of *A Hazard of New Fortunes*, and Conrad's father, dogmatic and unpleasant as he is, is treated very tenderly at the end. Lemuel Barker of *The Minister's Charge* has all the limitations of the countryman. His silence and his stubbornness and his inability to adjust are such that one often wishes to shake him, yet he is admirable too. He is fair to Sewell even after having been, as he sees it, let down by him. He is conscientious, incapable of deliberate evil, and shows considerable capacity for growth. Mr. Milray of *Ragged Lady* bears "a name shadowed by certain doubtful financial transactions," yet Howells presents him as a humane man. In *The Quality of Mercy*, Matthew Hilary, son of the president of the board whose duty is to punish Northwick, is a liberal much like Conrad Dryfoos but considerably less impractical. He loves Suzette Northwick, and her father's crime does not prevent his proposing to her. Both his father and his mother (conventional as the woman's social outlook is), accept his decision without question.

"I'm not ashamed of your choice, Matt [says his father]; I'm proud of it. The thing gave me a shock at first, because I had to face the part I must take. But she's all kinds of a splendid girl. The Board knows what she wished to do and why she hasn't done it. No one can help honoring her. And I don't believe people will think the less of any of us for your wanting to marry her. But if they do, they may do it, and be damned."

Hilary himself plans to resign from the Board at once, and if Northwick returns to the States, he will himself pay his debt, if necessary, to keep him out of prison. Surely this is not the conventional treatment of a "capitalist" by a "Socialist" writer! And surely it involves a generous reading of human character!

Howells saw that character, of course, as the result of an interaction between heredity and environment. He was never willing to go the whole way with the determinists in viewing a man as the *product* of his environment, for that would have been to rob life of moral meaning (and, incidentally, to deprive fiction, which is a study of human behavior, of all moral significance also). A man was often better than his environment; because he has a will of his own he can transcend his environment; otherwise, says Mr. Homos, we would all still be savages "without the instinct or wish to advance." The principle operated in small things as well as great ones: *Ragged Lady* was suggested by an Ohio girl who grew up in squalor yet was chic and ladylike, and Howells once reminded the New Hampshire Forestry commissioner that you cannot prevent hungry people from selling their trees to the lumber interests unless you arrange to relieve their hunger by other means. He summed it all up in an article on Poe about as well as he ever did anywhere: "A man is partly what God has made him, partly what he has made himself, partly what his fellow men have made him." Or, as Basil March puts it: "We can't put it all on the conditions; we must put some of the blame on character." But he immediately adds that "conditions make character." [13]

In other words, Howells prays William E. Barton's prayer: "Help us to make it easier for men to do right and harder for them to do wrong." He knows that whatever human character may be in its inmost essence, evil environment makes it much worse than it would need to be, and the fact that so much goodness as still exists in the world has survived under generally evil conditions proves that there is something there which is both worthy and capable of cultivation. In a cutthroat capitalistic society, where nobody is responsible for anybody except himself, and the wolf never camps far from the door, it is human nature "to hoard and grudge," but in Altruria, where survival does not depend on hoarding and grudging, this tendency disappears; there "it is human nature to give and to help generously." [14]

IV

Was Howells completely without racial prejudice? Perhaps this would be too much to say without modification of any man. But let us look at the record.

The importance of Italy for Howells's writings has been considered elsewhere. For the Italian people too he felt much sympathy. "In the quality of courtesy the Italians are still easily first of all men, as they are in most other things when they will." I am not sure that he cared more for the Italians than he did for the Spanish,[15] but he did find them more sympathetic; the more austere Spaniards would not "let you love them as the Italians do." "The uneducated Anglo-Saxon is a savage; the Italian, though born to utter ignorance, poverty, and depravity, is a civilized man."

For all that, I find a condescension in Howells's attitude toward the Italians; as Mrs. Clemens advised her husband to consider every man colored until he is proved white, so it is obvious that Howells will make allowances for an Italian which he would not care to make for an American. Mr. Homos may find the Italians in New York transformed from the friendly folk they are at home to a "surly" and even "savage" race—and blame New York conditions for the change—and Howells himself, in Cambridge, may write of one Italian woman that "she makes me ashamed of things I have written about the sordidness of her race." Yet he writes of Italy herself:

Most tourists have observed how things which are thought very shameful with us bring no disgrace among Italians. The poor do not blush to beg, and every one with whom the traveler comes in contact lies and cheats.

In 1909, in an address at the annual meeting of the New Society for Italian Immigrants, Howells, though showing his warm feeling for Italians, also spoke frankly of the Sicilian vendetta and other evils; in his address for the Gould Memorial Association in Rome itself, he called Italian children quicker and brighter and keener than other children, yet openly rejoiced that the Gould Home would supplement what the school gave with moral instruction which the children will not receive from their own parents, "to temper their Latin glitter with the sober hues of the Anglo-Saxon virtues."

If one were to judge by the attention she gets in his travel writings, compared to other countries, one would probably conclude that Howells was cold to France, but this is not wholly true. Though he says "I do hate a Frenchman" in *Italian Journeys*, he went out of his way on his seventy-fifth birthday address to pay homage to France as the home of all who care for the free spirit and the life of the mind. Jeff Durgin reports from his travels that "you don't know what a good-looking town is till you strike Paris," and in this matter at least the "jay" speaks for his creator, for Howells himself calls Paris "the most fascinating city in the world" and "a wonderful place, the only real capital in the world." In *A Traveler from Altruria* the only places in our world invoked to give an idea of the physical beauty of that utopia are the buildings of the World's Columbian Exposition at Chicago, Boston's Commonwealth Avenue, and "the prettiest and stateliest parts of Paris, where there is a regular skyline, and the public buildings and monuments are approached through shaded avenues."

Though Howells began to formulate his impressions of Germans and Germany as early as the time of his first visit to Europe, when he declared that "for my own part, I like not their over-ripe sausages and far-smelling cheese, nor their principle as developed in morals and aesthetics," most of the relevant material is in *Their Silver Wedding Journey*, a large part of whose action takes place in Germany. The Marches hate the women-and-dog teams used to drag light vehicles, the omnipresent hideous war memorials, the ugliness of *Under den Linden*, the solemnity of everybody except the children, the nasty habit of combing one's hair at table, and the German lack of taste in house decorations and clothes. But they enjoy and admire "the beautiful language of the *Ja*," the kindness and courtesy of the German people (they are always ready to be reconciled after a disagreement, and Mrs. March's expectations of being elbowed off the sidewalk by German officers are not realized), and the plain good faces of the large flat-footed dancers in the circus ballet. In itself the Rhine is not as beautiful as either the Hudson or the upper Ohio, but "the quaint towns and the ruined castles" on its banks give it an advantage. In the 'nineties, Weimar had been the only town in Germany where Howells could possibly see himself living, but in Mainz the Marches now confess that, except for the presence of shops in the residential streets, they have found a city of "more proper and dignified presence than the most purse-proud metropolis in America."

What of the oppressed races of the time?

There is nothing to indicate any particular interest in Indians, for Howells says practically nothing about them except in *Stories of Ohio*, where the subject could not have been avoided. Admitting that neither the French nor the English "had any right to the Ohio country which they both claimed," he admits also that "if it belonged to any people of right" (why "if"?), it belonged to the Indians, but concludes that "all that is left for us to ask at this late day is which could use the land best and most." The principle involved is that "the earth is for those who will use it, not for those who will waste it, and the Indians who would not suffer themselves to be tamed could not help wasting the land," which is just about what Theodore Roosevelt said in *The Winning of the West*. Howells did not blame the Indians for this; they were "not bad-hearted so much as wrong-headed, and they were mostly what they were, because they knew no better." When white men behave like Indians, he does blame them, and he describes the massacre at Gnadenhütten as "The Wickedest Deed in our History." His final decision (more pragmatic than moral) is that though "much that was beautiful and kindly and noble was possible" to the Indians, "they belonged to the past, and the white men belonged to the future; and the war between the two races had to be." In *Imaginary Interviews* he speaks of Indian Summer as "a stretch of time which we have handsomely bestowed upon our aborigines, in compensation for the four seasons we have taken from them, like some of those Reservations which we have left them in lieu of the immeasurable lands we have alienated."

Howells complained of the denial of suffrage to the American Negro as early as February 1867, and this in a review of a book by H. C. Lea in mediaeval law! (The year before he had already given short, sarcastic shrift to a racist book which attempted to argue the inferiority of blacks to whites on scientific grounds.)[16] Yet I am not sure that he ever loved Negroes as Mark Twain loved them. It is true that Basil March calls them "the most amiable of the human race," and Olney of *An Imperative Duty* thinks that if we are ever to have a Christian civilization, it must come through them. Mrs. March professes herself quite in love with the "beneficent coal-black glossy fairy, in a white linen apron and jacket," who serves her in *Their Wedding Journey*. "I never saw such perfect manners, such a winning and affectionate politeness. He made me feel that every mouthful I ate was a personal favor to him." In *A Hazard of New Fortunes* she extends her favor to take in janitors: "I think we shall all be black in heaven—that is, black-souled." But these Negroes stay where they "belong," ministering to whites, and as late as 1919 Howells admits that it made him uncomfortable to have a white man wait upon him at table. Howells loved Negro minstrelsy, but he has much less than Mark Twain to say about the nobler Spirituals in which so much of the higher aspirations of the race are expressed. "The Pilot's Story" is a tearjerker about a mulatto who drowns herself off a Mississippi steamer because her master-lover has sold her, and much later there is a very attractive Negro girl in "Somebody's Mother." Howells praised Hayes for his championship of Negro rights, and in "Police Report" (*Impressions and Experiences*) he tells us how he enjoyed watching a Negro lawyer badger a white man.

At one time Howells believed that "perhaps the Negroes thought black and felt black; that they were racially so utterly alien and distinct from ourselves that there could never be common intellectual and emotional ground between us." Paul Laurence Dunbar's poetry cured him of that. "God hath made of one blood all nations of men: perhaps the proof of this saying is to appear in the arts, and our hostilities and prejudices are to vanish in them." By 1901 he proclaims that "there is, apparently, no color line in the brain," even wondering whether Negroes may not be more subtle than white folks have supposed. "What if their amiability should veil a sense of *our* absurdities, and there should be in our polite inferiors the potentiality of something like contempt for us?" In "Mrs. Johnson" of the *Suburban Sketches* he had long ago painted the portrait, not wholly free of racial stereotypes, of an amoral but thoroughly good-hearted Negress. In a 1901 article he is "sure that the negro is not going to do anything dynamitic to the structure of society. He is going to take it as he finds it, and make the best of his rather poor chances in it. In his heart there is no bitterness." But before the year has passed, he is finding and lamenting bitterness in a new book by Charles W. Chesnutt, finding justice in it, yet wishing it were not there. And I for one can detect no summons to what is now called "desegregation" in Howells's statement: "If the Afro-American could only realize the fact that many Anglo-Americans are not worth associating with, it might help him put the vain desire from him." [17]

When it comes to racial intermarriage, however, Howells is curiously ambivalent. In theory he is against it, if, for no other reason, because he felt "that there is a precious difference of temperament between the races which it would be a great pity ever to lose." Yet as early as 1869 he reviewed in the *Atlantic* a novel by Anna Dickinson, *What Answer?*, in which a white man marries a rich, aristocratic, beautiful, and high-minded girl, wholly white in appearance but partly Negro by inheritance. Howells did not think the man was making much of a sacrifice but proposed postponing discussion of the matter to the *Atlantic* for January, 2869! It would be interesting to know whether this book in any way influenced *An Imperative Duty*, where Olney does not think it necessary to intermarry with Negroes "but short of that I don't see why one shouldn't associate with them." Since Olney himself marries a sextodecimoroon[18] his creator must have been aware of the irony (and bitter humor) involved here. But there is no bitterness in the young man's almost jaunty handling of the problem, when Rhoda, who, despite her warm sympathy with Negroes, has been almost crushed by the revelation of her own racial inheritance, greets his proposal with a melodramatic: "I am a negress!" "Well, not a very black one," replies Olney. "Besides what of it, if I love you?" And Howells comments that "as tragedy the whole affair had fallen to ruin. It could be reconstructed, if at all, only upon an octave much below the operatic pitch."

In one of his travel books Howells remarks that there is "one human being more odious than a purse-proud Englishman— namely, a purse-proud English Jew." And in 1909 he wrote from Carlsbad of the "troops of yellow Jews with corkscrew curls be- fore their ears" whom he found with other undesirable types at that resort. These are about the only passages I have found which indicate anti-Semitic feeling in any degree. In *The Son of Royal Langbrith* the sculptor employed to do the memorial tablet is called a "little Sheeny" by Falk, but Howells himself describes him as "a beautiful, poverty-stricken young Jew, with black hair brushing out over a fine forehead, and under the forehead, mobile, attentive eyes." His cosmopolitanism in literature militated against his overlooking books by Yiddish writers,[19] and when he became familiar with the slums of New York he was favorably impressed by both the intelligence and the gumption of the Jews who were herded into the ghettoes there in contrast to the behavior of other immigrant groups. Pondering anti-Semitic feeling in 1905, How- ells wondered whether "the moral offal" of the human race had not always devoted itself to trade. This assumption might, he thought, account "for the low degree of favor enjoyed by a di- vinely chosen people, whom other men have driven into finance, and then abhorred for the development of traits inevitable under the circumstances." [20]

But the old-time Bostonians were much more concerned about the Irish invasion than the Jewish invasion, and Howells was not wholly unaffected by the prejudices of his neighbors. In his eyes the Irish were always inclined to take the wrong side in politics and in religion. They were truculent too, and he shrewdly ob- served that they were often unwilling to extend to other minority groups the privileges they were winning for themselves.

Irishmen must of course live somewhere [he wrote his father in 1869]; but they are very disagreeable neighbors; and when I have my window open the noise made by the boys on the vacant lot below puts an end to work. Besides an Irishman in the neighborhood communicates a species of dry rot to all the property: the price of it falls and does not rise again.

Once he wondered what would happen when the Irish encountered the Chinese, now approaching from the other Coast. "Shall we [that is, the native Americans] be crushed in the collision of these superior races?" Though more ironical, this seems about as sensible as Mark Twain's looking forward with dread to the day when the Christian Science Church organization would control America.

Even here, however, Howells tries to be fair, and though the Irishman whom Dr. Olney sends out with a prescription in *An Imperative Duty* is obviously an idiot, the same novel contains a not unsympathetic picture of the second-generation Irish in Boston. From their "hard work and hard conditions" in factories, the girls have acquired "pale, pasty complexions" and "an effect of physical delicacy . . . which might later be physical refinement." Yet as Olney watches them on their holiday, he thinks that "if they survived to be mothers they might give us, with better conditions, a race as hale and handsome as the elder American race," which they have, of course, long since achieved.

If Howells had a real national prejudice, however, it was against the English. At the outset this was determined by historical causes: we fought England in the Revolution, and she was unfriendly to us during the Civil War. When Howells was in England in 1862, he thought himself "constantly insulted by the most brutal exaltation of our national misfortune." He was not unaware of his own British backgrounds, but since these were Welsh and Irish rather than English, this did not help much. He thought Englishmen colossally ignorant of everything outside of England but none the less inclined to entertain and express opinions on that account; and he criticizes them for everything under the sun. Their houses are chilly, and they eat cabbage at every meal; they breathe soot and fog instead of America's "rarefied and nimble air, full of shining possibilities and radiant promises"; their doctors are a horror; they know nothing about art. When Lowell or Higginson or Mark Twain attacks them, he is delighted. And he credits Mrs. Macallister with "that freedom in alluding to her anatomy which marks the superior civilization of Great Britain" when the poor woman has only spoken about resting her weight on her own backbone.

It is their arrogance which is most intolerable. Even so great a man as Matthew Arnold has "the gift, not rare in his nation, of saying needlessly offensive things rashly." When he heard Dickens read, Howells told his sister humorously that it was "rather sad . . . for an American, who had naturalized Dickens's characters, to find that after all they were English," but he was not humorous at all when, as late as 1903, he thought Dickens had made "a dreary failure" of his American types. Of Rose-Black, the English painter in *A Foregone Conclusion*, Owen Elmore wonders

if, in his phenomenal way, he is not a final expression of the national genius,—the stupid contempt for the rights of others; the tacit denial of the rights of any people who are at the English mercy; the assumption that the courtesies and decencies of life are for use exclusively toward Englishmen.

Howells reminds us that

This was in that embittered old war-time; we have since learned how forbearing and generous and amiable Englishmen are; how they never take advantage of any one they believe stronger than themselves, or fail in consideration for those they imagine their superiors; how you have but to show yourself successful in order to win their respect, and even affection.

But surely the apology is even more insulting than the original charge.

To be sure, not all Howells's Englishmen are like that. Lord

Rainford, the democratic nobleman of *A Woman's Reason*, is an admirable man, but Howells makes him ugly physically and treats him much as Thackeray treated Dobbin in *Vanity Fair*. And even in the farce *A Letter of Introduction*, Roberts thinks his English caller not "a bad kind of fellow, for an Englishman," and "liked him as well as it's possible to like any Englishman on short notice."

It is commonly said that during his later years Howells became more friendly toward England, and the change is ascribed to the cordiality with which he himself was received in England, to the popularity of his books there, and even to his agreement with Mark Twain that the Boer War, about the same time as our adventures in the Philippines, had made the two nations "kin in sin." To a certain extent, all this is true. Howells did moderate his sniping at England during later years; he found English travel "pure joy—there is no travel like it"—and he excised certain critical passages from the proposed Library Edition. But the change may easily be overstated. Howells granted that "in England everybody seems kind," but he also says that "all classes of the English are rather simple, or at least far simpler than we Americans are." Their plays are superior to ours but not their fiction nor yet their poetry. And though the stateliness of London streets made New York "seem slight, and crazy, and trivial," he still did not "believe the English half know what they're doing things for," and that it was because they had not "thought it out" that they were "able to put up with royalty and nobility." On his 1899 lecture tour he amused his audiences by telling about the young lady who thought he was an Englishman and dead. "It would be no bad thing, I suppose, to be an Englishman if one were dead." Two years later, when Lord Roseberry suggested the reunion of Britain and America, he not only retorted that this could be achieved only on the basis of the whole Anglo-Saxon world becoming republican,[21] but even thought that the suggestion must inspire in Americans "some wish to take up arms again and fight the Revolution to its historical close." In *Their Silver Wedding Journey* the Marches find Canada "in a very silly attitude, the attitude of an overgrown, unmanly boy, clinging to the maternal skirts, and though spoilt and wilful, without any character of his own," though Howells does add that "it would be a pity . . . if it should be parted from the parent country merely to be joined to an unsympathetic half-brother like ourselves. . . ." Even when declaring for the Allied cause in 1915, Howells thought it necessary to remind England of all her past crimes and particularly of her offences against America. "There are indeed two Englands," and his criterion for distinguishing between them was a simple one. "The good one has always been our friend— and of late years the good one has been growing in power and control." Not until 1918 was he ready to declare:

In all history there has been nothing braver than the recantation of the English faith in aristocracy and their profession of democracy in terms worthy of the inspiration of Lincoln. The spectacle of the reunion of England and America is an event of moral greatness surpassing the measure of any natural catastrophe or material event of the wonder year [1917].

V

Referring to Howells's defense of the anarchists whom he regarded as having been judicially murdered in Chicago after the "Haymarket Riot" of 1886 (the "murderers" did not commit murder, the occurrence was not a riot, and it did not take place in the Haymarket!), his wife's cousin, Edwin D. Mead wrote Henry Demarest Lloyd, "His general standpoint, you know, is the Tolstoi one of non-resistance." Like most statements about Howells, this one oversimplifies. But it is not surprising that, being so strongly humanitarian as he was, the problem of war and peace should have interested him beyond all other political concerns.

Howells was conditioned to anti-militarism from his youth. In the section contributed to his father's book on early Ohio, Howells claimed that as editor his father opposed the Mexican

War "and the atrocity of the popular sentiment" and that this ultimately cost him his paper. Though the opposition was somewhat
qualified,[22] it did exist; many years later, Howells gave it to Owen
Powell in *New Leaf Mills*. In his campaign biography of Lincoln,
Howells makes comparatively much of Lincoln's opposition to
the Mexican War. As a child, he himself was a jingo, however,
wishing for war with England, but his father "would not have the
child honor any semblance of soldiering," even a boy's play-
company. When the Mexican War came, Howells "could not help
feeling that his father was little better than a Mexican, and whilst
his filial love was hurt by things that he heard to his disadvantage,
he was not sure that he was not rightly hated."

It would be easy enough to find statements by Howells which
commit him to complete pacifism: "we who are averse to all war";
battle is "murder on the large scale"; "all war and all the images
of it are cruel and foolish"; "soldiers are under the law of military
obedience, and are so far in slavery, as all soldiers are"; "war
makes imperative things essentially and immutably wrong"; "wars
come and go in blood and tears, but whether they are bad wars,
or what are comically called good wars, they are of one effect in
death and sorrow." He did not wish to go to West Point with
Mark Twain because he hated "the sight of a military factory."

These utterances might be reinforced by expressions of opinion
from Howells's intelligent characters. Mr. Waters of *Indian Summer* does not respect the Italians less for having lost a war. Even
the plays touch on this subject. In *The Mouse Trap*, Campbell
and Mrs. Somers argue about whether a woman can have physical
courage or only moral. She cites various examples, but in each
case he replies that only moral courage is involved. Finally she
asks: "If hers is always moral, what kind of courage does a man
show when he faces the cannon?" to which Campbell replies,
"Immoral." In *Priscilla* Elder Brewster takes up a more humane
attitude toward the Indians than Miles Standish—

> Render not evil for evil, for thence is continual evil.
> Good for evil and peace for war is our duty—

and the heroine, already pacifistic in Longfellow's poem, refuses to be married in a meeting house crowned with Indian heads.[23]

There are, however, contrary utterances. As a youngster, Howells extravagantly admired "the fine behavior of the Spartans in battle, which won a heart framed for hero-worship," and when he came to Washington Irving, he could not decide whether he loved the Moors or the Spaniards more and consequently "fought on both sides." In commenting on past wars, he is likely to be militaristic or pacifistic, depending upon his attitude toward the issue at stake. Napoleon was a "dreadful little man," and even a "little wretch," but when they came to the field of Naseby, both Howells and his wife "began by common impulse to say verses from Macaulay's stalwart ballad of the battle." [24] Though he elsewhere calls Lincoln our greatest president, there is a passage in which Howells puts Washington ahead of him, "for Washington was all that Lincoln was . . . with a vast breadth of military power and achievement beside and beyond," and once he makes the army a profession, along with medicine, law, literature, drama, journalism, and even the church. His account of the Battle of Lexington in *Three Villages* assumes the validity of the American cause in the Revolution, though he grants English readers the possibility of another point of view. In reporting Gibbon's attitude toward the Revolution, he makes it "our cause," and as late as 1904 he placed the Revolution first among "good" wars because it benefitted loser as well as victor. In *Stories of Ohio* all the state's war heroes are extravagantly admired. Considerably more surprising is Howells's admiration for General Custer, and when he reviewed Mrs. Custer's book, *Following the Guidon*, he permitted himself a passage which must cause many a modern reader's blood to run cold, for he speculates on the possibility of regenerating human nature through extending military type discipline to civil life. "If, as Ruskin fancies, the army should ever serve us as the norm of the civil state, and we should come to have 'soldiers of the ploughshare as well as soldiers of the sword,' it might not be long before we should be told that it was against human nature to act selfishly." And he notes that "those who have attempted to dress out a future brighter than this present have always had something like a military organization in their eyes."

The Civil War was the first military crisis he was required to face as a man. Though in retrospect it seemed to him to have been inevitable—"the time had a sublimity which no other time can know"—he had not really expected it. He dreaded it as ushering in an age of barbarism which must retard human progress, and his emotional response to it, as in his 1861 letters to the New York *World*, describing, among other things, the "splendid rapidity with which Ohio filled up her quota of thirteen regiments," may rouse antagonism as coming from a man who not only avoided the war but spent the war years in Venice, ostensibly in government service but actually holding a position which left him largely free to devote his time to cultural pursuits. Such a reaction would not be wholly fair to Howells however; like Mark Twain, he was quite unqualified psychologically for direct participation in the conflict, yet it would be absurd to argue that therefore he must not be permitted to entertain any views concerning it. And here, again, the truth about Howells is more complicated than most of his interpreters have tried to make it out.

To begin with, like Emerson and others who were much older and might have been expected to be wiser, Howells quite lost his head over John Brown. "If I were not your son," he wrote his father in 1859, "I would desire to be Old John Brown's—God bless him!" And it would be difficult to go further than he went in his poem "Old Brown," published in the Ashtabula *Sentinel*, January 25, 1860:

> Death kills not. In a later time,
>   Oh, slow, but all-accomplishing,
>   Thy shouted name abroad shall ring,
> Wherever right makes war sublime.

In a twenty-two-year-old this may be pardonable. But in his obituary for Matthew Arnold in 1888, Howells still listed John

Brown, along with Grant and a number of great writers, as exemplifying the glory of America. Oddly enough, he omits Lincoln from this list.

By the time he published *Stories of Ohio* in 1897 Howells seems wavering a little on Brown, but the emphasis is still on the credit side:

Some think that Brown was mad, some that he was inspired, some think he was right, some that he was wrong; but whatever men think of him, there are none who doubt that he was a hero, ready to shed his blood for the cause he held just. His name can never die, so long as the name of America lives, and it is part of the fame of Ohio that he dwelt many years in our state.

But it was not until Oswald Garrison Villard published his authoritative biography of Brown in 1910 that the scales really fell from Howells's eyes. For Villard caused those who

lived through the John Brown time in love and affection, to question our unqualified reverence and affection, and allow that if he was greatly sinned against he also greatly sinned. . . . If any of us truly believe peace is right and war is wrong; that no good end can justify bad means, that though without the shedding of blood there is no remission of sins, it is the blood shed by the martyr and not by the murderer which shall save us—then we must condemn Brown for what he did in the night on the Pottawatomie, or worse yet, made others do for him. . . . Not by smiting off the ear of the high priest's servant in his wrath at Jerusalem, but by dying for his faith at Rome, did Peter become the rock on which Christ founded His church. The lesson of all war is peace: when will the nations learn it? The lesson of the holiest war, if ever carnage can be hallowed, is no other than that of the wickedest war.

Howells's last word on the subject was spoken in *Years of My Youth*:

Men are no longer so sure of God's hand in their affairs as they once were, but I think we are surer that He does not authorize evil that good may come, and that we can well believe the murders which Brown did as an act of war in Kansas had not His sanction.

He owned that in days gone by he had adhered to a cult, "as certain fervent verses would testify if I here refused to do so." Villard's biography had proved the verses wrong. The people of Virginia "could no more have saved themselves from putting . . . [Brown] to death than he could have saved himself from venturing his life to free the slaves. Out of that business it seems to me now that they came with greater honor than their Northern friends and allies."

As for his own relationship to the war, perhaps Howells did not, at the time, see the whole thing so plainly as it has been set forth here. On May 22, 1861 he wrote to Oliver Wendell Holmes, Jr., hearing that he had enlisted. "For myself, I have not gone in. But who knows himself now-a-days?" But he goes on: "whatever valor I have had in earlier years has been pretty well metaphysicked out of me, since I came of thought," and it is hard to feel that he was ever in great danger. He was probably right when he wrote John Grant Mitchell (reputedly the youngest general in the Union army, who married Mrs. Howells's cousin, Laura Platt), "I do not think a certain *reluctance* (I am loath to call it by a harder name) in my blood at all unfits me for appreciating heroism in others, and I assure you that I heartily exulted and triumphed in yours." Howells's brother Sam enlisted, and when there was danger of Joe's being drafted, Howells contemplated, though unwillingly, the possible necessity of his coming home from Europe to take Joe's place in the family business. Another brother, John, in military school in Cleveland, died on April 27, 1864. Later that same year, when Sam was sick, Howells wrote his father, "I am very sorry to hear of dear Sam's sickness, but if it will only procure him his discharge, I hope he will be able to stand it." He did not crave heroism for a Howells, either in literature or in life.[25]

Setting aside all controversial questions concerning Lincoln's war policies, it may, I think, be said that the qualities which Howells admired in Lincoln are, for the most part, those that posterity has admired also. But in 1862 he showed no comprehension of what Lincoln was fighting for.

We *can't* treat with the South on the basis of our defeats, unless we mean to yield everything. We must conquer before we can think of peace. When we have gained two or three battles, I suppose we'd better stop and let the South go. I'm satisfied that the people of the North care more about slavery than about the Union, and so what's the use of keeping up the bloody farce any longer?

This is almost as silly as Hawthorne's views on the war.[26] Neither would fight to save the Union, yet neither was willing to stop fighting! Howells wished to win a victory and then throw it away!

By 1866 defeatism had been replaced by grandiloquence; it now seemed "our immutable destiny, as God's agents, to give freedom to mankind," and three years later "the hope of the world" lay in its "Americanization." The whole tone of Howells's review of Higginson's *Harvard Memorials*[27] was close to hysteria. The Harvard men who died in the war were "rich in youth and culture, and instinct with high feelings and purposes," and they "fell before the rifle of some Arkansas savage, or Georgian peasant, or Carolinian vassal." Bromfield Corey himself could not have better exemplified New England snobbery at its worst. "With what consciousness of perfection life passes from the man who dies for others, none of the heroic and good can turn back upon their ended careers to assure us." Such reckless idealization can hardly be overmatched by anything in the cheapest romantic novels which Howells detested. The Editha whom he so mercilessly excoriates in his most anthologized short story would have been thrilled by it.

After the war Howells lauded the Republican Party as embodying "the American idea, its steadfastness and generosity." It does not "send prize-fighters to Congress," and it has "the reason and the heart of the people." His review of Whitelaw Reid's *Ohio in the War*, in the *Atlantic* in 1868, could not be more "regular," [28] and when he reviews Charles Gayarré's *Philip II of Spain*, he goes out of his way to call it "the only book produced south of Mason and Dixon's line, within the last six years, which deserves notice."

As early as 1868 Howells declares that "we no longer desire to hang Jefferson Davis, or even John Surratt, but the next year, reviewing Greeley's autobiography, he can still speak of all Americans as responsible "for Davis's escape from justice." He was very severe, and for him uncommonly sarcastic, in his review of Admiral Semmes's memoirs: "We of the North can have no reasonable objection to Admiral Semmes's hating us; he did us a great deal of harm, and we crushed him." He saw Andrew Johnson thinking of America as "a nation of emancipated tailors," and though he was not rabid about the attempt to impeach him, he approved of it.

On the other hand, Howells used his position as *Atlantic* editor as a force toward conciliation by welcoming Southern writers back into the magazine earlier than the super-patriots would have approved. By 1874 he was pretty well disillusioned about Black Republican Reconstruction, and in 1875 his publication of "A Rebel's Recollections" by George Cary Eggleston marked a milestone. He rejoiced that the Civil War was not being commemorated by adequate monuments, "for we are not a military people, (though we certainly know how to fight upon occasion,)" and he preferred memorials to take a useful and wholly nonmilitary form, like a church or a school. Looking back upon the war from 1897, he rejoiced that when we forgave the vanquished, "in us for the first time in the annals of the race Christianity had governed the action of a Christian people."

Did Howells ever feel any twinges about his own Civil War record? On this point it is interesting to turn to the novels. The first words of *A Fearful Responsibility* are as follows: "Every loyal American who went abroad during the first years of our great war felt bound to make himself some excuse for turning his back on his country in the hour of her trouble." During the Civil War, the hero of the book occupied a position similar to Howells's own, and the author may have been thinking of himself when he wrote: "He would have been truly glad of any accident that forced him into the ranks; but . . . it was not his idea of soldier-ship to enlist for the hospital." When Lily Mayhew arrives to stay with the Elmores, it at once becomes clear both that the early romantic attitude toward the war in America has not survived the first heavy losses and that Americans are passing up no oppor-tunity to make as much money as possible. "Good heavens!" cries Elmore to his wife. "Is the child utterly heartless, Celia, or is she merely obtuse?" But it is clear that she knows the situation better than he does and that her attitude toward human nature is more mature. At the end of the novel, Elmore is recalled to his college as president, but it has now been transformed to "Patmos Univer-sity and Military Academy." Silas Lapham served in the war, of course, and carries a bullet in his body, and it is clear that his wife was a fire-eater even if he was not. In *A Hazard of New Fortunes*, Basil March suspects that "Dryfoos had an old rankling shame in his heart for not having gone into the war. . . . He felt sorry for him; the fact seemed pathetic; it suggested a dormant nobleness in the man." In *A Foregone Conclusion* Ferris goes into the Union army when disappointed in his love affair and is wounded. Later, after he and Florida have come together again, he tells her that it was not much of a wound (though it incapacitated him out of the army) but that he was not much of a soldier either. In the later fiction, the tone changes somewhat. Judge Kenton has a Civil War record and is collecting data concerning the conflict, but his daughter Ellen reports that "Poppa doesn't believe in war any more. . . . He isn't sure it wasn't all wrong," and that he thinks Tolstoy "the only man that ever gave a true account of battles." In the short story "A Difficult Case" (*A Pair of Patient Lovers*), Holbrook fought with credit in the Civil War but what he saw of death destroyed his faith in immortality. Afterwards he made up his mind that if there was another war in his time, he would go to Canada.[29]

Any sensitive man who escapes war service which others perform must suffer some discomfort afterwards, even if his refusal is firmly grounded morally and ideationally. The difficulty is not that he has done "wrong" but that he has escaped what others have endured. But if he had set aside his convictions and gone to war, he would have suffered on other grounds. In this matter we all have a Huckleberry Finn kind of conscience which goes after us when we do wrong and also when we do right—all, that is, except the born butchers who can slaughter without compunction. Howells considered himself a "toad" in many connections, and for all I know this may have been one of them, but he has nowhere so indicated with any greater force than I have already recorded. There is nothing to match John Burroughs's bitter remark, looking back upon the Civil War record of himself and his family: "We were all cowards, and that's the truth of it." Neither did he, like Burroughs, seem to feel that he must make up for his exemption by being as bloodthirsty as possible toward the wars which followed. In 1912 he thought that slavery itself should have been abolished more slowly and peacefully.

Between the Civil War and the Spanish-American War, the only real war scare which America experienced came when Cleveland rattled the sabres before Great Britain in the Venezuela Boundary Dispute. Howells did not permit his own anti-English spleen to becloud his judgment, and he handled the President's "turgid and clumsy" message, with its four relative pronouns in one sentence, with masterly sarcasm.[30] The trouble with patriotic emotion, he declared, was that "it took no account of things infinitely more precious than national honor, such as humanity, civilization, and 'the long result of time.' "

The settlement of the boundary line between the British and Venezueland Guianas may be a holy cause; I do not say it is not, and I am very far from saying that the Monroe Doctrine[31] was not handed down from heaven. My difficulty is in reconciling these notions with certain other doctrines, equally handed down from heaven, against killing, and in favor of loving your enemies, and blessing them which despitefully use you.[32]

Mark Twain did not wake up to the true character of the Spanish-American War until after the theater of hostilities had shifted to the Philippines, but Howells was alert to its iniquity from the beginning, and certainly one of the foremost among the many distinguished writers and publicists who served notably in the anti-imperialist cause.[33] "The most stupid and causeless war that was ever imagined by a kindly and sensible nation," he called it to Henry James, who quite agreed with him, and to his sister Aurelia he described it as "the weakest and wickedest [war] the country has ever had." "We are not the greatest people on earth; we are almost the meanest and the wickedest, for we had no need to do what we have done." And again to James: "Our war for humanity has unmasked itself as a war for coaling stations, and we are going to keep our booty to punish Spain for putting us to the trouble of using violence in robbing her."

He gave a reading for wounded Spanish prisoners at Portsmouth and became president of the Anti-Imperialist League. He vigorously attacked Kipling for "The Islanders":

To be a flanneled fool at the wicket or a muddled oaf at the goal is possibly very bad, but it is not so bad as bayoneting a Boer, or helping herd his wife and children from his burning farm into a concentration camp.

When it was over, he was painfully aware that an era in American history had ended. We had become "conquerors" with "an imperial empire," and never again could America be "the son of the morning," toward which the struggling people turned their eyes with the hope at least of sympathy. All through the early twentieth century, in his departments in the Harper periodicals, Howells kept up his sniping at "a war which still seems to me one of wanton aggression." Often, however, these barbs were

so veiled and subtle that a stupid or insensitive reader might
almost suppose that the war was being praised.

When the Russo-Japanese War broke out in 1904, Howells discussed "What Shall We Do with our Sympathies?" in *Harper's
Weekly*.[34] He weighed the respective claims of the two powers
intelligently and decided to save his sympathies for the common
people who were sure to suffer whoever won and for "those
sages and saints who have understood that war always corrupts
and depraves." But by January 1905 he was admitting privately
to T. S. Perry that he was "mentally and morally a Russophile."
In September, having watched the diplomats arrive at Portsmouth, he was not greatly impressed by either side, but he attended a dinner given by George Harvey to the Russian delega-
tion and reported delightedly to his sister that Count Witte and
his wife

have read my books from the first, and liked them. There is no doubt
of my European reputation, however little I sell in America. . . .
Harvey told me that when Witte was shown the list of guests, he said
of Pierpont Morgan's name, "Yes, I know him." When he came to
mine, he broke out, "Ah! Mr. W. D. Howells! Then I shall see him!"

I hope this was not the reason why Howells now seemed increasingly unsympathetic toward the "Japs," as he was likely to call
them, but in the Japanese crisis of 1907 he was anything but
pacifistic. In their "ideal of insensate loyalty to a monarch," he
now saw the Japanese as "the least advanced of the great powers."
Politically he was sure Americans had nothing in common with
them "except the instinct of graft." And though he still believed
that "all wars are bad," he was willing to grant that "a war for
the protection and independence of the Philippines against the
reactionary empire of the Orient, might be one of those sacred
duties, of which there seem so few left to us." The scarcity of
such duties would hardly seem to justify lamentation, and this
was surely one of the most unwise articles Howells ever wrote.
He was much more in character in an "Easy Chair" paper of 1911,

written when arbitration hopes were high. This takes its point of departure from the current statement of an unidentified bishop who had warned against the danger of carrying peace talk too far because war was necessary to prevent nations from becoming effeminate. Howells doubted that the virtues displayed by soldiers were developed by war itself. Many do not fight when a nation goes to war.

Even some bishops remain at home, and the great mass of citizens . . . deny themselves the ennobling occasions of battle. . . . They shunt the chances of moral development upon the fine fellows who have enlisted or been drafted, whose families are left to subsist on a soldier's pay, and whom they will begrudge their pensions to the last generation.

Then came 1914. Like the Civil War, the World War took Howells by surprise, and there are some striking parallels between his behavior in the two crises.

His first published utterance on the war seems to have been "The Archangelic Censorship" in *The North American Review* for October 1914. It is already bitterly anti-German and anti-Kaiser, but beyond that there is nothing to say of it. In the first "Easy Chair" devoted to the war, in the November *Harper's Magazine*, he confines himself to demolishing his old *bête noire*, the "country right or wrong" hypothesis, and advancing world unification as the hope of peace. "National honor" he dismisses as "a figment of romance, which co-exists with national greed, national falsehood, national dishonesty, and all the other things that dishonor a man."

On February 1, 1915, the New York *Sun* printed a very bitter, ironical letter from Howells, expressing his indignation that the paper had tentatively considered the possibility of the United States entering the war on the German side as an outcome of our current controversy with Great Britain over her "right" to search American ships.[35] Nobody who saw this letter can have been surprised when Howells formally declared for the Allies in "Why?"

in the May *North American*. If, however, they had had the privilege of reading the letters he had been writing to his sister Aurelia,
they might well have wondered over his mildness. In the third
month of the war he had told Aurelia that if Germany conquered
Europe it would be our turn next, and in December he added, "I
think murder when I think Kaiser." By 1915, too, he was talking
about the possibility of our going in and nervous about how Ger-
man- and Irish-Americans would behave should we do so.
"Why?" declares Germany responsible for the evil that has been
wrought and hails the Allied cause as that "of liberty, of humanity, of Christianity," and "something like a last hope of mankind,"
but stops far short of interventionism. Howells would have this
country "bear everything from the belligerents short of invading
our shores after sinking our ships." "Till the German submarines
attack our home-keeping navy and their Zeppelins infest our
atmosphere and begin dropping bombs on Boston," it is only "our
will" that must go with the Allies; we must not "cast our lot"
with them. But in August he wrote Brander Matthews that we
seemed to be "holding up our heads so high that Germany may
spit in our faces more conveniently," and in December, when
Henry Ford invited him to a ride on the Peace Ship, he declined:

I wish you luck if the first conditions of peace are the abolition of
militarism, the restoration of the conquered countries to the people,
with full indemnity from the conquerors, and the establishment of
liberty and democracy.

In 1916 the "Easy Chair" grows more uneasy. Germany "has
forsaken the polite usages of Christian homicide for a riot of
bloodshed which it were gross flattery to call 'Hunnish.'" In
"The Little Children" [36] Germany is "the Anti-Christ of Schrecklichkeit"; another poem in the *North American* is a bitter protest
against the *Lusitania* outrage. Other "Easy Chairs" reminded
Americans of the debt they owed to France and speculated about
the possible republics to come out of the war, the remarks on
Russia being particularly suggestive. In December, sending his

autograph for the Canadian Booth at the Allied Bazaar in Boston, he praised Canada for "the heroic part she has borne in the great war for civilization." He adds: "May she prosper with the other allies in the struggle for Mercy and Justice and for a Lasting Peace!" [37]

But in 1916 Howells had other villains besides the Kaiser. For he now had to turn about and spank England for taking "a leaf from the German classic of Schrecklichkeit" and rousing "the moral sense of mankind against her" when she slew Sir Roger Casement and the Irish rebels.

What a pity, what an infinite pity! She has left us who loved her cause in the war against despotism without another word to say for her until we have first spoken our abhorrence of her inexorable legality in dealing with her Irish prisoners.

And there was now another villain named Woodrow Wilson, who floundered "from bad to worse" as the year went on, until at last he could not even "write his ridiculous notes intelligibly." On the other hand, he could send American soldiers into Mexico and threaten that country with a war which would be "wickeder" and "more stupid and objectless" than the first Mexican War.

Some excuse can be made for his German policy, but none for his Mexican muddling. There is some comfort in the overwhelming prospect of Hughes's election. The Roosevelt men have come back, and if the Republicans get into power, our troops will be withdrawn from Mexico, where they ought never to have been sent.

He was almost indignant to think that Aurelia could have thought he might vote for Wilson. "I think he is the falsest and basest politician since Buchanan." For all that, he was glad that the boys in the Howells family were "far off from soldiering yet."

In 1917, the year America entered the war, Howells made no statement of importance. But in 1918 he reached heights of hysteria comparable to those attained in the Higginson review of

1866. Germany was now "the murderer nation" and "the arch-foe of the human race," with her troops "the murderers embattled against all mankind," whom the Allies fight to prevent "the home of our race" from being "turned into a howling wilderness, the lair of ravening beasts." It is impossible to decide what her "worst wickedness" has been; the range of choice is too great. And he adds, with unconscious humor: "Nothing seems too abominable to believe of the Germans, if only it is bad enough." Surely nobody had ever really believed that we could stay out of the war! Even Wilson now had to have his halo.

The patriotism which shrank from the dictates of national pride and ignored the repeated affronts to the national honor had gathered through its very patience the power upon the hearts and minds of the people until far less than its nobly spoken demand for action was needed.

Conscription was defended as, even upon an Altrurian basis, a token of "justice, a supreme expression of equality." While as for the conscripts themselves, Howells saw them

with that look of goodness in their faces which was as if reflected from their mothers' faces, but was yet their very own, and which, if it could be kept somehow, would remain the composite likeness of the embattled nation.

Is this the author of *The Rise of Silas Lapham* or the author of *St. Elmo*? Surely one may at this point be permitted to doubt. But here, as in the case of the Civil War, the gas soon comes out of the balloon, for though in 1919 the "Easy Chair" is still wondering what to do with "that Unspeakable Wretch," the Kaiser, the very last paper in the series (April 1920) shows Howells explaining the human situation to Martian visitors who cannot understand "multiple murder." "We did not mince our terms," he says, "as we should have done while the war was still going on, when we should have been obliged to differentiate the facts and phases of heroism and patriotism." And when, that same year, he revised and reprinted portions of *Their Silver Wedding Journey* as a travel book, *Hither and Thither in Germany*, he wiped the war out of existence altogether, not only ignoring it but even excising passages critical of Germany from his own original narrative.[38]

Howells cannot, then, be called a complete pacifist (he succeeds rather neatly in begging the question in his utopia),[39] but except when he lost his head he came pretty close. He was not given to dogmatizing on any subject—it was always his tendency to leave a question open—and perhaps the closest he comes to a categorical statement on this point is when he says:

The idea of force is repellent to me. I would not use it when it can be avoided. The extreme to which Tolstoi would carry non-resistance to violence, I cannot, of course, share in. Yet there have been, and are, cases of those who either as individuals or sects, have held to non-resistance and have not been exterminated. Think of the persecution of the Quakers. Yet, despite it, they have thrived.

When, in *The Winning of the West*, Theodore Roosevelt lamented the destruction of the Moravian Indians, who were massacred because they had not been taught how to defend themselves, Howells was quick to point out that "at no moment of their most pathetic history . . . would war have availed them. It was in virtue of literally doing the word of Christ that they existed at all." In *New Leaf Mills*, Owen Powell is not quite satisfied with the effect of his forebearance upon the miller Overdale, who hates him and whom his wife fears. But he is entirely satisfied with the effect upon himself. "Whatever his feeling toward me was, I was aware of liking him better because I was still wishing to do him good in spite of himself." Howells would have liked to see nonresistance tried in the Homestead Strike of 1892.

I come back to my old conviction, that every drop of blood shed for a good cause helps to make a bad cause. How much better if the

Homesteaders could have suffered the Pinkertons to shoot them down unarmed. Then they would have had the power of martyrs in the world.

Later he called the attempted assassination of Henry Clay Frick by the anarchist Alexander Berkman a "wicked and foolish mistake," which "makes a blood mist through which the situation shows wrong."

CHAPTER FIVE

MR. HOMOS

I

We come now at last to Mr. Homos, or Howells as the Altrurian, the Spiritual Man. Like other phases of his personality, it involves varied aspects.

Most men find that the chief barrier standing in the way of spiritual development is the self. Howells was a highly-developed, even specialized, individual, but I do not believe anyone who knows him well would think that he thought of himself more highly than he ought to think. Though it would of course be absurd to call him a saint, his spiritual humility often suggests that of the saints. Thus he speaks of "what a toad I am and always have been," and he told Edward Everett Hale, "I am all the time stumbling to my feet from the dirt of such falls through vanity and evil will, and hate, that I can hardly believe in that self that seems to write books which help people." He took no comfort to himself from his aesthetic sensitiveness: "I do not regard the artistic ecstasy as in any sort noble. It is not noble to love the beautiful, or to live for it, or by it; and it may even not be refining." Surely there never was a more faithful husband or loving father than either Howells or Mark Twain, yet both saw themselves in Bartley Hubbard! Howells gives his own humility to both Helen Harkness and her father in *A Woman's Reason*, who apologize to each other for the wrongs they have committed, though he has been an excellent father and she a model daughter. Howells was so awed by his own daughter Winifred that he

221

could not bear to look into her eyes and think of what he was, and when Mark Twain sent him a picture of his Susy, it had much the same effect on him. "I wonder how any one can be at once so innocent and so sinful, as I am." He agreed with Mark Twain too that no man can dare to tell the truth about himself save under the veil of fiction, and he says, "I don't admire myself; I am sick of myself; but I can't think of anything else." He found it hard to believe that other people rated him more highly than he rated himself, and he suffered endless self-reproach over the thought of people who had been kind to him at one time or another and whom he had afterwards neglected. When Grinnell students serenaded him he refused to come out for fear of being guyed, and when he picked up his Doctor of Letters at Oxford, he reported happily to his sister that he "got not a single jibe."

When Howells was a boy, his father told him "that he regarded me as different from other boys of my age; and I had a very great and sweet happiness without alloy of vanity from his serious and considered words." Looking back upon his early years, it seemed to Howells that his brother had had "an ideal of usefulness" while he himself had "only an ideal of glory." His hair had begun to turn gray "before he began to have any conception of the fact that he was sent into the world to serve and to suffer, as well as to rule and enjoy." He credited himself with a hot temper in those days and regretted having given himself offensive journalistic airs. The Governor of Ohio invited him to his mansion, and he went, but when he got there, he was offended to learn that the Governor did not recognize him: "at twenty-one men are proud, and I was prouder than I can yet find any reason for having been." The interesting thing about this, of course, is not that it should have occurred but that Howells should have remembered and related it. When he was working on his autobiographical writings, he told Arthur Sherburne Hardy that "I am living over the dreary commonalities of my early life, and I loathe and despise the whole business." [1]

As a mature man, Howells certainly did not tend to overestimate his achievements either and always kept his masterpiece before him. His *bête noire* seems to have been people who referred to *Venetian Life* as "Venetian Days," which, apparently, he thought would indicate a more casual or less significant book. Did he intend irony or bravado when he declared of his life of Lincoln: "I wrote the Lincoln of Lincoln which elected him"? (He could never bring himself to examine the copy which Lincoln annotated and corrected.) When it was suggested that Mark Twain's letters to him might be published he approved heartily and added that it would do no harm if his were published with them. "It was not possible for Clemens to write like anybody else," he says, "but I could very easily write like Clemens." [2] In 1896 he wondered whether "this poor old fellow's style, his careful whimsicality, his anxious humor" is not "all rather out of date," [3] and in the case of this particular example, I should have to admit that I think it was. Once, answering a query—"Why is Mr. Howells's democracy less convincing to the imagination than Tolstoy's?"—he writes:

As for Mr. Howells, we hardly feel authorized to speak for him; but it may be tentatively said that his democracy does not convince the imagination so much as Tolstoy's because it is incomparably less powerfully imagined than Tolstoy's.[4]

Howells did not, like Whitman, Mark Twain, and Ernest Hemingway, create literature by dramatizing his own personality or keep himself in the foreground of the reader's attention, but there are a number of figures including Basil March to whom he gave some of his own characteristics. These are all rather ordinary fellows; none are painted larger than life. In his later years, when it was becoming very difficult for him to get a novel serialized, and new fashions were coming into fiction with which he did not pretend to have much sympathy, Howells was tempted to feel that his day was done, but he was always philosophical about this. The year before his death he referred to himself as

an aged author, mainly a novelist, who lived in a dream of wide, if quiescent, recognition. He was fearful that modern editors and their public did not want him, and that the general reader's generalship did not extend to his novels and other things, but he soothed his sense of isolation with the belief that if people did not know his work they knew about it.

But even this delusion was shattered when he received through the mail an invitation to enroll in a course to learn short story writing by correspondence!

II

In a late short story[5] Howells says that

Every one of us has a grain of sand on him that keeps him a kind of sick oyster. He coats it over with his juice and hides it away in his shell somewhere; and that's what turns into a Pearl, they say. . . . It costs a man his peace, but it keeps him merciful to others. Why, if a man had nothing on his conscience he'd be a perfect devil.

Whatever Howells may have had on his conscience, it is clear that most of the grosser temptations of men made no appeal to him. When his much loved younger brother, John Butler Howells, went away to school, Howells wrote him from Venice:

I suppose in Cleveland you'll have some temptations and trials which you've never met in Jefferson. Don't be taken with the shallow folly that anything which your conscience tells you is bad can be brave or fine. You'll find a great many brilliant fellows in the world who are also vicious. You must not believe that it is their vice that gives them brilliancy.

Poor Johnny did not have much time either to heed this advice or disregard it, for he died the next spring, and Howells wrote his brother that he wished he were as ready for death as Johnny had been. "But I am not, and never was since I was a little child."

Brought up a water-drinker, Howells afterwards embraced vintages, but there is no indication that he passed the bounds of moderation. He never smoked. As to food, he tells us that "he preferred feasting to fasting at any time," and the bulk he began to achieve fairly early in life suggests that this may have been true. In Cambridge we hear of him and H. H. Boyesen raiding the cellar in the middle of the night and regaling themselves upon "cheese and crackers and . . . a watermelon and a bottle of champagne," and when his old chief Godkin, of *The Nation*, saw him again in 1871, he found him "as sweet and gentle and winning in all ways as ever. . . . Howells *grows* steadily, I think, and in all ways, for he has become very stout." But feasting is never the symbol of good fellowship in his books that it is with Dickens, for example, who may well have eaten considerably less himself. If his worst gormandizers are the disgusting Mr. and Mrs. Landers of *Ragged Lady*, overeating and unwholesome food play their part in a number of other books including *Silas Lapham* and *April Hopes*. In *Indian Summer* he speaks of the doughnut as having "undermined our digestion as a people." In Venice in 1862 he looked back to his steak breakfasts at home; in "Breakfast Is My Best Meal" he makes fun of a man who does not drink or smoke but ruins his health by overeating, and "A Feast of Reason" is a very critical examination of dining out, or dining as a form of hospitality, with no holds barred.[6] When Howells saw how meat was displayed in English markets, he was tempted to vegetarianism, and in Altruria he made the mushroom staple, with "wonderful salads" and "temperate and tropical fruits" for dessert. The Thanksgiving dinner served in New York by Mrs. Makely in *Letters of an Altrurian Traveler* seems burlesque, but there are records of actual dinners of the time which are quite as monstrous. Howells was a connoisseur of tea, preferring Souchong to Oolong and, in general, Chinese to Japanese. The only dietetic curiosity recorded is that he says he liked fresh radishes with his coffee.

Beer is "vile stuff" in Howells's first extended work of fiction, "The Independent Candidate." There is a passage in praise of lager in his *Nation* column in 1886, but this is on the ground that it gives Americans relief from hard liquor. He praises Sted-

man's "The Ballad of Lager Beer" in a mixed *Atlantic* review of
his poems. In Columbus he was such a Germanophile that he
tried lunching at a German beer-saloon, "but it made me very
sick, and I was obliged to forego it as an expression of my love
for German poetry." In *Literary Friends and Acquaintance* he
tells us that he did not drink beer when he visited Walt Whitman's hangout, Pfaff's, in New York, and disclaims a "learned
palate" even at the time of writing. In *A Little Swiss Sojourn*
he speaks of his wife and himself as refusing from a Swiss host the
wine which was being given even to the children. In *Stories of
Ohio* he speaks of the Woman's Christian Temperance Union
Crusade in Hillsborough, Highland County, Ohio, in 1873, as one
of "the fanaticisms or enthusiasms which flourished among our
people," but he grants that "there has been far less drunkenness
in the region than before" and that public opinion has been
"roused to enforce the laws against liquor selling." In a 1905
"Easy Chair" he declares bluntly that "all drinking is excess,"
and toward the end of his life he more than once spoke respect-
fully of prohibition.

On the other hand, Howells sometimes speaks of ordering wine
on his travels, and it is clear that during his later years he sometimes used whiskey as a soporific. This happened on the painful
lecture tour of 1899, from which he wrote home to his wife that
they were "all terrible water drinkers" in the West, seeing no
half-way house between "topers or temperance (sic)." But he
does not say whether or not he thinks this has any connection
with the feeling of "*intolerance* in the air" which oppresses him.
"We are *freer* in the East, and say what we think. In the West,
I sh'd be first mobbed with praise and then, if I differed, with
rotten eggs."

He was disgusted that there were ninety saloons in two miles
of Sixth Avenue, and he denounced the domination in the mu-
nicipality of the liquor interests. Without private trade in drink,
he thought, "there would be far less poverty than there is." But
he had no sympathy with those who would attribute the woes
of the worker to his intemperance and make this an excuse for

withholding his just due from him, and he admitted that the saloons had "a cheerful and inviting look, and if you step within, you find them cosy, quiet, and, for New York, clean." They were, in fact, the only clubhouses the poor man had in New York, and

if he might resort to them with his family, and be in the control of the State as to the amount he should spend and drink there, I could not think them without their rightful place in an economy which saps the vital forces of the laborers with overwork, or keeps him in a fever of hope or a fever of despair as to the chances of getting or not getting work when he has lost it.

The qualification is significant, and when his statement is carefully examined, it becomes clear that he has only given the saloon a place in a diseased and unjust society.

Though wine at table is a kind of status symbol in the Howells novels (Bromfield Corey is shocked that the Laphams do not serve it, and when Lapham dines at the Coreys, he disgraces himself by getting drunk on a beverage to which he is unaccustomed), but it does not, generally speaking, play an important part in his fiction. Kitty Ellison first tastes champagne at the picnic at Chateau-Bigot and is surprised that she likes it, having thought that it was a cultivated taste. In *The Shadow of a Dream*, however, Basil March is shocked to find Nevill, a clergyman, smoking and drinking claret-punch. "I was very severe in those days."

In *Years of My Youth* Howells tells us that he once tried to smoke cigars flavored with cinnamon-drops which had been made by the father of a companion. But the decisive experience seems to have been his getting "drunk" on chewing tobacco, which gave him enough of the weed to last through his lifetime. In the English Boston he was attracted by a brilliantly illuminated building which he at first took for a printing office and felt "shame and grief" when he learned the next morning that it was a cigar factory and that cigar- and cigarette-making was almost the chief industry of the town. Yet he tries so hard to be fair that he sometimes leans over backwards, as when, shocked by the smoking by women reported in English novels, he first doubts whether there is as much of this in England as is reported, then admits that "in the vices, as in the virtues, there is no sex," and ends by declaring that he is "not saying that smoking is a vice." When he was at the height of his fame, he apparently allowed his name and his portrait to appear on a cigar box label. Commenting on Horace Mann's telling Hawthorne he could never feel quite the same about him after having learned that he smoked, Howells says, "We have gone far since then, and whether we smoked or read *Don Juan* or not ourselves, we should hardly renounce or condemn those who did, in ever so slight a measure." Yet he admits "a kind of reason" as well as "a rigid grotesqueness" and "inflexible absurdity" in Mann's point of view and does not try to decide "whether New England civilization was the more enviable in its flowering or in its going to seed."

In *Italian Journeys* Howells speaks of smoking by Italian women and comments that "there is, without doubt, a certain grace and charm in a pretty *fumatrice*." But he adds, either naïvely or cuttingly: "I suppose it is a habit not so pleasing in an ugly or middle-aged woman." The tone is sharper in an 1895 Christmas fantasy, where he has the Christmas Muse come to him as the New Woman and light a cigarette on the ground that she could always talk better with one, to which he replies that he had never noticed that women had any difficulty in talking without it. No woman in Howells's novels smokes, though Grace Breen rolls cigarettes for Libby when they go sailing together. Charmian Maybough, the rather "wacky" art student of *The Coast of Bohemia*, would like to smoke, because it is bohemian and because "Bernhardt does" (which she didn't), but really hates the smell of tobacco. In the farce *Self-Sacrifice*, a "nice" girl pretends that she smokes and drinks to deceive an admirer, for one of those high-minded but wholly irrational motives by which Howells females are often actuated, but it makes her deathly sick. She says, "There must have been something poisonous in those cigarettes," to which her admirer replies, "Yes, there was tobacco."

But Howells's primary concern as a moralist is not with such elementary matters as these. He is the analyst of scruple, the novelist of the "New England conscience," the moral examiner of self-assertion and self-sacrifice. It would be tedious to enumerate the novels and stories in which his characters torment themselves over ethical problems, and it is noteworthy that these are quite as prominent in such light novels as *The Kentons* and *Ragged Lady* as in *The Quality of Mercy* and *The Shadow of a Dream*. Sometimes real problems are involved, sometimes only hyper-quixotic scruples, but both may appear in the same novel, and one may cause as much agony as the other. We can all understand the elder Hilary's uneasiness of mind over whether, as chairman of the board, he was right or wrong when he gave Northwick a chance to get away (and also to make up his losses), as we can also the fact that when he reads of the accident and remembers having told Northwick that a good railroad wreck on the way home would be the best thing that could happen to him, he feels illogically as though he had killed him, but his son Matt seems worse than quixotic when he worries over whether Jack Wilmington, who had once been interested in Sue, or the clergyman Wade, has a claim on her which must be cleared up before he can propose. In *An Imperative Duty*, again, we can sympathize with Mrs. Meredith's struggles over whether or not she is bound to tell Rhoda that she is of Negro descent, and certainly with the girl's own agony as to where her duty lies when she learns the truth, but when Olny, having decided that he loves Rhoda, fears that he must honor Bloomingdale's claim upon her, he seems utterly fantastic.

Brice Maxwell in *The Story of a Play* struggles with the question of the respective "rights" which the actor Godolphin and others have acquired in his work. Ellen Kenton and Cornelia of *The Coast of Bohemia* agonize over the fancied necessity of telling their lovers about a previous attraction, though neither has violated any conceivable moral code. Wallace Ardith of *Letters Home* almost gives up America Ralson, whom he loves, because he has, almost innocently, allowed Essie Baysley to fall in love

with him. David Gillespie's sister in *The Leatherwood God* feels
called upon to leave her good husband Laban when her rascally
first husband Dylks, whom she had supposed dead, turns up in
the settlement, though nobody knows her story. Her brother tells
her she is living in mortal sin, and when she wishes Dylks were
dead, he accuses her of having murder in her heart. The whole of
The Son of Royal Langbrith revolves around the ethical problem: Should Mrs. Langbrith and Dr. Anther, who loves her, tell
her son James that his dead father, whose memory he worships,
was a moral monster, and, having learned the truth, is James
honor-bound to share it with society? But even this is not enough.
Dr. Anther would not have felt free to ask Mrs. Langbrith to
marry him if he had felt attracted to her during her husband's
lifetime, and she expects him to despise her when she tells him
that she did care for him during that time. In addition to all this,
Anther must face the question whether it is right for him to try
to cure Hawberk of opium addiction, knowing that should he be
restored to his normal state, he will probably remember the truth
about Royal Langbrith. The Shaker lovers in *The Day of Their
Wedding* worry about whether they sinned when they fell in
love with each other's looks rather than their characters. And
even the little girl in that inconsequential story "The Daughter
of the Storage" meets her ordeal when she cannot decide what
to give the little boy who wants to give her all his toys, and therefore does nothing. She would like to give him all of hers, but
since they were given to her by her parents, she is not sure that
she has the right. "Dear little tender conscience!" says her mother.
And her father adds, "Yes, conscience. And temperament, the
temperament to which decision is martyrdom."

This is the kind of thing in Howells which caused H. L.
Mencken, Sinclair Lewis, and others who had never read him
to dismiss him as an old-maidish writer who concerned himself
only with tea at the vicarage. Howells's preoccupation with moral
struggle may well go back to the neuroticism of his boyhood.
He wrote more than one "Easy Chair" paper about etiquette, he
wrestled with the conventional lie, and he has a tendency to treat

hyper-conscientious people with more sympathy than some of us would feel they deserve. But his conclusions on these matters are far from being Miss Nancy-ish. Instead he commits himself to a slate of four eminently unsentimental propositions:

1. Sacrifice for sacrifice' sake is not a virtue; it may even be a form of self-indulgence.
2. To torture oneself over unintended evils that have resulted from well-intentioned acts is insane.
3. People should marry for love, not because they fancy they owe an obligation to persons who may wish to marry them.
4. Problems involving self-assertion and self-abnegation should be tested by the utilitarian principle of "the economy of pain."

The first of these rules was enunciated by Lydia Blood as early as *The Lady of the Aroostook*: "I don't see why any one should sacrifice himself uselessly." The fact that you do it nobly is no excuse unless you also do it intelligently. Howells knew that it is very difficult to be clear-sighted in these matters. In *The Quality of Mercy*, Adeline Northwick worries herself to death over her fancied obligation to turn over her property to her father's creditors, and it is interesting that her sister Sue, who is more clear-sighted in the matter, finally does surrender hers, though by that time the sacrifice has been cushioned by her marriage to Matt. Howells believes that "it is only the exceptional few who can or may sacrifice themselves; it is an aristocratic privilege; a prerogative of the upper class; for others self-sacrifice involves a wrong." He thought John Woolman more "incarnate scruple" than "incarnate conscience"; "in his endeavors to make his life Christ-like and blameless he went, like other ascetics, further than Christ himself taught by example." He was even harder upon Laurence Oliphant, who sacrificed himself to a religious imposter. Even confession may be a means of throwing the responsibility for one's actions upon somebody else and taking a kind of moral bankruptcy law, and the "spasms of paroxysmal righteousness to which our Anglo-Saxon race is peculiarly subject" are more likely to lead to legal crimes like the hanging of the Chicago anarchists or indefensible wars like our war with Spain than to anything useful or constructive.

Howells rejected James A. Herne's *Sag Harbor*, for all his admiration for that dramatist, because

The motive was the tattered superstition that a woman may, can, will, or ever did marry the man she does not love and refuse the man she does love, because the man she does not love has been good to her, and will be broken-hearted if she does not marry him. Of course, it is strictly her sole business, and her supreme duty to marry the man she loves, unless he is an unreformed drunkard. Any other marriage is treason to her nature and pollution to her womanhood.

When he saw *Arizona* he would have liked its author Augustus Thomas to show his awareness that the hero who consents to blacken himself to cover for a worthless woman is an ass. She is "spoiled and lost already, for it is not the adultery, but the adulterous heart that counts in these things." And he himself wrote a farce, *A True Hero*, to show up an idiot who wishes to make such a sacrifice for a woman (the issue this time is theft, not adultery) because she was a woman and a mother and therefore had a sacred claim upon every man.

The situation here is farcical but the problems involved in this business of self-sacrifice are nevertheless interestingly explored. And similar situations presented in the novels are not farcical at all. Imogene Graham creates endless pain and trouble for Colville, Mrs. Bowen, and herself when she conceives the idiotic idea of "making it up" to the man for a disappointment of his youth. In "A Pair of Patient Lovers" Basil March suggests to the Bentley girl's lover, whose marriage to him has been indefinitely postponed because of her selfish mother's invalidism, that the sensible thing would be for them to elope. "I have never heard of a clergyman's running away to be married; but they must have sometimes done it." But the really serious situations are developed in *The Rise of Silas Lapham*, where Penelope cannot at first bring herself to accept Tom Corey's love because all the family had supposed him to be in love with her sister Irene, and in *The Minister's Charge*, where Lemuel Barker has allowed himself to become innocently involved with a girl whose only fault is that she lacks his capacity for development, so that marriage between them could only result in misery for both.

In *Silas Lapham* it is the mother of the girls who formulates the best statement of the "economy of pain" principle:

"No! If there's to be any giving up, let it be by the one that shan't make anybody but herself suffer. There's trouble and sorrow enough in the world, without *making* it on purpose!"

Unfortunately Mrs. Lapham is not quite able to live up to her own light, and it is Irene's common sense that finally solves the problem. In *The Minister's Charge* the situation is even more difficult, for Statira does not have Irene's common sense, and the "poor, silly girl's" health seems to hang in the balance. But Sewell insists on being clear-minded even here.

"There is no more pernicious delusion than that one's word ought to be kept in such an affair, after the heart has gone out of it, simply because it's been given. . . . The trouble comes from this crazy and mischievous principle of false self-sacrifice that I'm always crying out against. If a man has ceased to love the woman he has promised to marry—or *vice versa*—the best possible thing they can do, the only righteous thing, is not to marry."

Sewell is not afraid that if Lem marries Statira he will be unkind to her, but he knows too that "in marriage kindness was not enough." Even if the girl should die, Lem would not be responsible, for he has not willed her death. Dr. Morrell and Mr. Peck make the same point when Annie Kilburn grieves over the death of a child she had sent to the seashore:

". . . what we intend in goodwill must not rest a burden on the conscience, no matter how it turns out. Otherwise the moral world is no better than a crazy dream, without plan or sequence. You might as well rejoice in an evil deed because good happened to come out of it."

And Dan Mavering's father tells him in *April Hopes*:

"Harm comes from many things, but evil is of the heart. I wouldn't have you condemn yourself too severely for harm that you didn't intend—that's remorse—that's insanity; and I wouldn't have you fall under the condemnation of another's invalid judgment."

And it is significant that all this is completely in accord with the teachings of Swedenborg.

Was Howells always faithful to these principles? In life I am sure he worried over much that ought not to have concerned him. In his fiction, I think he fails seriously in these matters only once. He certainly tried to apply his standards to the evaluation of other novels. That Lady Castlewood's attempt to marry Henry Esmond to Beatrix, however, unwise as it may have been, comes under the heading of "idiotic and detestable self-sacrifice," I must confess I have my doubts, and I have no doubt whatever that when Howells describes Sydney Carton's sacrifice in *A Tale of Two Cities* as "an atrocious and abominable act," he is talking very great nonsense. It is interesting that he should have viewed Casaubon's death as a flaw in *Middlemarch* because it provides

a mechanical means of extricating Dorothea from her difficulty. It is to be condemned for that, and it is to be regretted that George Eliot had not had the higher courage of her art, and the clearer vision of her morality, and shown Dorothea capable of breaking a promise extorted from her against her reason and against her heart.

Yet at the end of *The Shadow of a Dream*, Howells himself does something much worse than what he accuses George Eliot of having done (Casaubon was, after all, an elderly man in delicate health), by having Nevil crushed to death between a train and the stone jamb of an archway as a meaning of resolving the dilemma with which the whole book has been wrestling: Do

Nevil and Hermia have a right to marry in spite of her late husband's recurrent dream in which they appeared to him as in love with each and false to him long before either was aware of the other's attraction? Howells wrote Howard Pyle that he had first intended them to marry but was not able to do it. "Happy for all if they could die out of their difficulties." But it was not a "happy" solution of the ethical problem—or any solution at all, for that matter—and it was not "happy" for the book on any assumption except that anything that can happen in life is legitimate in a novel. After both Nevil and Hermia are dead, March says that he and his wife "have dealt with them as arbitrarily as with the personages in a fiction," and that is just what Howells did. But "the personages in a fiction" cannot be dealt with arbitrarily without destroying what Galsworthy called "the spire of meaning" in a work of art, nor could Howells logically have availed himself of the excuse I suggested here without also accepting a great deal of what he considered unconvincing in romantic fiction and unsparingly condemned.

III

As we have seen, there were mixed strains in Howells's religious heritage on his father's side, but Swedenborgianism predominated. His Irish-German mother, a descendant of Conrad Weiser, derived from both Catholics and Lutherans. Quakerism came into the family with Howells's Welsh great-grandfather; his grandfather Joseph Howells, ran through Quakerism, Methodism, and even Millerism, but always "remained a Friend to every righteous cause," including abolition. It is no wonder that the novelist's father, William Cooper Howells, had drifted into infidelity before finding his haven in the "New Church" of Emanuel Swedenborg. It should be remembered too that the "rationalistic" ideas of the "Enlightenment" were strong in frontier Ohio, contributing to Howells's "reasonable," basically eighteenth-century outlook and causing him to underestimate the importance of the irrational or instinctual or super-rational faculties of man.

Howells and three or four brothers and sisters were received into the Swedenborgian communion by a passing New Church minister, but, since there was no visible branch of the church in their vicinity, they did not attend services but received "abundant," though "not very stated," religious instruction at home. For a time Howells attended a Baptist Sunday School, where (shades of Tom Sawyer!), he received "certain blue tickets and certain red ones for memorizing passages from the New Testament." And, though Swedenborgians made no more of Christmas than Quakers—or, for that matter, old-time Puritans—did, the children "sometimes huddled into the back part of the Catholic church and watched the service, awed by the dim altar lights, the rising smoke of the incense, and the grimness of the sacristan, an old German who stood near to keep order among them." This Howells enjoyed,

though he was afraid of the painted figure that hung full length on the wooden crucifix, with the blood-drops under the thorns of its forehead, and the red wound in its side. He was afraid of it as something both dead and alive; he could not keep his eyes away from the awful, beautiful, suffering face, and the body that seemed to twist in agony, and the hands and feet so cruelly nailed to the cross.

Swedenborgianism is a strongly mystical religion, but it carries a heavy, ethical, this-worldly emphasis. It added a whole fresh formulation of supernaturalism to that which other Christians accept, but it had no hostility to science (its founder was himself a scientist), and though it charted the hereafter as elaborately as Dante, it made judgment both automatic and self-determined, involving no hostility on the part of God. Of his father's belief in it Howells once wrote:

It was easy for him, whose being was in some sort a dream of love and good will, to conceive all tangible and visible creation as an adumbration of spiritual reality; to accept revelation as the mask of interior meanings; to regard the soul as its own keeper, and the sovereign

chooser of heaven and hell, but always master of the greatest happiness
possible to it.

His son could not, without qualification, be so described, but
he certainly never threw off his Swedenborgian conditioning.
Many years later, he speaks of his pleasure in seeing the elder
Henry James at the Saturday Club, "with the sympathy of a like
spiritual faith," and as late as 1912 he writes of Swedenborgianism
as "our faith." [7] He once sent Mark Twain a Swedenborg book,
and he thought it odd that Sir Oliver Lodge took no notice of
Swedenborg in *Raymond*. He mentions Johnny Appleseed's
Swedenborgian beliefs in his loving account of him in *Stories of
Ohio*. He corresponded frankly on spiritual matters with Howard
Pyle, who was reared in the same faith. In 1878 he was thinking
of sending his children to the New Church school at Waltham;
he had already been distressed by Winny's having picked up a
belief in hell from previous, non-Swedenborgian Sunday School
instruction. He seems never to have entirely ceased reading
Swedenborgian books: in 1871 this inspired reflections on "how
destructive are the sins that have almost eaten me up: vanity and
contempt," and in 1890 he found Swedenborg's *Heaven and Hell*
"often hard and mechanical in conception." But, he adds, "it seems
true." A good many of the characters in Howells's novels seem
to have read Swedenborg also, and Swedenborg-Howells cor-
respondences are pointed out here and there throughout this
volume.

About Quakers Howells wrote little except in his introduction
to Thomas Ellwood's *Life*. Though he took a dim view of Ellwood's poetry, he was charmed by his autobiography, and he
tells us unequivocally that though Quakerism had "its own follies
and excesses, . . . it swept more nonsense out of the heads and
hearts that received it than the rest of the world has yet begun
to get rid of, or is like to do for ages to come"; and in the introduction to the memoir of Lord Herbert of Cherbury, he adds
that though Quakerism as a movement "goes forward to an early

extinction, . . . its animating spirit can never die out of the world but "must prevail and rule at last."

But Quakers have their affinities with Shakers, Moravians, Mennonites, and Dunkers, and Howells has more to say of some of these than he does of them. Though Mrs. Dryfoos has a Dunkard background, the Shakers are much the most important in his fiction, appearing in *The Undiscovered Country*, *The Day of Their Wedding*, *A Parting and a Meeting*, and *The Vacation of the Kelwyns*. In the paper on Shirley, the Shaker village described in *Three Villages*, Howells says: "We saw in them a sect simple, sincere, and fervently persuaded of the truth of their doctrine, striving for the realization of a heavenly ideal upon earth." With their asceticism he had no sympathy, and he was too sophisticated and aesthetic to be a Shaker himself, but they attracted him on the side of their simplicity and their spiritually-minded Communism, which was quite free of violence and materialism. As for Moravians, though there are references to them in *Ragged Lady*, Howells's principal treatment of them is in his account of the ill-fated Moravian Indian village, Gnadenhütten, in *Three Villages*. This, his most elaborate piece of historical writing, is wholly sympathetic.

Puritanism was less directly a part of Howells's religious inheritance, but its cultural importance to him was great, and he was well aware that he lived in a Puritan country. Though he did not believe that Puritanism had hindered the development of American literature, he had no great love for it. The Puritans imagined they were abolishing episcopacy when they were actually destroying beauty, and though this was abominable, it was not contemptible, for they did not do it "for fun, though undoubtedly they got fun out of it." He knew that Puritanism always carried an anti-Puritan force within itself (as with Squire Gaylord of *A Modern Instance* and Dr. Mulbridge of *Doctor Breen's Practice*), but he also believed that its reading of human nature was in some aspects sound, and that it might well survive as culture long after it had perished as theology.

The Catholic Church, too, was largely a cultural phenomenon

so far as he was concerned. It gained an advantage with him as a boy when, because he greatly admired Alexander Pope, he wished to be a Catholic because his idol had been one, and when he was an old man visiting in St. Augustine "the nun's sweet voices rising in their matins over the gardens of the girls school " had a sweet and soothing effect upon him. But he seems to have felt that this was an aesthetic rather than a religious appeal, and so he had long before presented Kitty Ellison's emotion in her room in Quebec, overlooking a convent garden. In *Their Wedding Journey*, Isabel "would almost have confessed to any one of the black-robed priests upon the street" while Basil "could easily have gone down upon his knees to the white-hooded, pale-faced nuns gliding among the crowd." But the narrator adds: "I do not defend this feeble sentimentality,—call it wickedness if you like,—but I understand it, and I forgive it from my soul." And Howells himself adds, many years later, when he visits a church with the novelist Valdés: "He made me want to crook the knee with him at the high altar of a church we visited, but I stood firm—and ashamed."

In Venice he was greatly impressed by "the grandeur of the Catholic faith" at Mass, where

a sense of Christ's exceeding triumph came almost with tears; and all the story of his lowly birth and bitter death and his final victory passed through my thoughts, while a keen pang for my own Christ-lessness smote me.

Yet he also found religious services in Italy performed "without a touch of religious feeling or solemnity of any kind," though he sometimes wondered why the whole thing did not become even more mechanical than it appeared. Pope Piux X was a "gentle priest whom all men speak well of for his piety and humility," but Cardinal Antonelli had "the very wickedest face in the world. . . . As he passed out he cast gleaming, terrible, sidelong looks upon the people, full of hate and guile." In *Modern Italian Poets* he calls priests bad in theory, though he adds that in experience he generally finds them very amiable. Certainly the young

French-Canadian Père Etienne, in *The Quality of Mercy*, is very attractive, but the only priest who is important in Howells's fiction is the one who falls in love with Florida Vervain in *A Foregone Conclusion*, and he is a priest without faith until toward the end of the book, when, after the collapse of his hopes, he suddenly achieves it (Howells does not really explain how or why), finds his whole life absorbed by the religion which had hitherto been only a form to him, and dies.

In his review of Tennyson's *Queen Mary*, Howells speaks of "the liberties never wholly safe from . . . [the] pretensions of the Catholic Church." He praised General Sheridan, condescendingly, for being "liberal and democratic-minded,—Irish and Catholic as he was by blood and faith." In a very unfavorable review of Vincenzo Botta's *Dante as Philosopher and Poet*, he rejects Dante's "scheme of universal empire" very decidedly and adds that "the wisest part of his policy was that of steadfast opposition to the growth of the temporal power of the papacy."

Though not all of Howells's strictures on the Catholic Church are early, there was, I think, a decline in animus as he grew older. Reviewing Lea's *History of the Inquisition*, he refused to regard religious persecution as something distinctively Catholic, viewing it instead as the fruit of an impulse distinctively human which time and chance merely gave Catholics a better opportunity to gratify than it gave Protestants. When he visited the home of St. Catherine of Siena, he was moved by a sense of reverence, but since he permits himself to use such words as "illusion" and "hallucination," he evidently respected her character more than her faith. In 1914, only six years before he died, Howells slipped into a *North American Review* article a reference to "the church, which is the Mother Church, even of rebellious and disobedient children."

Toward a very different kind of "Mother" Church he was much less tolerant, for he always treats Christian Science with extreme contempt. To him that religion was a "superstition" and its textbook a piece of "illiterate twaddle" and "vacuous vulgarity." He speaks of Christian Scientists as "comfortable people, cheerful in the least and lowest of the least spiritual precepts of the gospel, and more eager to save their bodies than their souls alive." When Mark Twain published his book on the subject in 1907, Howells "read your Mrs. Eddy massacre . . . and gloated on every drop of her blood." Actually he was much less sympathetic than Mark Twain, for though Mark Twain despised Mrs. Eddy as a person, he saw considerable value in the ideas she had got hold of and built her organization around. With the single exception of Mormonism, which he regarded as the same kind of imposture as Dylks perpetrates in *The Leatherwood God*, I can think of no other religion which Howells treats so unsympathetically as Christian Science.

All in all, the church he treats most sympathetically would seem to be the Episcopal Church. In 1868 he wrote Aurelia that he liked to go to the Episcopal church in Cambridge because the service was beautiful and the sermon shorter there than elsewhere, but perhaps we should not forget that the very next year he was attending a prayer meeting at a Methodist chapel, where he "heard more bad grammar and good religious feeling than I supposed to exist in Cambridge." Margaret Vance of *A Hazard of New Fortunes* is Episcopalian, and Howells says of her that "she was of the church which seems to have found a reversion to the imposing ritual of the past the way back to the early Christian brotherhood." Conrad Dryfoos is an Episcopalian also, and when old Lindau dies, nobody knowing what religion he had, if any, the Anglican service is read over him, "so often the refuge of the homeless dead." During his later years, when Howells summered at Kittery Point, he attended the Congregational church, and one Sunday morning, when the "supply" failed to materialize, he occupied the pulpit, reading one of his Altrurian papers. In 1889, he wrote a very interesting letter to R. Heber Newton, Rector of All Souls' Church in New York, expressing his enthusiasm over one of his sermons.

I found myself wishing I knew how many they [Newton's words] put to shame (as they did me) for the comfort we dare to take while there is a hopeless want in the world. I thank you for my share in the humiliation.

But he adds that "I must not let you infer that my interest is that of one inside of any creed. (I've a dread of not always being outright about this)." Yet, "in a loose and stumbling way," he has thought about such things "from my early instruction in Swedenborgianism—I've had some doctrine concerning it." When he died in 1920 he was buried from Percy Stickney Grant's Church of the Ascension at Fifth Avenue and Tenth Street.[8]

As a Swedenborgian, Howells had little to do with clergymen during his youth; later he was well acquainted with such men as Edward Everett Hale, Henry van Dyke, and Joseph H. Twichell; he talked earnestly about religion with all three, and all were impressed by the Christianism of his spirit. There are a good many clergymen in his novels, of varying affiliations and degrees of attractiveness. In *Ragged Lady*, Orson Landers is a contemptible, self-seeking lickspittle, and Gregory, though admirable, is a fanatic. It might not be unfair to call Mr. Peck of *Annie Kilburn* a fanatic, but he holds too many of Howells's own ideas to be treated unsympathetically, and Mr. Sewell of *The Minister's Charge* is hardly less conscientious though he is certainly much more sensible. William Baysley, the poor country Baptist minister of Iowa, plays a very small part in *Letters Home*, but Howells leaves no doubt in the reader's mind that he is a saint and that the author admires him as much as Chaucer admired his Parson. Ewbank of "A Difficult Case" wears out his health and strength in struggling with the doubts of an aged parishioner. As for Breckon, whom we meet on shipboard engaged in falling in love with Ellen Kenton, since he is "merely the leader of a sort of forlorn hope in the Divine Goodness" cherished by a nondescript Ethical Culture Society, not much needs to be said about this delightful young man as a shepherd.

In a sense, the most elaborately studied cleric in Howells's fiction is the backwoods rascal Dylks of *The Leatherwood God*, who technically was probably not a clergyman at all. But it is ridiculous to call Howells's portrayal of Dylks "a veiled attack upon the dogmas of revealed religion." [9] Dylks was an historical character, and *The Leatherwood God* is an historical novel. Howells gives us a subtle intermixture of fanaticism and imposture. As the rascal himself says in one of his more clear-sighted moments, "You are tempted on, step by step, all so easy, till you can't go back, you can't stop." And again: "Their faith puts faith in you. If they believe what you say, you say to yourself that there must be some truth in it." At the end he is treated compassionately, both by the author and by his own son Joey.[10]

IV

Howells has often been called an agnostic; there are even times when he applies the label to himself. The natural gravitation of his mind was toward the concrete, and he always tended to hold that "the formulation of any faith in a creed is the beginning of question." He once told S. Weir Mitchell that his only "deepening conviction," as he grew older, was that of "absolute helplessness," and the beautiful poem "The Bewildered Guest" in *Stops of Various Quills* would seem as perfect an expression of agnosticism as could be devised:

> I was not asked if I should like to come,
>   I have not seen my host here since I came,
>   Or had a word of welcome in his name.
> Some say that we shall never see him, and some
> That we shall see him elsewhere, and then know
>   Why we were bid. How long I am to stay
>   I have not the least notion. None, they say,
> Was ever told when he should come or go.
> But every now and then there bursts upon
>   The song and mirth a lamentable noise,
>   A sound of shrieks and sobs, that strikes our joys

> Dumb in our breasts; and then, some one is gone.
> They say we meet him. None knows where or when.
> We know we shall not meet him here again.

Nevertheless, the term agnostic is wrong as applied to Howells, and even if its denotation is correct, its connotations will not fit.

It is true, of course, that "agnostic" is one of those slippery labels that mean all things to all men, but when Van Wyck Brooks, in his study of Howells, applies it to men like Longfellow and Lowell, it is robbed of all reasonable meaning. In a sense, to be sure, we are all agnostics.

> We have but faith; we cannot know;
> For knowledge is of things we see;

and without this condition faith could have no meaning nor even exist as faith. But this is not the usual meaning of the term. For though agnosticism is not atheism, its drift *is* toward denial, and this does not suit Howells, who was an earnest seeker always. When he uses it, he gives it his own accent: "it can . . . be said that agnosticism is not an unpromising or unhopeful frame of mind. It may be only one remove, and it is only one syllable from a Gnosticism wiser and not less trusting than the old; and perhaps the present psychologism is the beginning of it." And, again: "agnosticism is a perpetual toleration of mystery as thinkable." But by 1919 he is ready to declare "that agnosticism is as dead as the faith it seemed to slay," and if we are not yet "on the verge of a revival of belief in a life hereafter," he does say that when "we universally want to know whether we shall live again, we shall know, on the simple principle that people always get what they want."

The *Quills* themselves assert the reality of Deity.

> Dark prophet, yes! But still somehow the round
> Is spiral, and the race's feet have found

The path rise under them which they have trod.
Your facts are facts, yet somewhere there is God.

And the last poem in the book conveys a stern warning:

If I lay waste and wither up with doubt
The blessed fields of heaven where once my faith
Possessed itself serenely safe from death;
If I deny the things past finding out;
Or if I orphan my own soul of One
That seemed a Father, and make void the place
Within me where He dwelt in power and grace,
What do I gain by that I have undone?

When he reviewed Oliver Wendell Holmes's *Mechanism in Thought and Morals* in 1871, Howells was noncommittal, but two years later he struck out against a "brutally Huxleyized" treatment of religious belief, though none such had appeared in the book he was reviewing.

If the word agnostic is to be applied to Howells at all, it applied no more to religious than to unreligious matters; thus J. M. Robertson, comparing him with Turgenev, finds that "the one writer has made up his mind about life; the other has not." But Howells in a sense replies to Robertson when he says that in *Macbeth* Shakespeare makes us question evil while in *Ghosts* Ibsen only makes us question the good, and in *My Literary Passions* he prefers Björnson to Ibsen on much the same grounds. Commenting on the implications for faith of an English scientist's denial of the possibility of life on other planets, Howells finds that what the author's investigation really adds up to is that "he tells the Soul that Science cannot answer its questions, because it has no experience of the facts; and science is experience." This, of course, is exactly what John Fiske argued, and Howells was friendly with Fiske, and influenced by him in these matters, as he was by *The Will to Believe* of William James. And, to come back to the troublesome word again, Howells calls Fiske an agnostic and then declares that he has "done more than any other to repair the ravage of research in the region of accepted beliefs." Fiske was an apostle of Evolution, and it was not until after he had become dissatisfied with the "psychological outcome" of the evolutionary philosophy "that he began to speak as one having authority, and to say those things, new and glad, of God and of the Soul which are possibly more important than anything [else] said of either in our darkened day." Reviewing *The Idea of God* and *The Destiny of Man*, Howells was impressed that though Fiske was not technically a Christian,

he was unable to language his thoughts of infinity at supreme moments except in the words of the old book of those Semitic tribes so remote from Darwin; and it is remarkable that modern light and knowledge have no hope or type more sublime than Christ and His millennium.

It is quite true that Howells had a temperamental dislike of formulated creeds and ecclesiastical systems. In defending *Paradise Lost* against Albert Mordell, he admits frankly that its "scheme" is "preposterous," but he felt thus about formularization in non-religious matters also. Since Marxism has now become the tightest orthodoxy to rule men's minds since Calvinism, this may seem a strange thing to say about a "socialist." But Howells's socialism too was experimental; he never joined the party.

Howells stressed the religious origin of the American settlements ("it was not Thomas Jefferson who first imagined the first of the self-evident truths of the Declaration, but George Fox"), and in 1902 he still thought of Americans as "a very biblical people." He saw "the human conscience" as "God in us," but he found no sanction even for fraternal love in nature. "Fraternity is supernatural, as all civility is." Hester's experience in *The Scarlet Letter* caused him to doubt the possibility of solving moral problems without "the help of the mystery 'not ourselves, that makes for righteousness,' and that we may call Chance or that we may call God, but that does not change in essence of puissance whatever name we give it." "Implanted goodness" was what saved —"the seed of righteousness treasured from generation to generation, and carefully watched and tended by disciplined fathers and mothers in the hearts where they have dropped it," and it is quite clear that he intended to indicate that Marcia Gaylord's lack of religious training contributed importantly to her share of the responsibility for the failure of her marriage.

Clem in *Ragged Lady* does not consider herself a religious person; if she went out as a missionary, it would be for Gregory's sake, not for God's, but when he asks her whether she *believes* in God and the Bible, she replies, "Why, certainly!" and "Why, of cou'se!" Florida Vervain, repelled by her Catholic surroundings in the Italy of *A Foregone Conclusion*, wonders whether religious faith might be a mistake—"perhaps there might not be any other world, and . . . *our* church as well as the rest . . . might be only a cruel blunder, a dreadful mistake. Perhaps there isn't even any God!" But when she asks Ferris, "Do *you* think there is?" he replies, "I don't *think* it. I *know* it."

Howells's leading skeptic is Matthew Braile of *The Leatherwood God*, who reads Tom Paine and is called an infidel. But Braile is definitely theistic, and he always knows the difference between right and wrong. Howells himself denied that Lord Herbert of Cherbury was a Christian on the ground that he denied revelation, but when he reviewed Ward Lamon's book on Lincoln, he thought the author dwelt too much on the fact that Lincoln was not "theoretically a Christian." Of Mark Twain he says that he "arrived at the first stage of the scientific denial of the religious hope of mankind; he did not reach that last stage where Science whimsically denies that she denies nothing," but elsewhere he writes that with Mark Twain and Livy both, "Christianity ceased to be a creed and remained a life." [10]

In *New Leaf Mills*, Owen Powell goes out into the night to sense not only the unity but the harmony and friendliness of creation.

The sky bristled with stars, and he thought how the coals would bristle in the morning. He felt the sweet unity of creation, the little things and the great things, and he felt that life and death in the measureless scheme were the same.

Howells knew that what literary critics call "poetic justice" did not reign in this world, that divine justice is "averse to melodrama" and "strong effects," and that the moral law is much less regular or automatic or definable in its operations than physical law, yet many of his characters do retain a faith in Providence. Jeff Durgin in *The Landlord at Lion's Head* sees no meaning in life because he wants it that way, but Ferris of *A Foregone Conclusion* thinks God "lets men learn Him from their own experience of evil. I imagine the kingdom of heaven is a sort of republic, and that God draws men to Him only through their perfect freedom." Ellen Kenton comes pretty close to existentialism when she tells Breckon that "we have to make believe before we can believe anything." And we have Howells's own word for what he believed. He did *not* believe that goodness always produces pleasure or unhappiness, but he *was* sure that "it brings peace and rest to the soul, and lightens all burdens: the trial and the sorrow go on for good and evil alike; only those who choose the evil have no peace." He knew that "there are times when a rush of evil seems to sweep across the world and overwhelm us, but it isn't often. When we all seemed to go down before agnosticism, we didn't really all go down, and even those who did held fast to the greatest of the virtues, Charity." All in all, Henry van Dyke would seem to have stated the matter accurately enough when he said of Howells:

He was an inveterate questioner, a temperamental skeptic in the old Greek sense of the word, which means an inquirer, a searcher. But underneath all he was a mystic, unwilling to surrender realities invisible and eternal, or to

Deny the things past finding out.[11]

V

Aside from theism itself, what about the Christian religion appealed to Howells most? I should say the figure of Jesus Christ himself and the Christian faith in immortality.

For Howells the life of Christ was "the supreme human event," the only life ever lived without failure, and the Crucifixion "the supreme tragedy of the race." With him "something came into the world . . . that was then and will be forever irreconcilable with the world as the world was and is." Reading Renan's naturalistic life of Jesus for the first time in 1892, he wondered how "this mild, sentimental thing" could once have so stirred Christendom. Three years earlier he had scolded Mark Twain for giving Christ less than his due in *A Connecticut Yankee* and for failing to acknowledge that wherever he had been given a chance in society, great good had been done. But he adds: "I don't mean the fetish, the fable Christ, but that great, wise, serious, most sufficing man. Read [Charles Loring] Brace's *Gesta Christi*, and you'll get it all." He was fascinated by Howard Pyle's modernization of the Christ-story in *Rejected of Men*, though he was troubled by the miracles. And we hardly need the testimony of *My Literary Passions* to attest the rapture with which he received the reaffirmation of Christian principles in Tolstoy.

Tolstoy gave me heart to hope that the world may yet be made over in the image of Him who died for it, when all Caesar's things shall be finally rendered unto Caesar, and men shall come into their own, into the right to labor and the right to enjoy the fruits of their labor, each one master of himself and servant to every other.

In 1916, Albert Mordell inquired,

Why should millions of people pattern themselves after an ascetic and self-martyrizing idealist who lived in a different age and under circumstances very different from our own? If the world were populated by Christ types we should have few great inventors, philosophers, and scientists; great industrial and diplomatic activities would be at a standstill.

Howells admitted that this was true at least as far as diplomacy was concerned and went on to enumerate some of the other things we should lack:

there would be no exploitation of labor for the making of millionaires; no wars, no white slavery, no caste—none of those things which the civilized world seems so much concerned in perpetuating.

He challenged Mordell to prove by the Gospels that Christ was "an ascetic and self-martyrizing idealist," himself seeing him rather as a man who

bade sinners do no more than cease to do evil, and not to seek to punish sin in others unless they were themselves without it; who was in every way so divinely right and just a man that the witnesses believed he must be God.

This is much like Halleck in *A Modern Instance*, who believed that "if Christ never lived on earth, some One lived who imagined him, and that One must have been a God." For that reason, "the historical fact oughtn't to matter." [12] Howells himself does not seem to have believed in the Divinity of Christ, however, nor to have been much concerned with the Atonement. In *A Hazard of New Fortunes* Conrad Dryfoos is a true Christian martyr, dying for the sins of the people (and especially for the salvation of his own father) as Christ died for the sins of the world; in a way this is the most Christian passage in all Howells's fiction. Generally speaking, however, he revolted against the "bloody" element in Christianity, even as represented in ecclesiastical art, as he revolted also against the whole conception of hell. He would not pretend to feel anything but "loathing" for Orgagna's painting.

If I am told that I ought at least respect the faith with which the painter wrought, I say that the faith was not respectable; and I can honor him more if I believe he was portraying those evil dreams in contempt of them—doing what he could to make faith in them impossible by realizing them in all the details of their filthy cruelty.

As to the Divinity of Christ, he writes his father in 1872 that he is disappointed in his current reading of Swedenborg

because I find that he makes a certain belief the condition for entering the kingdom of heaven. I always tho't it was a good life he insisted upon, and I inferred from such religious training as you gave me that it made no difference what I believed about the trinity, or the divinity of Christ, if only I did right from a love of doing right. Now it appears to me from the Testament that Christ was a man directly, instead of indirectly, begotten by a divine father; and for this persuasion, which I owe to the reason given me of God, Swedenborg tells me I shall pass my eternal life in an insane asylum. This is hard, and I can't help revolting from it. I am not such a fool as to think that I can do the highest good for myself, or that I am anything in myself; but I don't see why I cannot be humble and true and charitable, without believing that Christ was God. I am greatly disappointed, and somewhat distressed in this matter. At times I'm half minded never to read another word of theology; but to cling blindly to the moral teachings of the gospels.

That Howells passionately desired immortality is shown by the energy he devoted to discussing it. Sometimes he speaks of "us poor believers" or of those who are "now with God" or looks forward to "when we meet Yonder." And the longer he lived the more was he "persuaded that the problems of this life are to be solved elsewhere or never." More characteristically, however, both he and his characters ask questions or express a hope, as "I wonder if father is somewhere that he can sympathize as he did life long with the resurrection of the year" or, of his daughter: "And where is she, and shall I ever see her again? The world has largely resolved itself into this question for me." [13] Or, as Basil March puts it: "Perhaps there's something else, something better—somewhere." When Susy Clemens died, Howells tried to comfort Mark Twain with the hope of immortality. When he found that Valdés believed in it, he was pleased, and he found Tolstoy's denial of it "like a survival, a projection into the hopefulness and ardor of . . . early Christianity . . . of the vast, passive Asiatic melancholy which seems to tinge all Russian character." But we may see how uncertain and yet how sensitive he was when he tells Howard Pyle, "I do not always feel sure that I shall live again, but when I wake at night the room seems dense with spirits."

He knew that there was no satisfying substitute for faith in immortality. When he found himself growing "more ancestral than individual" with age, with "father's figure and bearing in mine," he wondered whether we might all be "gathered into our race at last, and hereafter will have only little gleams of personal consciousness." And he adds, "Well, it is all right," but he did not really think so. The idea of an immortality of influence was noble, but neither George Eliot nor Robert Dale Owen was able to satisfy him that it was enough. And though Egeria of *The Undiscovered Country*, rebelling against her mediumship, wishes she could stay in the world, and rejects her father's idea that "death is the condition of our advancement," Howells himself felt that one life here was quite enough; indeed he was by no means sure that he would have accepted that if he had been consulted. Thus the idea of the transmigration of souls did not attract him, and when Thomas L. Harris professed to have discovered powers of renewal within himself, he was neither impressed nor attracted. In 1903 he reported on a symposium on the question whether one would wish to live life over. Though many had replied in the affirmative, Howells doubted the report. What they must really want, he thought, was to live *on*, not *over*.

Like John Fiske, Howells could see no very significant *a priori* difficulty in the way of believing in immortality. Continuity is "the lesson of experience" and its "instinctive expectation." "The sense of this is so pervasive that humanity refuses to accept death itself as final." And again:

Isn't it imaginable that when a certain anthropoid ape went wrong and blundered into a man, he also blundered into a soul, and as a slight compensation for having involuntarily degenerated from his anthropoid ancestor, came into the birthright of eternal life?

We dream of the dead as alive and get messages from them. May not this "be a witness" that we have not really lost them, and that "there is something there" in the darkness "which answers to our throe with pity and with longing like our own?" Even more, is not the fact that we think of them as being more alive than we are ourselves a testimony?

There is a buoyant sense of their escape, of their release to the unknown, the untried. If they are at all, they are in the gracious presence of new conditions, new chances, new deeds. The miracle of creation has been wrought afresh for them; they have entered upon immortal youth; they have parted with age; they have turned their faces from death forever. Death, their own death, abides with us who call ourselves alive.

It is true that old Holbrook in "A Difficult Case" (*A Pair of Patient Lovers*), which is Howells's most elaborate discussion of the immortality question in fiction, does not *want* to live forever. "I'm tired. I've had enough. I don't want to do anything more, or have anything more done to me. I want to *stop*." Yet when he suffers himself to be persuaded by his pastor Ewbank, he takes a new lease on life, and when he loses his faith again, he dies. Howells never made the mistake of supposing that faith in immortality was incompatible with a keen interest in social religion. Describing the sad conditions which existed in Altruria before the great change, Mr. Homos says, "Religion ceased to be the hope of this world, and became the vague promise of the next." But he also says that "the presence of the risen Christ in our daily lives is our assurance that no one ceases to be, and that we shall see our dead again. I cannot explain this to you; I can only affirm it."

Though Howells did not believe in the old-fashioned heaven and hell, he was convinced that belief in immortality gives human life a sanction it otherwise loses, and, other things being equal, he felt that the decline of this faith would have a bad effect upon morality. Whatever he may have believed about Swedenborg's elaborate attempts to chart the future world in his youth, he certainly did not take them literally in later life, but they did retain considerable suggestiveness for him. It is interesting that though the desire to meet loved ones again was probably his strongest motive for desiring immortality, he should also have associated the thought of dread with this—in his mother's case because he was no longer the boy who had begged her to live to a hundred but a man much older than she was when she went away, and with Winny, apparently, because he had always been a little in awe of her even here. Sensitive as he was of his own shortcomings, he did not look forward to being punished, yet when Verrian of *Fennel and Rue* raises this question with Miss Shirley, he says, "I expect to be got even with." In *The Seen and Unseen at Stratford-on-Avon*, Shakespeare, who expresses a good many of the ideas Howells liked to play with in these connections, says that "there *is* a sort of hell. But there is no punishment; there is only consequence, and there is the relief of doing penance." But when he is asked whether it will last forever, he replies: "How do I know, with my little three centuries' experience?"

In his later years, Howells's faith in immortality grew stronger, not only, as he says, because "age is the time to trust," but because the climate of scientific opinion was now more spiritually-minded than the science which had disturbed his inherited faith in his youth. In 1917 he wrote a friend that "after long unbelief," he was "getting back some hope again" and "getting back peace, which seemed gone forever."

Five years before he had published in *Harper's Weekly*[14] an odd story called "The Fulfilment of the Pact," about a dead man who came back to his wife. He knows very little about the life beyond, and he is able to tell her much less than she wishes to know. But "I am absolutely sure now that life as you have it

on earth is not a trick of the Giver. That it's a pledge. That it's
a promise in itself that life will never be taken away." When she
suggests killing herself to come to him, he opposes the suggestion
on the ground that "it's an offence against the order of things."
He is not sure she would be punished for it. "There doesn't seem
to be anything like punishment, though I don't know exactly.
But there's consequence. If you interrupt the universal order
there's confusion—disease that you have to recover from." Three
years later, in the "Easy Chair," [15] Howells published a dialogue
between himself and the Human Soul, who had been away for
some time. The Soul asks the Easy Chair whether he did not once
believe in him.

"Unquestioningly."
"When and how did you lose faith in me?"
"Hm, we don't know; but as to when, it was about the year 1870,
when most other cultivated people gave you up."
"But you now believe in me again?"
"We must."
"And what made you return to a belief in eternal life?"
"Death."
The word was surprised from us, but we could not take it back.

This leads to a declaration from the Soul, which is the most elo-
quent thing Howells ever wrote on this subject, or perhaps on
any other:

". . . it may be that in the fullness of eternity it shall be seen on
earth that death was only another form of life. It seems to rend your
very soul; it tears apart every fibre of your being when it comes to
your beloved. You said that you could not bear it when it came; but
you bore it, as all the innumerable host of men have borne it from the
first. In the very ecstasy of your anguish there was somehow peace,
there was refuge, there was escape. If here you can outlive, is it not a
sign that you shall live on?"

Howells's most carefully considered word on the subject, however, is "A Counsel of Consolation" in the *Harper* symposium,

In After Days, to which Henry James and a number of less illustrious writers also contributed.

I cannot truly speak to the stricken from the absolute faith which some others can speak from. I am of those who patiently wait for the fulfilment of the hopes which Christianity has worded from the Greek philosophers rather than from the Hebrew prophets. . . . There are many things that I doubt, but few that I deny; where I cannot believe, there I often trust; and as all faith is mystical, I would have the bereaved trust their mystical experiences for much truth which they cannot affirm. In their darkness it will be strange if there are no gleams of that outer light which wraps our whole ignorance of this life. These will penetrate it sometimes in what seem preternatural experiences of the waking hours, and sometimes in visions of the night, which I would have the sorrower at least passively accept, or not positively refuse.

For comfort he advises the Bible, Plato, and Socrates, and such modern poets as Tennyson in "The Two Voices" and *In Memoriam.* He would have the dead remembered, not forgotten, and remembered with

the foibles, the frailties, which in every human being help make up his sum, and endear him equally with his virtue. And though passion will finally resolve itself into patience, there is, in the last analysis, no surer source of comfort than "the voice of One who taught as if with authority, 'If it were not so I would have told you.' " [16]

It must be obvious that a man with such interests as these could not, in Howells's day, have avoided being interested in spiritualism. "The belief in ghosts is almost universal among the people," he writes in *Seven English Cities*; "as I may allow without superiority, for I do not know but I believe in them myself." There was considerable interest in ghostly matters in his early Ohio; later this was reinforced by the "rappings" out of Rochester and the spiritualistic movement which they spawned. In 1912 he devoted an "Easy Chair" to spiritualism, and in 1919 he dedicated another to the revival of interest which came out of the war.

Like everybody else in 1919, he read Sir Oliver Lodge's *Raymond*, finding it "not very important, but very touching, and not uninteresting."

In one of his essays Howells remarks that he never encountered a dishonest publisher. "I have heard of other people meeting them . . . just as I have heard of people seeing ghosts, and I have to believe in both the rogues and the ghosts, without the witness of my own senses." Yet apparently he did see a ghost (or what is generally called a ghost) on at least one occasion,[17] and, according to Van Wyck Brooks, he told S. Weir Mitchell that all the psychic "Romances" in *Questionable Shapes* and *Between the Dark and the Daylight* were from his own experience. I think we may be sure of this in the case of "His Apparition" at least, for though the story deals not with psychic belief but with the purely human complications which result from Hewson's relating his experience, neither the ghost nor the man to whom it appears behaves at all the way one might expect in fiction.

He had always supposed that if anything of the sort happened to him he would be greatly frightened, but he had not been at all frightened, so far as he could make out. His hair had not risen, or his cheek felt a chill; his heart had not lost or gained a beat in its pulsation; and his prime conclusion was that if the Mysteries had chosen him an agent in approaching the material world they had not made a mistake.

The "Romances" are not all ghost stories, strictly speaking, nor is it only in these collections that Howells deals with psychic matters. In *The Landlord at Lion's Head*, Jackson Durgin and Mr. Whitwell are devotees of planchette, and Mrs. Durgin has a "spirit picture" of two children she lost. What we now call extrasensory perception is referred to in *Miss Bellard's Inspiration*. In "The Face at the Window" (*A Daughter of the Storage*), which was based on an experience of friends of the Howells family, a father's ghost comes home to tell that his son is dying, and in *The Flight of Pony Baker* a dead boy returns to play with his comrades on the Fourth of July. "A Presentiment" is a story about a man leaving home for a trip who is sure that he will never see his wife again. Upon his return, he is informed of her death.

But did Howells "believe" such things? I should say Howells knew that phenomena occur for which there seems to be no naturalistic explanation and that he kept his mind open. In his introduction to a collection of psychic stories, *Shapes That Haunt the Dusk*, he finds Americans particularly adept in dealing with this kind of story.

The collection is like a group of immortelles, gray in that twilight of the reason which Americans are so fond of inviting, or, rather, they are like a cluster of Indian pipe, those pale blossoms of the woods that spring from the dark mould in the deepest shade, and are so entirely of our soil.

He attended at least one spectacular seance[18] and had some contact with the Society for Psychical Research. He believed that exposing fake mediums did nothing to lessen faith in spiritualism, and he had his fortune told by "an aging Italian sybil" in the fair at Buxton, but he was probably not serious about this. Like all who have tried to investigate psychic phenomena, he was often put off by both the puerility of the "messages" and the character of the witnesses, but when he read Tolstoy, this great realist felt that nothing else was "so wonderful as his power upon us in the scenes of the borderland where his vision seems to pierce the confines of another world."

In *The Seen and Unseen*, Shakespeare and Bacon "materialize" to visit Stratford, but this is a fantasy. The serious treatment of spiritualism in *The Undiscovered Country* is not very enthusiastic, for though Dr. Boynton is treated very tenderly, he is both dupe and self-deceiver, and at last he thinks of himself as having imposed mediumship upon his daughter as a kind of vampirism. Finally he agrees with Hawthorne that spiritualism is objectionable because of its materialism.

"All other systems of belief, all other revelations of the unseen world, have supplied a rule of life, have been given for our *use* here. But this offers nothing but the barren fact that we live again. If it has had any effect upon morals, it has been to corrupt them. I cannot see how it is better in its effect upon this world than sheer atheism."

The Undiscovered Country suggests both *The Blithedale Romance* of Hawthorne and *The Bostonians* of Henry James, but Boynton himself is like Orestes A. Brownson in his courage and sincerity, his rashness in drawing radical conclusions from insufficient data, his willingness to scrap them as soon as new data appear, and his general, self-willed absurdity. When he dies, Ford remarks that he has now verified his theories one way or the other, and the doctor replies, "Yes, and in the old way,—the way appointed for all living." The auctorial comment which closes the book gives us Howells's own view at the time he wrote it: "If Boynton has found the undiscovered country, he has sent no message back to them, and they do not question his silence. They wait, and we must all wait." [19]

VI

When all is said and done, Howells came closest to being Mr. Homos not in his theological speculations but in his passion for social and economic reform. While important clues to his social ideals may be found in his Altrurian romances,[20] it must be remembered that these are works of art in the utopian tradition, not blueprints for a new society. They cannot, therefore, stand as the full index of his mind.

The Altrurian, Mr. Homos, made his first appearance as the guest of the American novelist Mr. Twelvemough in the November 1892 issue of *Cosmopolitan*.[21] Mr. Homos finds it very hard to understand the inequalities of American life. Why should people be discriminated against, for example, because of the kind of work they do? Mr. Homos creates a sensation when he helps the baggage man with his luggage or tries to carry a heavy tray for the waitress, and the strange thing about it is that those he is trying to help are the most shocked of all. Why should a landowner be permitted to denude his land of timber clear to the water's edge, because he wants or needs the money the timber will bring, thus spoiling the country for everyone about? Would it not be more sensible to have the state buy the land, paying a price which would include the full value of the timber? Neither does Mr. Homos ever understand why his question about where laborers go for their summer vacation should arouse mirth. Surely they must need a rest as much as anybody else. Mr. Homos soon learns that he cannot think of America as either a civilized or a Christian country, though it contains many civilized people and "abounds in good people, who love one another, and lead lives of continual self-sacrifice." Neither is it a democratic country, for its representative government has now become little but a form.

The Altrurian commonwealth was founded by St. Paul, but fell away from the ideals of the founder (the parallel to an America which has departed from the ideals of the Founding Fathers is clear) until it finally achieved a state of affairs very much like that which now prevails in the United States. But when economic warfare and monopoly finally became intolerable, the voters inaugurated public ownership.

Complete social and economic equality now prevails in Altruria. Everyone does physical work three hours a day. The rest of his time is free for creative work, which is rewarded only by itself. There is no money in Altruria. No one "is asked to do work that he hates, unless he seems to hate every kind of work. When this happens the authorities find something for him that he had *better* like, by letting him starve till he works." The greatest man is he "who has been able for the time being, to give the greatest happiness to the greatest number—some artist, or poet, or inventor, or physician."

Life in Altruria is organized around small towns, not cities, and swift transport between them is furnished by electric power. Mr. Homos is shocked that in America the transportation companies are required to pay nothing for the privilege of ruining the property of the people through whose streets they run their trains, as in the case of the New York City Elevated, for example.

There are several forms of religious ritual in Altruria, but there is no prescribed creed, and "our religious differences may be said to be aesthetic and temperamental rather than theological and essential." After the work of the day is over, services are held in the temple; this involves a hymn and a march in the course of which an offering from the woods or fields is laid upon the altar. Afterwards, anyone is at liberty to speak—or to leave without offence. Funeral services are not held over a corpse, though there is a brief rite at the interment, "where it is wished that the kindred shall not be present, lest they think always of the material body and not of the spiritual body which shall be raised in incorruption." People are not allowed to marry until they have given reasonable evidence of the sincerity and durability of their affections, including a test by separation. When a marriage is unsuccessful, divorce is granted freely, but it is regarded as a blot on a person's record and an injury against the state. The marriage ceremonial is much like that now employed by the Quakers.

Crime, though not unknown, is rare, since practically all the incentives to crime which prevail in capitalistic countries are absent in Altruria except murder for jealous rage. Since "you cannot recreate one life by destroying another," there is no capital punishment.

Equality is the keynote in Altruria. "Equality is such a beautiful thing that I wonder people can ever have any other ideal. It is the only social joy, the only comfort. If you meet an inferior or a superior, you are at once wretched." Howells told Joyce Kilmer that equality was "the best thing in the world" and "the thing for which the Best of Men lived and died." Fraternity cannot be achieved by destroying even those whose greed and selfishness stand in the way of its realization, for if destruction could achieve it, we should have had it long ago.

The millennium, the reign of Christliness on earth, will be nothing mystical or strange. It will be the application of a very simple rule to life, which we find in no wise difficult or surprising where the economic conditions do not hinder its operation. The members of a family live for one another as unconsciously as they live upon all others.

Howells did not undervalue the political freedom upon which Americans in general pride themselves, but he gives cold comfort to those who thought that once it had been secured, there was nothing else to be desired. For "liberty is never a good in itself, and is never final; it is a means to something good, and a way to the end which its lovers are really seeking." Liberty is no good, for example, to a man who is starving, nor does it have much value unless "security from want and from the fear of want" go with it. The Altrurians

thought it the drollest thing in the world that men should be willing to give their own lives and take the lives of other men for the sake of a country which assured them no safety from want, and did not even assure them work, and in which they had no more logical interest than the country they were going to fight.

None of this means that Howells wanted to put humanity into a copper kettle and boil it down until all constituents had been reduced to a dull uniformity. He distinguishes sharply between natural inequalities and those artificial inequalities which are created by differences in means and opportunity. One was remediable; the other was not. "Every ideal that presupposes an inequality among men, except such as their conduct creates, is a vulgar superstition."

As things stand, life is a horror for the "have's" as well as for the "have not's." It is only by the character-destructive means of resolutely shutting the needs of others out of one's mind that a sensitive person can have any peace in this world, and even the insensitive are often much less comfortable than they appear. In *Through the Eye of the Needle*, Mr. Thrall found his wealth a burden to him, all the more because he could not be sure he was not doing more harm than good with it even when he gave it away, and his problem was not solved until he reached Altruria, where wealth had neither meaning nor power. But the grotesqueries that we encounter here would be funny if they were not so tragic. Look at the tragi-comic to-do in *Annie Kilburn* about whether the poor of Hatboro are fit to be invited to the affair that is being put on for their benefit. Nor is it only the upper classes that struggle with such distinctions. Lemuel Barker will not meet Statira in the Public Garden because he does not wish her to be taken for "one of these servant-girls." When he goes home to the country after his stay in Boston, he is ashamed of his relatives, and Howells makes us see the inevitability of this. "He felt the self-reproach to which the man who rises without raising with him all those dear to him is destined in some measure all his life." When he asks his employer, Miss Vane, for the number of her pew in church, she has not the heart to withhold it, but she questions her pastor as to whether it is proper for him to sit there. "I don't know," confesses Mr. Sewell wearily. "It may lead to great abuses. If we tacitly confess ourselves equal in the sight of God, how much better are we than the Roman Catholics?" [22]

VII

Where did it all come from? and how did Howells get that way? In later life he was inclined to think that he had witnessed equality in frontier Ohio and only there. In *The Coast of Bohemia* Mrs. Burton says that "lines are drawn just as hard and fast" in a New England village as in the city. "You have to live in the West to understand what equality is. . . ."

This was partly a matter of necessity—what William Cooper Howells called "the general dependence of all upon the neighborly kindness and good offices of others"—but some of it derived from the temper and ferment of the frontier, the egalitarian ideals of the still young republic and, in the case of the Howells family, their Quaker and Swedenborgian connections. Quakers, though sometimes guilty of spiritual snobbery, have never as a class paid any regard to distinctions of race, class, or rank, and Ohio Swedenborgians not only had a considerable specific interest in Fourieristic settlements but must also have known that Robert Dale Owen had a communal establishment at New Harmony, Indiana.[23] After the collapse of the Dayton *Transcript*, Howells's father and his brothers undertook to establish a communal settlement of their own on the Little Miami River, but about all that came out of this was one of Howells's last novels, *New Leaf Mills*.

This is the kind of thing that Robert L. Hough had in mind when he remarked of Howells that his socialism was "essentially a barn-raising, house-warming kind of cooperation between rural neighbors." It may well have been so, but there is much radical material in the Ashtabula *Sentinel*:

From time to time poems and little articles of the most radical sort appeared. They demanded revolt against all oppression, reapportionment of property and complete political and economic liberty. One of the most startling things about this material is the casual way in which it was treated.[24]

Nevertheless there are elements which do not quite fit into the picture. The Howellses were poor, but they cherished their "Cymric," possibly royal, origins, and were often of the governing caste as things went in that time and place. If they did not think of themselves as "better" than their neighbors, they were certainly aware that their manners were different. And the young Howells is often considerably less of a rebel than we might have expected him to be. He tells us that as a small child, he was ashamed of his grandfather's abolitionism. On his first trip to New England, the spirit in which he contemplated the factory girls entering the mills at Lowell was far from being that of a walking delegate, and when he returned to Venice in the 'eighties he was appalled by the misery he had failed to observe when he was there as consul. Can it be that the explanation of this paradox is that Howells's early tendencies toward radicalism were buried during the early years of his literary success and personal ambition, and that they did not importantly revive until after his contacts with Tolstoy, Gronlund, and others?

Howells himself encourages us to believe something like this. "What I had instinctively known before, I now knew rationally," he writes of the period following his discovery of Tolstoy. He also says that Tolstoy brought him back to "the light of that human conscience which I had falsely taught myself was to be ignored in questions of art," and he adds that he now read the life of Christ "with a rapture such as I have known in no other reading." Perhaps, then, the Russian's primary value to him was not that he taught him something new or different but rather that he interpreted him to himself.

Howells read *The Cossacks*, the first of Tolstoy's books that he encountered, in 1885, and it was quickly followed by *Anna Karenina*. By April 1887, when he described the Russian as "precisely the human being with whom at the moment I find myself in the greatest intimacy," he claimed to have read most of the writings then available in English. The two never met, and Howells apparently never wrote to Tolstoy until the latter had sent him a message, to which he responded. When Tolstoy's seventieth birthday was celebrated in New York, Howells wrote a letter in which he declared that "his writings and life have meant more to me than any other man's."

The point has been made elsewhere in this volume that the influence was primarily ethical, not aesthetic. As he himself told William Lyon Phelps, "my pace was set long before his giant strides overtook me." [25] But perhaps it is even more interesting to note that he preserved his independence even in his spiritual and ethical discipleship. Incapable of extremism, Howells was necessarily also incapable of both fanaticism and sainthood, and though he was often troubled by his own way of life, he never followed Tolstoy to the fields or the cobbler's bench. In the poem "Parable" the Young Man of the Gospels follows Christ's command to sell all and give to the poor, but the expected results do not follow.

Then some of them to whom he gave his wealth
Mocked at him for a fool or mad, by stealth
Or openly; and others he could see
Wasting his substance with a spendthrift glee;
And others yet were tempted, and drawn in
The ways of sin that had not dreamed of sin:
Others, besides, that took were robbed and killed:
Some that had toiled their whole lives were unwilled
By riches, and began the life accurst
Of idleness, like rich men from the first.
Some hid the money in the earth, a root
From which should grow a flower of deadly fruit;
Some kept, and put it out as usury,
And made men slaves with it that had been free.[26]

Howells did not believe that the solution of his personal problem which Tolstoy had worked out in his own life was necessarily binding upon others, nor that we must each of us try to lead "a poor, dull, and ugly" life because Tolstoy felt that he must do this to atone for the "worldly, sensual, and violent" life he had led before his conversion. It seemed to him that there was an element of almost comic histrionism involved in Tolstoy's trying to live the life of a peasant, while his wife, who did not share his views, kept her hold on the family fortune; when the chips were down, Tolstoy did not stand on a plane of equality with the poor, and nothing that he could do would put him there. But the weakest part of Tolstoy's gospel, in Howells's eyes, was that it contemplated a purely personal salvation. The world, after all, is God's world, and man is a creature of society. He cannot separate himself from it; if he is to be saved, he must be saved in society, and society must be saved with him. Otherwise, he will never be saved at all.

Howells's social views were also influenced by his adventures with the Chicago anarchists. Unless literature and scholarship are themselves heroic (Browning thought so when he wrote "A Grammarian's Funeral"), writers are not often called upon for heroic behavior. One such opportunity came to Howells, and he rose to it, jeopardizing his position with the Harpers and his popularity as a novelist to do so. No other American writer stood up with him. It was his finest hour.[27]

The meeting on Desplaines Street, just off the Haymarket, on May 4, 1886, grew out of a strike at the McCormick Reaper works, and was called to protest police brutality. Because the weather was threatening, it had not been heavily attended. Mayor Carter H. Harrison, Sr., I was present, and when he went home he apprehended no danger. After his departure, only a little while before everything would have been over, a police captain, John Bonfield, went in literally looking for trouble, and a bomb was thrown which killed one man and mortally wounded seven others.

Confident that the anarchists were getting ready to blow up the city, and illogically convinced that hanging some of them might prevent this, panic-stricken Chicago now proceeded to illustrate the truth of George Bancroft's saying that "the fears of one class of men are not the measure of the rights of another." All the radicals the police could lay their hands on were rounded up, and eight were indicted for murder. At the time the bomb was exploded, as Howells afterwards pointed out,

one was at home playing cards with his family, another was addressing a meeting five miles away, another was present with his wife and little children, two others had made pacific speeches, and not one, except on the testimony of a single, notoriously untruthful witness, was proven to have anything to do with the throwing of the Haymarket bomb, or to have even remotely instigated the act. . . . Spies was convicted of murder partly because he conspired against Society with men some of whom he was not on speaking terms with. Among the crimes for which Parsons was convicted of murder was quoting in his paper General Sheridan's belief that a dynamite bomb might kill a regiment of soldiers; and the Supreme Court of Illinois, reviewing the testimony, located him at two points, a block apart, when the bomb was thrown, and found him doubly privy to the act upon this topographical conceit.

Seven of the eight were condemned to death. One, Louis Lingg, committed suicide in his cell. Two had their sentences commuted.

The other four were hanged on November 12, 1887, and buried under a spectacular monument at Waldheim Cemetery in Forest Park, which still promises the passer-by that "the day will come when our silence will be more powerful than the voices ye are throttling today."

Howells entered the case on November 6 with a plea to the readers of the New York *Tribune* that they urge the Governor of Illinois to commute the sentences of the condemned men on the ground that no murder guilt had been established. That he realized the dangers he faced in thus baiting a public and a press hungry for blood is shown not only by his hesitation (Judge Pryor, chief counsel for the anarchists, had urged him to act as early as September) but by his consulting his wife beforehand and securing her agreement with him that he could not honorably longer remain silent. He did not consult Harper and Brothers, who, to their honor, raised no objection at any point, though they printed no news of his action in any of their magazines. "Great as your work is," wrote Harriet Prescott Spofford, "you never wrote more immortal words than those in behalf of these men who are dying for free speech."

The language that Howells used in connection with the anarchists shows that he became as emotionally involved with them as he ever did with anybody. He wrote Francis Fisher Browne, editor of *The Dial* in Chicago (and his letter was printed, with sarcastic commentary, in the Chicago *Tribune*) that "for many weeks, for months," the case had "not been for one hour out of my waking thoughts; it is the last thing when I lie down, and the first thing when I rise up; it blackens my life." He cherished a note of August Spies which was given to him by the leader of the Chicago Ethical Society—"an intelligent, earnest, *good* face! And that man hanged! Incredible!"—asked for photographs of all the victims, and expressed indignation that Johann Most had been imprisoned for a speech defending them. He also urged the publication of a book to do justice to the memory of the martyrs, and offered himself to contribute a letter, which was all his contract with the Harpers permitted him to do. On November 13 he wrote his father:

All is over now, except the judgment that begins at once for every unjust and evil deed, and goes on forever. The historical perspective is that this free Republic has killed five men for their opinions.

One commentator has stated that the case led Howells "to a sympathetic consideration of philosophical anarchism," but aside from his having subscribed to Parsons's paper, *The Alarm*, there is no evidence of this. On the contrary, he considered the opinions of the anarchists "frantic," and though he felt that a free society in which each man would govern himself was the ultimate goal, he also believed that that goal was a long way off and that men would have to go through socialism first. Under present conditions, the anarchist was "the Individualist gone mad." What Howells did believe was what Voltaire believed—"I do not agree with a thing that you say, but I will defend to the death your right to say it"—and that the injustice which the country had committed would help, not hurt, the anarchist cause. "All over the world people must be asking themselves, what cause is this really, for which men die so gladly, so inexorably? So the evil will grow from violence to violence." The effect of the whole Haymarket case upon both Howells and his wife was a lasting one. As he wrote his sister Annie on November 18:

Elinor and I both no longer care for the world's life, and would like to be settled somewhere very humbly and simply, where we could be socially identified with the principles of progress and sympathy for the struggling mass. . . . The last two months have been full of heartache and horror for me, on account of the civic murder committed last Friday at Chicago. . . . Some day I hope to do justice to these irreparably wronged men.

But there were others, languishing in prison, whose wrong was not irreparable. In 1892 John Peter Altgeld was elected Governor of Illinois, and the next year he pardoned Neebe, Schwab, and Fielden, issuing a state paper which virtually indicted the community of judicial murder. Once more the wolf pack was unleashed. The Governor had vindicated Howells's judgment but only at the cost of political suicide. When he died in 1902 and his body lay in state in the Chicago Public Library, thousands of people lined up on Michigan Avenue in a cold spring wind blowing in off the lake, to pay their respects to the man whom the newspapers had described as the Nero of the twentieth century. But it was not until our own time that Vachel Lindsay's poem, "The Eagle That Is Forgotten" and the solid biographical studies which followed it restored Altgeld to the place he deserves to hold in the American mind.[28]

VIII

And what was it, then, that Howells's social consciousness finally added up to? Was it socialism? From the 'eighties on he was generally considered a socialist, and when Walter Hines Page wanted an authoritative article on the subject for *The Forum*, it was to him that he turned. At times he seems to have accepted the label gracefully; at other times he entered exceptions. He never joined the party, and as late as 1901 he declared that he did not wish to wear a label. When a Chicago paper called him a socialist, he asked them if they were sure. "Socialism, as I understand it, is not a position but a comparative thing; it is a question of more or less in which we have already, and not a question of absolute difference."

The motive of course was humanitarian. "After all, we are our brother's keepers, though a Cainic society has been denying it ever since the first murder." By 1896 he was convinced that though human misery might not be growing, it was "growing intolerable, if not to the sufferer, then to the witness," and that a man who denied humanitarian claims was "in danger of truly becoming a devil." We had no choice about taking care of the weak; all there was left to us to decide was whether we should do it as brothers or as jailers.

The derelicts in the Boston police courts contributed, the smell of poverty in New York, the lost creatures of the London slums. But not all the influences came from the left. Both Lowell and Henry James wrote very critically about dangerous tendencies in American life, and Howells once told an interviewer that so conservative a man as President Hayes first called his attention to the fact that in some areas socialism was already in operation, citing the post office as an example. Howells was certainly strongly impressed by the papers which J. B. Harrison contributed to the *Atlantic* under his editorship, and which were later collected as *Certain Dangerous Tendencies in American Life*. Since Harrison at this time viewed even the eight-hour day with alarm, he can hardly be called a radical, but the interviews included in his articles gave voice to much more advanced views than his own, and Howells was printing other articles by such writers as Robert Dale Owen, Richard T. Ely, and Henry Demarest Lloyd. The Panic of 1873 was a great shock to him, as it was to many Americans. Though he must have known who Karl Marx was as early as 1871, we have no evidence that he ever read *Das Kapital*, but the Americanized, Christianized Marxian, Laurence Gronlund, was important to him. He tells us that he first became interested in socialism when he heard Gronlund speak in Buffalo in 1888, and that he then read Gronlund's book, *The Co-operative Commonwealth*, the article by Kirkup in the *Encyclopaedia Britannica*, and some of William Morris's tracts.[29] In 1888 he wrote Henry James that "after fifty years of optimistic content with 'civilization' and its ability to come out all right in the end, I now abhor it, and feel that it is coming out all wrong in the end, unless it bases itself anew on a real equality," and in 1890 he described himself and his wife and Mark Twain and his wife as "theoretical socialists, and practical aristocrats."

As to how it was to come, the one thing he was sure of was that it could not come by violence. In 1912 T. S. Perry found him, though "the tenderest and most amiable of men," revelling "in anarchy, and social upheaval and all modern improvements," but this is a misinterpretation. It is true that in *Roman Holidays* he reports having witnessed a two-day strike:

I beheld in it a reduced and imperfect image of what labor could do if it universally chose to do nothing. The dream of William Morris was that a world which we know is pretty much wrong could be put right by this simple process.

But this was a very special sort of strike, without violence or the threat of violence; when these entered, Howells was swiftly antagonized. He admired John Hay's anonymously published novel, *The Bread-Winners*, considerably more than it deserved as a work of art, for while he apparently had no terror of the possible tyranny of a socialist state, he was quite sure "that the workingmen *as* workingmen are no better or wiser than the rich *as* the rich, and are quite as likely to be false and foolish." Like Putney in *Annie Kilburn*, Howells is forever crying to the workers: "Why, you fools, . . . what do you want to boycott for, when you can *vote?* What do you want to break the laws for, when you can *make* 'em?" He hated violence because it was wrong, because it disregarded the public welfare, and because it militated against the workers' cause. As Basil March says of the streetcar strike in the *Hazard*:

What amuses me is to find that in an affair of this kind the roads have rights and the strikers have rights, but the public has no rights at all. The roads and the strikers are allowed to fight out a private war in our midst—as thoroughly and precisely a private war as any we despise the Middle Ages for having tolerated . . . and to fight it out at our pains and expense, and we stand by like sheep and wait till they get tired.

But Howells himself was not amused at all.

Among the specific reforms which Howells advocated at one time or another, looking toward the remaking of the social and economic order, Robert Hough, whose *The Quiet Rebel* is the most elaborate study we have of this aspect of his thinking, stresses:

1. nationalization of natural monopolies (railroads, express lines, telegraph lines, gas and water works, telephone and electric power circuits)

2. preservation of the public domain[30] and the establishment of national parks

3. government aid and subsidies to farmers

4. public employment for relief purposes

5. public control of housing

6. a government-subsidized theater

7. old-age pensions

8. state-managed inns along state roads.

Though Putney in *The Quality of Mercy* is a Georgeite, and though Mrs. Camp says in *A Traveler from Altruria*, "Perhaps no one has a right to earn any portion of the earth," Howells had no enthusiasm for the single tax (this was his principal disagreement with Hamlin Garland). In 1888 he wrote his friend and disciple that

I can't as yet bring myself to look upon confiscation in any direction as a good thing. The new commonwealth must be founded in justice even to the unjust, in generosity to the unjust rather than anything less than justice.

Ten years later, he indicates that he does not believe the single tax would do the job required in an otherwise unsocialized world:

Wherever there is competition there will be the oppression of the weaker by the stronger, and wherever there is unequal wealth there will be the world, the flesh and the devil.

As a matter of fact, Howells expected the nationalization of land to come late in the socializing process.[31]

Howells's humanitarianism being what it was, it was natural that he should be specially concerned with our penal system. It made his heart sick to see people being sent to jail even when they were guilty, partly because the jail term seemed far more likely to make the offender worse than better, and partly because the state itself became a thief when it robbed him of his time, his liberty, and his labor without compensation or protection for his family. "We have no courts of justice now," he cries; "we have only courts of statute. As it is, far more injustice is done than if all offenders were frankly forgiven." Of course he was too realistic to believe that that could be achieved, and like many of us, he was far more sensitive to the inequities of the present system than prepared to outline in detail what should be substituted for it.[32]

In the 'sixties, when he was writing his "Minor Topics" for *The Nation*, Howells could find nothing too harsh to say of the sentimentalists who interfered with the execution of justice upon murderers. He hailed the execution of Dr. John Webster in Massachusetts as "the most impressive vindication [of justice] the country ever saw."

Is crime to be punished? that is the real question. Hanging is by some called judicial murder; but the murders which difficult convictions and pardoning executives encourage—what sort are they, theorist?

Quite in line with this kind of thinking is his praise of Rutherford B. Hayes in his campaign biography:

His promptness in quelling the riots of the striking coal-miners in Ohio, during the present year, is an earnest of what his action would be on a larger theatre in any greater emergency, and the following letter to the adjutant-general, who was sent with troops to crush out the riots, shows the temper of a ruler not disposed to dally with his duty, or to address a murderous mob as his "friends."

By 1883, however, when the American Irish in Congress wanted the United States to intervene with Britain for the Irish Sinn Feiner, Patrick O'Donnell, the terms of Howells's protest, as expressed in a letter of Edmund Gosse, show that he had already undergone a change of heart, and, as Hannah Belcher has remarked, capital punishment was one of the few things about which he ever quite changed his mind.

I think no man should be hung [italics mine]; but that man was a cruel and pitiless assassin, and rightly suffered under the law. If he had been a man of any other nationality Congress would not have dreamed of interfering; how then can I explain that this Irish forcing of our national action appeared merely grotesque to us? Congress is "Democratic"; by seeming to befriend O'Donnell it could capture the Irish votes for its party; and by making a Republican president its instrument it could foist any disagreeable consequences upon him.

Nor did "Execution by Electricity" seem more humane to Howells. In 1888, when its introduction was being seriously considered upon these grounds, Howells wrote a bitterly sarcastic letter to *Harper's Weekly*,[33] suggesting that perhaps the Governor himself "might touch a little annunciation-button, and dismiss a murderer to the presence of his Maker with the lightest pressure of the finger." Or he might invite a distinguished company to be present, and one of the ladies might do it or even a little child. Seven years later, he declares bluntly that "murder is murder, and I myself believe that the murder the State does in punishment of killing is the worst murder of all," and in 1903 he objects to capital punishment on the ground that it glamourizes the criminal and makes a hero of him.[34]

Did Howells really expect socialism to triumph, then? This seems to have depended upon his mood and the current state of social progress. In the unpublished Preface he wrote for the utopian romances in the "Library Edition" he spoke confidently of "his vision of idealities, which in some similitude must one day be the actualities of the world." Perhaps the fact that Swedenborgians believed that Christ's Second Advent had already occurred helped Howells to realize that, in some part and in some degree, the socialist state was already here. Hayes had cited the postal service, but he saw the same thing in the public parks, in the World's Columbian Exposition at Chicago, where co-operation for the time being replaced co-operation to produce a fleeting White City fairer than all the dreams of men before it, and in the authority given, even under a capitalistic society, to such bodies as the Board of Health. Some day, he hoped, an American might have a country "as palpably his own as Central Park is, where his ownership excluded the ownership of no other."

In 1909 he found New York "not so bad a monster" as it had threatened to become when he was writing the *Hazard*, and in 1912 he called Lloyd George "that greatest living Englishman, who is Welsh," because, by providing pensions for the old, the sick, and the jobless, he had "taken the sting from charity by making it justice." When the government took over railroads, telephone, and telegraph during World War I, Howells thought socialism was almost here, but he was swiftly disillusioned, and his last "Easy Chair" was the work of a very discouraged socialist. Even then, however, there was no trace of the bitterness with which Mark Twain hailed the "giddy gait" at which the Kingdom of God marched on "from age to age," and I can well imagine party members, whether Socialist or Communist, sighing over his dereliction when they find him writing in *Certain Delightful English Towns* that

I think every one ought to earn a living, and when past it ought to be pensioned by the state, and let live in comfort after his own fancy; but failing this ideal, I wish the rich with us would multiply foundations after the good old English fashion.

Foundations, certainly, have had a much larger share in American enterprise these latter years than Howells ever saw, and every administration beginning with Hoover's has taken measures which commit us more firmly to Howells's ideal of the welfare state. If the peaceful revolution is still far from complete, it has certainly gone farther than any but the most misty-eyed dreamer ever believed it could go in his time.

I have denied Howells sainthood, and I have, in a sense, turned the denial to his advantage by trying to show that sainthood is, in a sense, excess, and that there was no excess in him. In closing, I must permit myself one personal word. I have written at length of no person with whom I was unable to sympathize, but I must confess that even among those I admire most, there is more than one whose society I would rather enjoy at a comfortable distance. There is none of whom I feel more strongly than I do of Howells that not to have known him was a great loss or with whom I feel more certain that I might have been at home. One might feel ashamed before him, to be sure, but one would know too, as John Buchan said of Scott, that "he gathers all things, however lowly and crooked and broken, within the love of God," and it may be that this is itself a species of sainthood. William Dean Howells may not have understood everything that needs to be done to bring in the millennium, but it is the plain, cold truth to say that if all men were like him, it would have been here long ago.

NOTES

Reviewers of my books have sometimes remarked that my documentation is "inconsistent." The word is ill-chosen. In the sense in which that term is properly employed, my books are not documented at all. I could not document them without attaching a reference to virtually every sentence, and many sentences would require three or four references. I use my footnotes primarily to treat marginal and supplementary matters and to refer the reader to fuller discussions of many of the matters under consideration than I have space for; sometimes, when the information given is highly specialized, or when it derives from a source which the student of the subject being treated in my book could not normally be expected to consult, I indicate its origin.

In the volume in hand, a great deal of information is drawn from Howells's unpublished letters and from his multitudinous unreprinted magazine and newspaper articles, and at one time I hoped that it might be possible to document all such statements, but as time went on, I accumulated so much material that I soon saw that this was altogether impracticable. The first draft of my manuscript, including references, will be deposited in the Mugar Library at Boston University, where it may be consulted by interested persons.

The following abbreviations are employed both in the Notes and in the Bibliography which follows it.

ABC	American Book Company	AL	*American Literature*
	pany	AQ	*American Quarterly*
ACC	Appleton-Century-	Atl	*The Atlantic Monthly*
	Crofts (and their prede-	Bkm	*The Bookman*
	cessors)	Ce	*Century Magazine*

CE	College English	NEQ	New England Quarterly
ColUP	Columbia University Press	NYUP	New York University Press
D	Doubleday and Company (and their predecessors)	OAHQ	Ohio Archaeological and Historical Quarterly
Du	E. P. Dutton and Company	OUP	Oxford University Press
DUP	Duke University Press		
"EC"	"Editor's Easy Chair"	PBSA	Papers of the Bibliographical Society of America
ELH	English Literary History		
"ES"	"Editor's Study"	PMLA	Publications of the Modern Language Association
GR	Georgia Review		
H	Howells		
Ha	Harper and Brothers	RUP	Rutgers University Press
HB	Harper's Bazar		
HLB	Harvard Library Bulletin	S	Charles Scribner's Sons
HM	Houghton Mifflin Company (and their predecessors)	SAQ	South Atlantic Quarterly
		SFR	Scholars Facsimiles and Reprints
HM	Harper's Magazine		
HUP	Harvard University Press	TSLL	Texas Studies in Language and Literature
HW	Harper's Weekly	TWASAL	Transactions of the Wisconsin Academy of Sciences, Arts and Letters
IUP	Indiana University Press		
JRUL	Journal Rutgers University Library		
"LL"	"Life and Letters"	UKCR	University of Kansas City Review
LinL	Mildred Howells, ed., Life in Letters of William Dean Howells		
		UMP	University of Minnesota Press
M	The Macmillan Company	UNCP	University of North Carolina Press
MQ	Midwest Quarterly		
NAR	North American Review	UTSE	University of Texas Studies in English
NCF	Nineteenth Century Fiction	WDH	William Dean Howells
		YUP	Yale University Press

HOWELL'S LIFE AND READING

1 He even spent one year (1850) in a log cabin, near Xenia, in Greene County, where his father was interested in developing a communal settlement. See the factual record in *My Year in a Log Cabin* (1893) and compare *New Leaf Mills* (1913) for the use the novelist made of the experience.

2 July is the date generally given, but in a letter to Edward Eggleston (March 11, 1872), H says October; see *NEQ*, XXXIII (1960), 240–42. However, there is a letter to his father (January 29, 1871) in the Houghton Library, in which H says that on July 1 he will become editor of the *Atlantic* at a salary of $5,000. He also reports that *The Independent* is flirting with him.

3 H also had a career as a dramatist, largely a writer of one-act farces, but this is sufficiently covered elsewhere.

4 E. H. Cady, "WDH and the Ashtabula *Sentinel*," *OAHQ*, LIII (1944), 39–51.

5 Rudolf and Clara Kirk, "H's Guidebook to Venice," *AL*, XXXIII (1961), 221–24. See H's reviews of Ellen Frothingham's translation of *Hermann und Dorothea*, *Atl*, XXV (1870), 761–62, and of Bayard Taylor's *Faust*, XXVII (1871), 158–60, and XXVIII (1871), 124–25.

6 H's vigorous attack on Albert Mordell, when he published *Dante and Other Waning Classics*, *HM*, CXXXII (1916), 958–61, is notable both as a testimonial to his interest in Dante and because it affords evidence of his ability to differentiate between literary art and ideational content. There is an amusing reference to Francesca da Rimini in a comment on a contemporary divorce case in "Letter from New York," Cincinnati *Gazette*, December 2, 1865: "O friends! who take up the paper so lightly," etc.

7 See also "Recent Italian Comedy," *NAR*, XCIX (1864), 264–401, and the discussion of Paolo Bellezza's *Humour*, *NAR*, CLXXXIII (1901), 709–20, where H shows an impressive range in his comments on the humorists of many nations.

8 William W. Betts, Jr., "The Relations of WDH to German Life and Letters," in Philip A. Shelley, Arthur O. Lewis, Jr., and W. W. Betts, Jr., eds., *Anglo-German and American-German Crosscurrents*, I (UNCP, 1957).

9   See Cady's comment on p. 215 of the edition of *The Shadow of a Dream* and *An Imperative Duty* published by Twayne, 1962.

10   Jumping the line into Denmark, H thought Hans Christian Andersen's poetry worthless and felt that his autobiography revealed him as "a sentimental snob" but was not sure that it was fair to apply Anglo-Saxon standards to a Continental figure. One Norwegian, Björnson, he placed near the top.

11   See Edwin S. Morby, "WDH and Spain," *Hispanic Review*, XIV (1946), 187–212; Stanley T. Williams, *The Spanish Background of American Literature* (YUP, 1955), Part III, Ch. 8; and, for Blasco-Ibáñez, also "EC," *HM*, CXXXI (1915), 957–60.

12   Bacon, of course, appears in this book along with Shakespeare. In "Experience of a True Baconian in Shakespeare's Town," *NAR*, CXCV (1912), 120–27, the Baconian hypothesis is reduced to absurdity through the pretence of being "a firm, even violent, supporter" of it; see also "The Psychology of Plagiarism," in *Literature and Life*. For the rest of the Elizabethan dramatists, especially Ben Jonson, H cared little or nothing; see *My Literary Passions*, Ch. XXXIII; "Reading for a Grandfather," *HB*, XXXVII (1903), 1153–57; "EC," *HM*, CXI (1905), 633–35, which last is on Shakespeare and G.B.S.

13   "EC," *HM*, CV (1902), 479–83; see also "LL," *HW*, XL (1896), 319.

14   Among the H manuscripts at Houghton is "Old Clothes," a very Thackeryean essay (b MS Am 1784.2–47).

15   Or so Walter Brooks reports, *Author*, I (1889), 105.

16   *L in L*, II, 291–92.

17   For a much fuller consideration of "Longfellow and Howells" than can be given here, see the article of that title by the present writer, in an issue of the *Emerson Society Quarterly* which, at the date this note is proofread (April 11, 1969) is still forthcoming.

18   *HW*, LIII, January 16, 1909, p. 12.

19   "Impressions of Emerson," *HW*, XLVII (1903), 784. Howells's review of *May-Day and Other Pieces*, *Atl*, XX (1867), 376–78, has a very fair evaluation of Emerson's virtues and shortcomings as a poet. For a considered allover view, see also his review of James Cabot's *Memoir*, "ES," *HM*, LXXVI (1888), 476–78.

20   See Jean Rivière, "Howells and Whitman after 1881," *Walt Whitman Review*, XII (1966), 97–100. Howells knew that Whitman's form had been influenced by the Old Testament: "But if any worship-

ping critic had turned to his Bible . . . he would have found the Psalmist of the King James version writing a good deal like Walt Whitman at his best. Of course the subjects were different. The American poet celebrated man and adored himself; the Hebrew poet celebrated God and deplored himself." Since the King James Bible prints all the poetic books of the Old Testament as prose, this was penetrating, despite its ungracious qualifications. In his introduction to Stuart Merrill's *Pastels in Prose*, Howells speaks of Job, Ecclesiastes, etc., on the other hand, as "prose poems."

21   See Aubrey H. Starke, "WDH and Sidney Lanier," *AL*, III (1931–32), 79–82. It is not true, however, that Howells *never* mentions Lanier; see Arms-Gibson bibliography, *98–15*, p. 127.

22   See George Perkins, "H and Hawthorne," *NCF*, XV (1960–61), 259–62. James W. Mathews, "The Heroines of Hawthorne and H," *Tennessee Studies in Literature*, VII (1962), 37–46, finds many common characteristics which I cannot grant. Elaine Hedges, "H on a Hawthornesque Theme," *TSLL*, III (1961), 129–43, is excellent on *The Shadow of a Dream*.

23   See the letters to James T. Fields (Aug. 24, 1869 and Sept. 22, 1869) in *LinL* for H's difficulties with Mrs. Stowe over her Byron article, which he never saw until it was in type but which appeared in the *Atlantic* while he was in charge. Though he has obviously been annoyed by her eccentricities, he does not regret having printed the article, and he gives no sign of fear that it may wreck the magazine.

24   See Robert W. Ayres, "WDH and Stephen Crane: Some Unpublished Letters," *AL*, XXVIII (1956–57), 469–77.

25   Much has been made of H's failure to encourage Theodore Dreiser, who is himself responsible for the story that H once brushed past him with "You know, I don't like *Sister Carrie*." It is true that H refused to sign a petition designed to counteract efforts to suppress *The "Genius"* on the ground that he had not read it, but he was probably the first person to anthologize anything of Dreiser's when he reprinted "The Lost Phoebe" and praised it highly in his *Great Modern American Stories*. In 1914, Mark S. R. Reardon 3rd tried to draw H on Dreiser, but he would not rise to the bait; see *Mark Twain Quarterly*, Vol. VIII, No. 2, Summer-Fall, 1948, pp. 5, 11. When Dreiser interviewed H in 1900 he called him "the great literary philanthropist" and "the look-out on the watchtower . . . straining for

the first glimpse of approaching genius," but the only kind word he gave him in later years was when he told Dorothy Dudley that *Their Wedding Journey* was his one good book, "really beautiful and true." See Fryckstedt, *In Quest of America*, p. 268, for a convincing argument that Dreiser misspoke himself, meaning to exempt *A Modern Instance*.

26 See Jack Brenner, "H and Ade," *AL*, XXXVIII (1966–67), 198–207.

27 For comment by H on a number of other later American fictionists, see "EC," *HM*, CXXX (1915), 796–99, 958–61.

28 One suspects Mark Twain's influence in H's account of how pilots learned the Mississippi in "Captain Dunlevy's Last Trip" (*The Daughter of the Storage*), and there is a suggestion of Mrs. Clemens in "Though One Rose from the Dead" (*Questionable Shapes*). H, of course, preserved his memories of his friend and reprinted his reviews of his books in *My Mark Twain*, which was prepared for the press soon after the humorist's death. See also "The Surprise Party to Mark Twain," *HW*, XLIV (1900), 1205, and the review of Paine's biography, "EC," *HM*, CXXVI (1913), 310–12. In "EC," *HM*, CXXIII (1911), 310–13, H speculates as to whether Holman Day is to inherit Mark Twain's mantle.

29 For H on James, see, especially, "Henry James, Jr.," *Ce*, XXV (1882), 25–29, and "Mr. Henry James's Later Work," *NAR*, CLXXVI (1903), 125–37. James's writings on H are adequately described and reprinted in part in F. O. Matthiessen, ed., *The James Family* (Knopf, 1947). Oscar Cargill gives a detailed account of the personal relations between the two in "Henry James' 'Moral Policeman': WDH," *AL*, XXIX (1957–58), 371–98, but some of his tentative conclusions about influences are questionable. See Kermit Vanderbilt, *The Achievement of W. D. H.*, p. 47n, p. 73n for interesting examples of the possible influence of James on H.

CHAPTER ONE: MR. TWELVEMOUGH

1 In the Introduction to *Their Wedding Journey* in the "Selected Edition," John K. Reeves has made a careful study of H's use in this work both of his own experience and of previous records he had made of it. See also Clara M. Kirk, "Reality and Actuality in the March Family Narratives of WDH," *PMLA*, LXXIV (1959), 137–52.

2   James Woodress has exhaustively documented H's use of his Italian experiences in *H and Italy*. "In his earliest fiction he used Venetians for the leading characters, but as his foreign sojourns receded into the past, he switched to American protagonists and showed them against the background of American life." The proportion of works to which the Italian materials contributed is very high. John K. Reeves covers a smaller, domestic area in "The Way of a Realist: A Study of H's Use of the Saratoga Scene," *PMLA*, LXV (1950), 1035–52, and there are two studies of his journalistic backgrounds: Earl B. Braly, "WDH, Author and Journalist," *Journalism Quarterly*, XXXII (1955), 456–62, and B. A. Sokoloff, "Printing and Journalism in the Novels of WDH," *TWASAL*, XLVI (1957), 165–78.

3   See W. M. Gibson, *AL*, XIX (1947), 160.

4   The apparently wild yarn about the man who thought he had registered at the Kaiserin Elisabeth, but had actually been taken to another hotel which he had great trouble in finding again, was an experience of H's own; see "Overland to Venice," *HM*, CXXXVII (1918), 837–45.

5   See Virginia Harlow, *Thomas Sergeant Perry, A Biography* (DUP, 1950).

6   See *Three Villages*, pp. 94–95.

7   See Richard H. Taneyhill and R. King Bennett, *The Leatherwood God, 1869–70: A Source of WDH's Novel of the Same Name, in Two Versions*, Introduction by George Kummer (SRF, 1966); Haskell S. Springer, "*The Leatherwood God* from Narrative to Novel," *Ohio History*, LXXIV (1965), 190–202, 212. Springer finds that H "establishes a defining point of view, creates Dylks the human being, delves into the psychology of religion, makes all the elements of the story completely realistic, and affirms the vital role of sex in human affairs." He also thinks that H drew on the Mormon experience in Ohio, intending to suggest resemblances between Dylks and Joseph Smith. For a fuller study, see Eugene H. Pattison's University of Michigan dissertation, " 'The Leatherwood God': Genesis, Artistry and Reception."

8   "*Cesar Birotteau* and *The Rise of Silas Lapham*: A Study in Parallels," *NCF*, XVII (1962–63), 163–74.

9   William J. Free, "H's 'Editha' and Pragmatic Belief," *Studies in Short Fiction*, III (1966), 285–92.

10   Walter L. Fertig, "Maurice Thompson and *A Modern Instance*," *AL*, XXXVIII (1966–67), 103–11.

11   George Arms, "A Novel and Two Letters," *JRUL*, VIII (1944), 9–13.

12   F. C. Marston, Jr., "An Early H Letter," *AL*, XVIII (1946–47), 163–65.

13   Walter Fuller Taylor, *The Economic Novel in America* (UNCP, 1942) is very good on this element in Howells; see especially pp. 221–22, 247, 249, 273–74.

14   In a letter to Henry James (March 10, 1873), H did, however, admit that Kitty Ellison went more or less her own way, especially in the second serial installment, and in "The Unsatisfactoriness of Unfriendly Criticism" (*Imaginary Interviews*), where Eugenio must surely stand for at least part of his auctorial self, he writes that even if an author "knows that he has done it well, if the testimony of all his faculties is to that effect, there is somehow the lurking sense that it was not he who really did it, but that there is a power, to turn Matthew Arnold's phrase to our use, 'not ourselves, that works for' beauty as well as righteousness, and that it was this mystical force which wrought through him to the exquisite result."

15   Part of H's dissatisfaction at the time he wrote this to his sister Aurelia in 1898 was his feeling that "I am an elderly man, and I ought to deal more with things of spiritual significance." And though his next long novel, *The Kentons*, was a return to his earlier, happier, lighter manner, he wrote a number of short pieces during the next few years that dealt with psychological, psychic, or spiritual matters. See Ferris Cronkhite, "H Turns to the Inner Life," *NEQ*, XXX (1957), 474–85.

16   Bennett, *WDH: The Development of a Novelist*, pp. 43–45, shows conclusively, I think, that the basic reason for H's failure to bring out *Private Theatricals* (later known as *Mrs. Farrell*) in book form was not fear of a libel suit, as we had previously been told, but his own dissatisfaction with it. He wrote Aldrich (March 3, 1876) that he knew there were bad breaks in it and that he must change it greatly before reprinting, but as late as August 13, he wrote Lowell that he was planning to revise the work for book publication, and promised that Miss Norton should have one of the first copies.

17   I do not agree with Herbert Edwards, "The Dramatization of *The Rise of Silas Lapham*," *NEQ*, XXX (1957), 235–43, that H refused to go in for practical playwriting in partnership with Herne because "he felt the scenes backstage would be too rough and crude for him to face." Neither do I feel that "actors are portrayed very

unfavorably" in *The Story of a Play*. The reason H declined Herne's overtures was surely that he knew his forte and his range and did not propose, as a successful novelist, to undergo a highly speculative apprenticeship to a playwright and producer.

18 He was wonderfully temperate and generous too in his comments on Alexander Harvey's silly book about him in 1917. He did not like Harriet Prescott Spofford's article about him when Bliss Perry, as *Atlantic* editor, submitted it to him, but he objected vigorously when Perry proposed not printing it on that account.

19 *Silas Lapham* must be the novel referred to in the discussion of business and business ethics in *A Traveler from Altruria* (Ha edition, p. 203), and the unnamed novel in *Their Silver Wedding Journey* (Ch. XXXV) must be *April Hopes*. When, many years after *Silas* had been published, Henry Rood asked H if Irene had ever married, he talked about her exactly as if she were a real person: "It seems to me that she married one of the West Virginia brothers who had a paint mine—but I'm not sure."—*Ladies' Home Journal*, XXXVII, September 1920, p. 154.

20 See Robert W. Walts, "WDH and His 'Library Edition,'" *PBSA*, LII (1958), 283–94. Much of what Mr. Walts says about the reasons for the failure of this edition are sound, but he ignores the fact that, at the time and for many years after, both Scribners and Houghton Mifflin successfully marketed by subscription collected editions of many British and American writers. Many of these were quite as expensive as the Howells would have been, and some (the Henry James, for instance) involved arranging for including copyrighted material published by more than one house.

21 On H's views concerning money in general, see three articles in *HW*, XLVII (1903): "To the Jews a Stumbling-Block and to the Greeks Foolishness" (p. 189); "The Unreality of Reality" (p. 229); and "Tainted Money" (p. 468). He dissented from John D. Rockefeller, Jr.'s interpretation of the story of the Rich Young Man in the Gospels before his Sunday School class, maintaining that it is no harder to take Christ literally now than it was in his own time. The point is simply that his standards have been found too high for human nature and the church has permitted a compromise. He doubted that there can be a good millionaire but granted that though "property can no more be defended without question of its sanctions," neither can it be "attacked without great misgivings."

22   See David J. Burrows, "Manuscript and Typescript: Material Relating to H's *The Son of Royal Langbrith*," *JRUL*, XXIX (1966), 56–58.

23   Rudolf and Clara M. Kirk, "*Niagara Revisited*, by WDH: The Story of its Publication and Suppression," in Rudolf Kirk and C. F. Main, eds., *Essays in Literary History Presented* to J. Milton French (RUP, 1960).

24   After this contract had been signed, H figured out for his daughter that he would have, all in all, an annual income of $16,500. "My net income would be about $14,000 . . . and if I chose I could run it up to $20,000 by writing outside." It is surprising that he should have figured royalties on his old books as worth only $1,500 a year. The executor's report gives the net estate at death as $167,552.63, but this does not seem to have included all real estate. (I am indebted to Professor Arms for this information.)

25   One of the most famous scenes in *Silas Lapham*—that in which Lapham gets drunk at the Corey dinner—accomplishes nothing and is almost unrelated to what precedes and follows. After Silas is sober again, nobody except himself ever pays any attention to what happened, and even he soon forgets it. Neither his own fate nor that of any member of his family is affected by it.

26   "I began to compose by imitating other authors. I admired, and I worked hard to get, a smooth, rich, classic style. The passion I afterwards formed for Heine's prose forced me from this slavery, and taught me to aim at naturalness. I seek now to get back to the utmost simplicity of expression, to disuse the verbosity I tried so hard to acquire, to get the gift of compact, clear truth, if possible, informal and direct. It is very difficult. I should advise any beginner to study the raciest, strongest, best spoken speech, and let the *printed* speech alone; that is to say, write straight from the thought without bothering about the manner, except to conform to the spirit or genius of the language. I once thought Latinised diction was to be invited; I now think Latinised expression to be guarded against." WDH, in George Bainton, ed., *The Art of Authorship* (ACC, 1890).

27   See Edd Wingfield Parks, "H and the Gentle Reader," *SAQ*, L (1951), 239–47.

28   The unpublished "Geoffrey Winter" is a tissue of Thackerayean commentary: "I am perfectly conscious of the commonplaceness of the character which I sketch with touches so rude and coarse."

"No—the movement of the story is not spirited. I confess that I have not brought my reader acquainted with people entertaining or instructive." And much, much besides. (A small part of "Geoffrey Winter" is published as "A Dream," *Knickerbocker*, LVIII [1861], 146–50.)

29 There are two special characteristics of H's narrative art which I do not propose to discuss, the first because I have nothing to add to what has already been said again and again, the second because its serious study is just getting under way. The Marches are the most important characters which he carries over from one story to another, but many others are similarly handled, including Ferris, Putney, Sewall, Clara Kingsbury, and Bromfield Corey. See Everett Carter's general comment in *H and the Age of Realism*, pp. 128–32, and Clara M. Kirk's much more detailed and specialized study: "Reality and Actuality in the March Family Narratives of WDH," *PMLA*, LXXIV (1959), 137–52. This habit makes for a homely informality, as the old stock company did by giving its patrons a chance to see the same actors, week after week, in different roles. On H's symbolism there are good comments in Carter, pp. 132–36, and in William M. Gibson, *William D. Howells*, but there is more in William McMurray's *The Literary Realism of WDH* and in Kermit Vanderbilt's *The Achievement of WDH*.

Though Mark Twain praised Howells as an inerrant stylist, this was never true in an academic sense. For his theory in the matter see *Criticism and Fiction*, XXII, and his two amusing papers on neologism: "LL," *HW*, XXXIX (1895), 1037, and "EC," *HM*, CXXXIV (1917), 594–97. O. W. Firkins, *WDH*, pp. 304 ff., considers his coinages, slang, and provincialisms. Except for his use of "Jap," the slang is less likely to cause trouble nowadays than such monstrosities as "occiputs," "memoriferous," "rectiliniosity," "contemperamental," and "pluriscience." In *The Vacation of the Kelwyns* he writes that "only one thing happened in the interval now following to divert the girl's thoughts from their centripetal tendency."

He misspells "Emily Dickenson," "Finley Peter Dunn," "Alice Browne," "Sheherazade," "Lydia Bennett," heroine of *Pride and Prejudice*, "Spencer," for the author of *The Faerie Queene* and "Spencerian," "James A. Hearn," the author of "*Margaret Flemming*," and "Clements" consistently for Clemens in the famous *Atl* review of *The Innocents Abroad*. Other errors in titles are *The Bigelow Papers*,

The Connecticut Yankee, The Tales of a Wayside Inn, The Strange Case of Dr. Jekyll and Mr. Hyde, The History of Lincoln, by Nicolay and Hay, and *London Illustrated News.*

In *My Mark Twain* he misdates his first meeting with Mark Twain. In the Prefaces to the "Library Edition" he does not always date his own work correctly. He speaks of "The Houghton Mifflin Company" and calls Elizabeth Stuart Phelps, whose husband's name was Ward, "Mrs. Stuart Phelps." There is one egregious blunder of fact when, commenting on a sketch by Edward Everett Hale, H says that Poe might possibly have written it, "but we cannot imagine Poe having been born in Boston." He would not have needed to imagine it but only to remember it. In Chapter I of *The Leatherwood God* we are told within a single paragraph that Dylks was bare-headed and that he was wearing "a tall beaver hat."

He employs the broken construction "The reason was because" (*The Flight of Pony Baker*) and writes "At the lunch which we had so good in the dining car . . ." (*Familiar Spanish Travels*). He writes "Rev. Kimball," "Rev. Bruce," and "The Reverend Clarke," and in *The Seen and Unseen at Stratford-on-Avon* he makes Shakespeare guilty of a similar barbarism. He writes:

. . . the fresh morning air, and the content of their own hearts, gifted our friends, by the time the boat reached Albany, with a wholesome hunger. . . . (*Their Wedding Journey*)

"My name isn't Merriam," he resented, at last, a misnomer which had annoyed him from the first. (*Fennel and Rue*)

He suffered at times from indigestion; but he was indefatigably industrious, and had thought the blond hair thin on his head in places; he wore a reddish mustache. (*The Vacation of the Kelwyns*)

. . . being a lady, and very well off, they [Annie Kilburn's opinions] were received with deference.

By that time the English summer has suffered often if not severe discouragements. (*Seven English Cities*)

Once, at a great junction, my porter seemed to have missed my train, and after vain but not unconsidered appeals to the guard, I had to start without it [his luggage]. (*Seven English Cities*)

CHAPTER TWO: MR. DEAN

1   ". . . romanticism was the expression of a world-mood; it was
not merely literary and voluntary; it grew naturally out of the political, social, and even economic conditions at the close of the eighteenth century. . . . In its day it was noble and beautiful, it lifted and
widened the minds of people; it afforded them a refuge in an ideal
world from the failure and defeat of this. . . . Romanticism belonged
to a disappointed and bewildered age, which turned its face from the
future, and dreamed out a faery realm in the past; and we cannot have
its spirit back because this is the age of hopeful striving, when we have
really a glimpse of what the earth might be when Christianity becomes
a life in the equality and fraternity of the race, and when the recognition of all the facts in the honest daylight about us is the service which
humanity demands of the humanities in order that what is crooked
may be made straight, and that what is wrong may be set right. The
humanities are working through realism to this end, not consciously,
for that is not the way of art, but instinctively; and they will not work
to that other end, because so far as it was anywise beautiful or useful,
it was once for all accomplished by the romanticists of the romanticistic period." "ES," *HM*, LXXIX (1889), 641. H is less temperate,
however, when he goes on to speak of the Romantic Period as belonging "to the childhood and the second-childhood of the world, when
people believed in the grotesque creatures of their own imagination,
and then when they made-believe in them."

2   Leonard Lutwack, "WDH and the 'Editor's Study,'" *AL*,
XXIV (1952), 195–207.

3   In 1904 H told A. S. van Westrum that "what I say today I
may deny tomorrow. Our opinions are changed for us inevitably by
the ever-varying procession of life. I have always claimed the right to
revise mine, and always exercised it. Moreover what one says on the
spur of the moment, in conversation—and an interview is nothing
more—should certainly not be tortured into a lifelong conviction."
And in 1912, looking back on his "Study" years, he wrote that he was
not sure now that he had been right about romance, though he had
been sure then.

4   See the letter "Anachronism," *Ce*, XXIX (1885), 477, where
he replies to a reproach for having spoken of "Daisy Millerism" in
The Rise of Silas Lapham, though the date of the story was a year

before *Daisy Miller* was published: "it is the effect of contemporaneousness that is to be given, and the general truth is sometimes better than the specific fact."

5   "I never insist on material reality, and it would be a matter of indifference to me if Cooper had placed the Giardini Publici on top of the Campanile if he had only dealt more airily and less tediously with human feeling."

6   Like Irving Babbitt, H saw considerable kinship between romanticism and naturalism.

7   In "LL," *HW*, XLI (1897), 1297-98, which describes H's annual encounter with the Christmas Muse, she brings Santa Claus to him on the ground that, being wholly fantastic, H could not possibly object to him on principle!

8   Parthenope Brook, in *The Vacation of the Kelwyns*, "had never observed among her acquaintance that girls were really nicer than young men, but she believed that they ought to be won by heroes who sacrificed or ventured a great deal for them, rescued them from some sort of peril, or risked their lives for them even when they were not in danger; if not, they must fall a prey themselves to some terrible accident, or be seized with some sickness in which the heroines could nurse them up from the brink of death to the loftier levels of life in happy marriage." Clem's reading experience in *Ragged Lady* is on a somewhat loftier level. When the rector lends her novels by Austen, Edgeworth, and Burney, she reads her own Yankee experiences into them, "and it seemed the consensus of their testimony that she had really been made love to, and not so very much too soon, at her age of sixteen, for most of their heroines were not much older. The terms of Gregory's declaration and of its withdrawal were mystifying, but not more mystifying than many such things, and from what happened in the novels she read, the affair might be trusted to come out all right of itself in time." The fullest discussion of the kind of fiction H disliked within any of his novels is the consideration of "Tears, Idle Tears" (which ought to have been called "Slop, Silly Slop") in *Silas Lapham*, Ch. XIV. See "EC," *HM*, CVI (1903), 972-73, for an amusing inventory of the museum of materials H would like to establish for the use of romantic writers.

9   I find it very puzzling that H should have thought the short story unqualified to deal with "the unreal." Bret Harte is the only author of "romanticistic" short stories whom he mentions. What about

ghost stories, his own among them? Ghosts may *be* real, of course, but surely not all the writers of ghost stories have "believed" in them. Incidentally, the book Boyne Kenton is reading in *The Kentons*, Ch. XIV, would seem to be certainly George Barr McCutcheon's *Graustark*. And in connection with this whole realistic-romantic-romanticistic debate, I think one cannot help asking how it could possibly be more harmful than much of the material H tolerates or than his own farces, for example. Surely nobody would be more likely to take it seriously.

10 "A Normal Hero and Heroine Out of Work" (*Imaginary Interviews*) is an amusing dialogue, protesting against the use of abnormal characters in fiction. The girl says: "What I should like to ask the short-story writers is whether they and their readers are so bored with themselves and the people they know in the real world that they have no use for anything like its average in their fiction."

11 H's comment on Florentine history in *Tuscan Cities* illustrates his resistance to melodrama. "For my part, I find it hard to be serious about the tragedy of a people who seem, as one looks back at them in their history, to have lived in such perpetual broil as the Florentines. They cease to be even pathetic; they become absurd, and tempt the observer to a certain mood of triviality, by their indefatigable antics in cutting and thrusting, chopping off heads, mutilating, burning, and banishing." There are very few human beings of whom he speaks so severely as Lorenzo de Medici.

12 "ES," *HM*, LXXIII (1888), 641–42, reprinted in Kirk and Kirk, *WDH, Representative Selections*, pp. 356–57, and in a revised form in *Criticism and Fiction*, Section XXI.

13 "A Note on H and 'The Smiling Aspects of Life,'" *AL*, XVII (1945–46), 175–78.

14 "WDH's Theory of Critical Realism," *ELH*, XVI (1949), 151–66. See also Carter's *H and the Age of Realism*, pp. 185 ff., where he describes the changes the passage underwent in subsequent revisions.

15 "The Smiling Aspects of Life and a National American Literature," in Alan S. Downer, ed., *English Institute Essays* (ColUP, 1950).

16 "The 'Brighter Side' of Fiction—According to H and Henry James," *CE*, XXIV (1963), 463–64.

17 *The Opposing Self* (Viking Press, 1955), pp. 100–103.

18 "Truth, Morality, and Swedenborg in H's Theory of Realism," *NEQ*, XXVII (1954), 252–57.

19 See John E. Hart, "The Commonplace as Heroic in *The Rise of Silas Lapham*," *Modern Fiction Studies*, VIII (1962–63), 375–83.

20 *The Round Table*, N. S. No. 13 (1865), pp. 200–201.

21 See *PMLA*, LXXIV (1959), 485.

22 Howells's dislike of Forster's *Life* of Dickens and the first collection of his *Letters* must have exercised considerable influence on his attitude toward the novelist. When the first volume of the biography appeared (*Atl*, XXVIII, 139–41), he was moved by Dickens's account of the blacking warehouse experience, then a new revelation, but suspected that some of the emotion described originated after the event; he also doubted that Dickens felt Mary Hogarth's death quite so deeply as he afterwards believed, and apparently questioned Forster's good taste in giving this story to the world. By the time he reviewed Volume II (XXXI, 237–39), H had made up his mind that the volumes were "bragging in tone, feeble and wandering in analysis, and comical in criticism," and that "the unamiable traits of the biographer combine with the unamiable traits of the subject to give the book as disagreeable a tone as a book ever had." Volume III (XXXIII, 621–22) held "comparatively little interest" for him, and he made one of the worst conditional prophecies on record when he wondered "whether it will be thought hereafter worth while for anyone to write another Life of Dickens." When the *Letters* appeared (XLV, 280–82), he was still unpleasantly impressed by Dickens's egoism. "He was a man who did not arrive at a Copernican conception of the universe." His horizon shut down "ten feet away from an observer who saw superficial generalities with preternatural keenness within that limit; though even within that limit, he did not see detail correctly, or was unable to report it correctly." Though Dickens became increasingly more true to life as he grew older, he was not "deep nor wise" nor very alert to the life of his time.

23 Cobley, "WDH, 1837–1920," *Manchester Quarterly*, LI (1925), 93–120.

24 "My Favorite Novelist and His Best Book," *Munsey's Magazine*, XVII, April 1897, pp. 18–25.

25 Vol. CLXXI, 935–48.

26 Clara and Rudolf Kirk, "Two H Letters," *JRUL*, XXI (1957), 1–7.

27 "The Evolutionary Foundation of WDH's *Criticism and Fiction*," *Philological Quarterly*, XL (1961), 91–103; "Evolutionary Literary Criticism and the Defense of Howellsian Realism," *Journal of English and Germanic Philology*, LXI (1962), 296–304.

28 "Mr. H and Romanticism," in *The Authority of Criticism* (S, 1899).

CHAPTER THREE: MR. PAPA

1 Aubrey Starke, "WDH Refuses an Interview," *AL*, X (1938–39), 492–94.

2 Franklin Walker, *Frank Norris, A Biography* (D, 1932), pp. 169–71.

3 Kjell Ekstrom, "The Cable-Howells Correspondence," *Studia Neophilologica*, XXII (1949), 48–61.

4 The quotations are from "From Generation to Generation," "Calvary," and "Conscience."

5 "Equality as the Basis of Good Society," *Ce*, LI (1895), 63–67. See also "The Superiority of Our Inferiors" and "The Whirl of Life in Our First Circles," in *Imaginary Interviews*; also A. Schade van Westrum, "Mr. H and American Aristocracies," *Bkm*, XXV (1907), 67–73.

6 M. A. DeWolfe Howe, *A Partial (and Not Impartial) Semi-Centennial History of the Tavern Club, 1884–1934* (The Tavern Club, 1934).

7 Many letters in Volume II of the *Mark Twain-Howells Letters* deal with the trouble the two friends took to try to collect some money owing to Charles W. Stoddard from one Fred Harriott. It is interesting that Howells should have lost his patience in this matter before his more mercurial friend lost his. A striking example of Howells's generosity occurred when Elizabeth Stuart Phelps outlined her novel *Doctor Zay* to him when he already had *Doctor Breen's Practice* partly in type. He encouraged her to proceed and wrote her a letter (October 28, 1881—Houghton Library) to clear her of all possible suspicion of having borrowed from him. But one of his most charming letters, and one of the best letters of its kind I have ever read, was sent to Kate Douglas Wiggin and her husband, along with a copy of *Venetian Life* (their honeymoon was to take them to Venice):

I am sending you with more love than I can say, or Mr. Riggs would let me, my book about Venice. I would write it all over again to make it worthy of the occasion, if there were time, but you have given us such short notice that I have not been able to do more than interline the old text throughout with the most earnest wishes for your happiness. They will be legible to no one but yourself and Mr. Riggs, for they are in sympathetic ink of a peculiarly confidential tint. It is the most beautiful of all your beautiful gifts, that you make people long to be of your own quality of friendship, and if these wishes of mine have any grace of the sort, it comes from you.

My book is in two volumes, but it is only one Life—like that now beginning for you both. Such a life began for my wife and me in Venice thirty years ago, and it fondly renews itself in our hearts at the thought of your joy.—Kate Douglas Wiggin, *My Garden of Memory* (HM, 1923), p. 275.

8   See his "WDH," *HM*, CXIII (1906), 221–25; reprinted in *What Is Man? and Other Essays* (Ha, 1917), pp. 228–39.

9   In 1860 H saw Blondin, the tightrope walker, cross Niagara Falls. He both admired and deplored him, but he thought the spectacle "evil." It would have been a relief to run away, but being unable to do this, he merely drove his nails into the palms of his hands. It seems odd that he never has anything to say about the aerialists who risk their lives somewhat similarly to entertain people at circuses.

10   "LL," *HW*, XLI (1897), 590.

11   The summary is that of James Woodress, *H in Italy*.

12   In addition to Howells's travel books, the following late articles should be noted: "A Bermudan Sojourn," *HM*, CXXIV (1911), 16–27; "Some Last Drops in Tunbridge Wells," *NAR*, CXCIII (1911), 879–92; "The City of the Royal Pavilion," *NAR*, CXCIV (1911), 602–11; "To the Waters of Blackpool," *NAR*, CXCIV (1911), 872–81; "Experiences of a True Baconian in Shakespeare's Town," *NAR*, CXCV (1912), 120–27; "A Pair of Pageants," *NAR*, CXC (1912), 607–17; "In Charleston," *HM*, CXXXI (1915), 747–59; "A Confession of St. Augustine," *HM*, CXXXIV (1917), 680–88, 877–85; "A Memory of San Remo," *HM*, CXL (1920), 321–27.

13   "The Rotational Tenants: A Hallowe'en Mystery," *HM*, CXXXIII (1916), 770–77.

14   Josiah B. Millet, ed., *George Fuller, His Life and Works* (HM, 1886). "I suppose that if I had been a painter I should not have wished, even if I could, to do those faces and figures and landscapes often teasingly withdrawn into their glows and mists; my liking, in literature at least, is to the strong, full light of day, to visages unsparingly distinct, to scenes in which nothing is poetically blinked. Yet I

enjoyed Fuller's work as I do Carpaccio's, or Botticelli's, or Tadema's. If it had not the earthly reality which I love, it had a heavenly sincerity, which is perhaps the celestial translation of reality."

15 For H's admiration for William Powell Frith, see Kirk, *WDH and Art in His Time*, Part III, Ch. II.

16 "The Chick of the Easter Egg," in *Between the Dark and the Daylight*.

17 There is some ambiguity about H's attitude toward ballet. In 1864 he wrote of certain nude pictures, sensual merely and lacking in sentiment, that to nobler art "they are as the ballet is to the opera—muscular merely and soulless." But elsewhere he describes the ballet as "everywhere delightfully innocent" and writes: "How beautiful it always was to have the minor coryphées subside into nebulous ranks on either side of the stage, and have the great planetary splendor of the *prima ballerina* come swiftly down the centre to the very footlights, beaming right and left."

18 When his brother Joe's son was engaged by Lew Dockstader, H was pleased. "It is not what one would have expected of a Howells exactly, but it is an honest calling, and much better than cheating somebody in trade."

19 H takes off the artificiality of the theater amusingly in *Saved, An Emotional Drama* and *A True Hero: Melodrama*. Technically the most interesting device in his plays is the effective use of the phonograph in *The Unexpected Guests*, where it almost takes on supernatural overtones. This is interesting to compare with the sea shell in Richard Strauss's opera, *The Egyptian Helen*.

20 In the country school exercises in *The Vacation of the Kelwyns*, the boys do a scene from *Rollo*. Emmerance, trying to improve the performance, not only shows H's realistic tastes but comes pretty close to what we now call "method" acting.

21 Meserve thinks that Miss Ramsey's comments on Gerda Bracy's Thistledown Dance in *Self-Sacrifice* (1911), which H cut when the play was revised from the *HM* version, refer to vaudeville dancers. "One hears such different opinions. Some people think her dancing is very spiritual; one man said that, anyway, her costuming was not very material." But I doubt that vaudeville dancers were discussed in quite this way. Could H have been thinking of Isadora Duncan?

22 *HM*, CXXXIII, 409–13.

23 H's only adverse criticism of either Julia Marlowe or her first husband Robert Taber is that they occasionally, and perhaps accidentally, echo Irving and Terry, which he thinks unfortunate because, good as they are in themselves, these players are not good models, and Marlowe and Taber do not need models. Actually, Marlowe's method was fully developed before she could possibly have been influenced by Ellen Terry. In a Houghton manuscript, "The Delicacy of Mr. Palliser," in which H tried to rework a discarded portion of *Ragged Lady* as a short story, he speaks of "the divine tenderness, the divine humor with which the actress [Marlowe] was rendering the part of Viola."

24 For H's use of the word "films" in *London Films*, see George Arms, "H's English Travel Books: Problems in Technique," *PMLA*, LXXXII (1967), 104–16, especially pp. 112–13.

25 There is much information about "The H Family" in a piece thus entitled by Richard J. Hinton, written in 1897, and edited and printed by Clara M. and Rudolf Kirk, *JRUL*, XIV (1950), 14–23.

26 In *My Mark Twain* H remarked of his old friend that "he was the most caressing of men in his pity, but he had the fine instinct, which would have pleased Lowell, of never putting his hands on you." This furnished William Lyon Phelps (*Howells, James, Bryant, and Other Essays*) with material for a discourse on H's own amazing delicacy. "Evidently the friendly arm on the shoulder, the added emphasis of touch was something horrible to Mr. H, and when I read that sentence, I wondered if, in the many conversations I had enjoyed with him, I had ever tortured him in that way. That is a curious aversion, most unusual; for Henry James, who seemed as an author so fastidious and distant, would put his arm affectionately round your neck at the first interview." But since both Charles Hanson Towne (*Adventures in Editing*, ACC, 1926) and Paul Laurence Dunbar (*Letters of Brand Whitlock*, ACC, 1936, p. 25) have recorded H's friendly touch, this seems overinterpretation. In any case, his reticence, which was great, was not wholly, or even mainly, a physical thing; rather, as George N. Bennett says, it reflects his "intense individuality," the "inner integrity and consistency which gave dignity to his life and work." If Mark Twain was correct in believing, as he told H after her death, that Mrs. Clemens thought he didn't like her, he must have been almost inhumanly reticent toward her, but in view of what he wrote about her in the letters he sent her husband during her life,

time, and the way she prized the letter he sent her when Susy died, this is hard to believe.

27   To paraphrase Sterne, one might say that H felt that they do these things better in Spain. Of a lover courting through a casement he writes, "I confess I thought it charming, and if at some period of their lives people must make love I do not believe there is a more inoffensive way of doing it." I wonder if he knew Hugo Wolf's charming song, "Auf dem grünen Balkon," which presents just such a situation.

28   Elsewhere H denounced "the evils which intelligent Italians believe to result from the celibacy of their priesthood" and "the anomalous position which the priest, isolated from mankind by an ascetic superstition of the middle ages, holds in the ameliorated society of this day." This drew fire from the editor of the Boston *Pilot*, John Boyle O'Reilly.

29   Kermit Vanderbilt, *The Achievement of WDH*, pp. 24 ff., 48, 64 ff. is important on H's treatment of sex. "Not only did he treat sexual neurosis again and again in his novels, but he understood its direct relation to the external disorders of a changing civilization." Walter J. Meserve seems to me to overstate H's prudery in "Truth, Morality, and Swedenborg in H's Theory of Realism," *NEQ*, XXVII (1954), 252–57.

30   "H knew of course that the path from evangelical excitement in camp meetings to powerful sexual stimulation was notoriously short and that the bushes around a revival full of 'power' were likely to be well inhabited."—Cady, *The Realist at War*, p. 267.

31   H was of course acquainted with the great architect Stanford White, who was murdered in 1906 in Madison Square Garden by a degenerate young Pittsburgh millionaire, Harry K. Thaw, who believed him to have been intimate with his wife, Evelyn Nesbit, before her marriage, and who escaped the electric chair on the insanity plea. The testimony given involved scandalous matters, and many were shocked by the newspaper reports. Though the Thaw-White case remained for many years the most famous American murder case, there seems to be only one veiled reference to it by H in print. This is in *HW*, LIII, April 10, 1909, p. 29, where he advises Italians about "assimilating" American manners: "Suppress such misleading passages of our life as our abominable voluntary madness, in which a man, on the mere warrant of a frightened or wanton woman's word, condemns

and puts to death another man whom he has refused any shadow of
defence." But there is an unpublished letter to his brother Joe (October 6, 1906), in which Howells discusses the case openly:

> You are right about Thaw. It is because he was brought up irresponsibly, and in the belief that he could buy anything with money, that he
> thought he had the privilege of murdering a man who was perhaps his immoral equal, but was as much above him intellectually as a god. White was
> one of the greatest Americans who ever lived; I knew him, and did not
> respect his life; no man could; but he could not have been worse than the
> worthless slut who put her husband up to killing him. The Thaws now think
> that it is only the form of acquittal which they have to choose; but it is
> most probable that he will be found guilty and executed. Certainly he would
> be found guilty if there were no capital punishment. It is quite time that
> Americans were stopped from taking a woman's word against a man's, and
> their trying, sentencing and killing him, by what our idiots call "the unwritten law." White was rather boyish, bad boyish, but compared with
> Thaw he was a hundred times worthy to live.

He repeated these views substantially in another letter to Joe (March
13, 1907), now adding that his wife was "really conducting the Thaw
trial, and she lives only from the morning till the evening editions of
the papers. She calls all the women concerned by their first names,
and she knows just what Jerome [the prosecuting attorney] and
Delmas [the chief defense counsel] are at, which is more than they do,
half the time." It is hard to see how White could have been both as
good and as bad as H would make him, and many will balk at
"worthless slut" as applied to Evelyn Nesbit. Even if it had been just,
however, to have her husband kill Stanford White would have been
about the last thing in the world that she could have desired.

32 See Arthur A. Adrian, "Augustus Hoppin to WDH," *NEQ*,
XXIV (1951), 84–89. H's objection to Ward H. Lamon's revelation
of "the spiritual squalor and the cruel suffering" of Lincoln's marriage,
which ought never to have been revealed while his widow and children lived, was entered upon similar grounds of delicacy. Edmund
Gosse says H once planned to write a novel whose scenes were to be
laid partly in Hong-Kong. When he complained "that he could but
faintly 'realize' the Chinese manner of life," Gosse sent him a privately
printed "report on the night-side of Hong-Kong," full of details, but
H did not acknowledge its receipt. "Being pressed, he admitted that
he had received it, but that it had horrified and disturbed him so much

that he had burned it, and had put away from him all thought of writing about Hong-Kong." This was probably a wise decision, for the material involved probably did not lie within H's range. But the story is a queer one altogether, and one wonders why Gosse thought the perusal of what he himself calls a "scabrous treasure" would help H to "realize" any kind of Chinese life that he could possibly have wished to write about. Gosse goes on to tell that H once remarked of a dingy house in Boston that he would be happy if he could see and hear everything that went on within its walls for a week, whereupon Gosse gave him "a rude suggestion" of what he might encounter, and H "put up his hand as if to ward off a blow. 'Oh! don't say that!' he cried. 'I couldn't bear it; I couldn't write a line if I thought such things were happening.' "

33 Vol. XXXVI, 956-60.

34 "Physical love, as sanctioned by marriage, was to H man's affirmation of faith in the good of nature. Love without its natural expression was as incongruous as faith apart from its ethical application."—James W. Mathews, "H and the Shakers," *Personalist*, XLIV (1963), 212-19.

35 "The Play and the Problem," *HW*, XXXIX (1895), 294; "EC," *HM*, CXXXIII (1916), 626-27.

36 "An Embarrassing Situation," *HW*, XLVII (1903), 916.

37 As early as 1879 H reviewed Mary Wollstonecraft's *Letters to Imlay* very sympathetically (*Atl*, XIV, 124-25). "They are the letters of a wife, though she was not Imlay's wife" and "the expression of a loving heart and a generous soul lavishing themselves in vain on an unstable and unworthy object." And though he is careful to repudiate her "mistaken theory of faithful love without marriage," he adds that her portraits are "lovely and interesting" and that she was "sincere in spite of her rhetoric" and "pure in spite of her error." In 1889 he was clearly shocked by Anne Reeve Aldrich's *The Rose of Flame and Other Poems of Love* but felt "bound to recognize the truth, the power" of her verse, and to draw attention to her "subtle perception" and "impassioned solemnity."—*HM*, LXXIX (1889), 639-43.

38 "The Dean," in *Prejudices* (first series) (Knopf, 1919).

39 In *A Chance Acquaintance* H writes: "Ladies have often to lament in the midst of their finesse that, really, no man is deserving the fate they devote themselves to prepare for him, or, in other words,

that women cannot marry women." And in *Their Wedding Journey*, Isabel, in a moment of enthusiasm, tells Basil that "a husband is almost as good as another woman!" The suggestiveness which these passages might carry to the mind of a modern reader was of course quite unintended by H, a point which is worth making only because of the attempts which have been made to find sexual significance in the scene in *The Rise of Silas Lapham* where Irene toys with the wood-shaving. In a modern, Freud-oriented author, the case would be very different, but if H had even remotely dreamed that such an interpretation might be made, he would never have used the incident, and if any contemporary editor had suspected such intention on the author's part, the scene would never have been printed. This, then, is one case where "resemblances" really are "purely coincidental." They have no more significance for interpretation than the patterns we sometimes discern in fire, leaves on the trees, or frost on the window-pane, and any attempt to read deep meanings into them is anachronistic criticism.

40 I do not believe H ever wrote a sentence which shows more about his respect for women than his writing a Mr. Salter after he had defended the Anarchists that the newspapers were classing him with George Francis Train (who made a lecture tour defending them) and Nina Van Zandt, the well-to-do New York girl who married one of them, August Spies, by proxy. (He immediately adds: "I say nothing against her.") On the other hand, an amazing vestige of snobbery survives in the piece "By Horse-Car to Boston" in *Suburban Sketches*, which contains strictures on men who sit while women stand. One conservative gentleman of H's acquaintance "has settled in his own mind that if the family cook appears in a car where he is seated, he must rise and give her his place. This, perhaps, is a trifle idealistic; but it is magnificent, it is princely."

41 Yet Lydia is as fine a girl as either Florida or Kitty; if she does not grip the reader's sympathy to quite the same extent, it is because until nearly the end of the book, she is not placed in anything like so difficult a situation as these other girls. When she is, and Staniford seems to have deserted her, she behaves splendidly.

42 Firkins (pp. 296–300) is interesting on what he considers certain inconsistencies in *Heroines of Fiction*; see also Annette Kar, "Archetypes of American Innocence: Lydia Blood and Daisy Miller," *AQ*, V (1953), 31–38. David H. Hirsch, "WDH and Daisy Miller," *English Language Notes*, I (1963), 123–28, suggests a certain ambivalence in H's mind toward Daisy and tries to draw some interesting

implications from it. John Roland Dove, "H's Irrational Heroines," *UTSE*, XXXV (1956), 64–80, argues that H's "characteristic heroine is a girl who, from the point of view of the rationalist, commits the cardinal vice of putting the heart above the head and considering impulse rather than reason." This article, though one-sided, is not without value. But there is no validity whatever in the contention of William Wasserstrom, "WDH: The Indelible Stain," *NEQ*, XXXII (1959), 486–95, that "H created very few feminine characters whose charm or beauty or virtue was not somehow vitiated." H has attracted very few critics who prefer to read into him rather than read him; of these Wasserstrom is the chief. Fortunately George Arms's reply, *NEQ*, XXXIII (1960), 243–44, is sufficiently cogent so that the matter need not be labored here; cf. Wasserstrom's weak rejoinder, pp. 144–45.

43 To be sure, he also says of Colville, that "at forty-one a man is still very much of a boy." He would not, I am sure, make a comparable statement of a woman.

44 *NAR*, CXCI (1910), 64–74.

45 Shakespeare is out of line with this when Howells makes him say in *The Seen and Unseen* that husbands and wives are together in eternity, marriage being "the only human relation that endures forever."

46 "Geoffrey Winter," Howells's first unpublished novel, is the story of an unhappy marriage; so is a long but uncompleted story at the Houghton Library called "A Love Match," in which we are told of the married pair that "it was simply their habit to hurt each other's feelings all they could." But the love of quarreling dies with age, and at last they really come to like each other somewhat better! Robert Louis Stevenson to the contrary notwithstanding, the treatment of the Maynards in *Doctor Breen's Practice* makes that much more of an anti-divorce novel than *A Modern Instance*, for Mrs. Maynard is such a selfish fool that it is hard to believe the marriage worth saving. "We had broken into each other's lives, and we couldn't get out again, with all the divorces under the sun." Howells was aware of this difficulty in connection with all human relationships. "There is always an unexpected wrench, a rending of fibres, a pang of remorse." When it comes to a showdown, the Kelwyns find they cannot even put the Kites out of their summer place, though they have quite failed to keep their part of the bargain, but prefer to get out themselves.

47 The Maxwells in *The Story of a Play*, the Kelwyns, the

Brandreths in *The World of Chance,* and the Lefferses in *Their Silver Wedding Journal* are only a few examples among many. But H does not give the impression of blaming women for this; on the contrary, marriage—and men—could hardly exist without it.

48   "Solitude" in *Stops of Various Quills.*

49   The question whether motherhood really possesses the peculiar sanctity which attaches to it in the popular imagination is raised but not really explored in "Somebody's Mother" (*A Daughter of the Storage*). In "LL," *HW,* XXXIX (1895), 604, there is an admirably commonsensical treatment of a recent symposium on whether or not a husband has a moral right to kill his wife's lover, which apparently was still being seriously considered in 1895. H finds the only safe guide in the Christian law of forgiveness and gives a pretty rough time to Chauncey M. Depew and others who had temporized in their answers.

50   Ethel F. Fisk, ed., *The Letters of John Fiske* (M, 1940), pp. 363–64.

51   Whitlock, *Letters,* p. 110.

52   If any year in H's life was worse than 1889, it must have been 1910. His wife's sister Mary died in March, Mark Twain in April, Elinor herself in May, and her brother, Larkin Mead, in October.

53   Van Wyck Brooks, not yet out of the shadow of *The Ordeal of Mark Twain,* said of H that "he wrote much more for her [his wife] than for anyone else, and his mind was unconsciously governed by her distaste for all that was disagreeable and unpleasant.—*A Chilmark Miscellany* (Du, 1948). What did Brooks know about Mrs. H's taste? Where did he get his information? In the same paragraph he ascribes H's "prudery" and "timorous over-niceness" to the writer himself, harking back to the period before he was married. When Matthew Arnold called at Howells's house and was told he was at Mark Twain's, he said, "Oh, but he doesn't like *that* sort of thing, does he?" Mrs. H replied: "He likes Mr. Clemens very much, and he thinks him one of the greatest men he ever knew."—Albert Bigelow Paine, *Mark Twain, A Biography* (Ha, 1912), II, 758.

54   *Ladies' Home Journal,* XXXVII, September 1920, p. 154.

55   F. C. Marston, Jr., "An Early H Letter," *AL,* XVIII (1946–47), 163–65.

56   One of the stories in this collection, "The Pony Engine and the Pacific Express," anticipates Carl Sandburg's *Rootabaga Stories.*

57   See Willis Fletcher Johnson, *George Harvey, A Passionate*

Patriot (HM, 1929), p. 88, for a letter to Dorothy Harvey, whom Howells had taken to see *Peter Pan*. It shows that his tenderness was not limited to his own children.

58   The passage is from H's pamphlet, *Winifred Howells*, which also contains portraits of Winifred and some of her poems. See, further, his reference to her in "EC," *HM*, CXXXVIII (1919), 832, and the letters concerning her in *Mark Twain-H Letters*. The fullest account of her illness and death is in Cady, *The Realist at War*; consult index. The first of H's quotations is from Henry James, in a letter to him. E. H. Cady, "H Bibliography: A 'Find' and a Clarification," *Studies in Bibliography: Papers of the Bibliographical Society of the University of Virginia*, XII (1959), 230–33, prints the text of *Don't Wake the Children*, music by Clemence Wilber Bowers, verses by WDH (Jefferson, Ohio, J. A. Howells & Co., 1895). This is not a good poem but is moving as a revelation of the author's love for his children and especially for its references to Winifred.

CHAPTER FOUR: MR. AMERICAN

1   See Louis J. Budd, "H's 'Blistering and Cauterizing,'" *OAHS*, LXII (1953), 334–47.

2   "The Latest Royal Scandal," *HW*, XLVII (1903), 137. The harmless Edward VII was another matter. H realized that though he "was very civil to Americans," it was "part of a constitutional king's business to be civil to everyone," and that since he was "probably not sentimental about us . . . we need not be sentimental about him." Still, he would have been sorry to leave England without seeing him. "All kings are bad, I knew that well enough; but I also knew that some kings are not so bad as others."

3   According to Morris Hillquit, *Loose Leaves from a Busy Life* (M, 1934), pp. 116–17), H made a contribution to the Debs campaign fund in 1908.

4   See H's letters to his father, November 12, 1876 and December 24, 1876—Houghton Library.

5   See L. N. Richardson, "Men of Letters and the Hayes Administration," *NEQ*, XV (1942), 110–41.

6   Why *Gabrielle de Bergerac* I have no idea, since not only is it a non-American story but it exemplifies the kind of romantic historical fiction that H generally detests.

7   L. Moffitt Cecil, "WDH and the South," *Mississippi Quarterly*, XX (1966–67), 13–24, argues, not wholly wrongly, that H never had a warm feeling for the South. But Cecil himself shows sectional feeling.

8   See Cady, *The Road to Realism*, p. 257, for a list of the books involving Ohio characters and locales.

9   John K. Reeves, "The Limited Realism of H," *PMLA*, LXXVII (1962), 627–28.

10   Though I know many critics admire Bromfield Corey as a characterization, I do not myself regard him as one of H's decided successes. Compared to Silas Lapham himself, he is a pasteboard figure.

11   *Fourscore* (HM, 1934).

12   *HW*, XXXIX (1895), 342.

13   Howells's most elaborate study of character and temperament and of the degree of responsibility which a person must carry for his actions is in the figure of Jeff Durgin in *The Landlord at Lion's Head*, certainly one of his most impressive characterizations.

14   For full discussions of this point, see Daniel Aaron, *Men of Good Will* (OUP, 1951); Robert W. Schneider, *Five Novelists of the Progressive Era* (ColUP, 1965); Max Westbrook, "The Critical Implications of H's Realism," *UTSE*, XXXVI (1957–58), 71–79.

15   He does, however, give a very unsympathetic picture of Spanish gypsies in *Familiar Spanish Travels*.

16   *Nation*, II (1866), 228–29; *Atl*, XIX (1867), 243–44.

17   See *NAR*, CLXXIII (1901), 280, 882, and cf. his review of a novel by his kinsman, Paul Kester, *His Own Country*, in which segregation is considered, *HM*, CXXXV (1917), 435–37.

18   I am indebted for the word "sextodecimoroon" to Anne Ward Amacher, "The Gentle Primitivist and the Semi-Tragic Octoroon," *NEQ*, XXIX (1956), 216–27. "Octoroon" is the term usually applied to Rhoda, but it is of course far from accurate. Miss Amacher establishes a primitivistic strain in *An Imperative Duty*, especially in H's analysis of Rhoda's appeal to Olney, which prefigures the treatment of the Negro in twentieth-century fiction. Thomas W. Ford, "H and the American Negro," *TSLL*, V (1963–64), 530–37, points out that the British reviews of *An Imperative Duty* were more favorable than the American, and concludes that H sympathized with Olney in being opposed "to any unrealistic interpretation of the Negro. He would not go along with the crusader or militant reformer who would make the

Negro something more than he is. Further, we have enough reform to make in our own race." (Mr. Ford writes from the University of South Carolina.) Howells does not approve of his heroine's temporary desire to live with the Negroes as a Negress, renouncing the white side of her heritage, because he always disapproves of quixotism and hysterical emotionalism. No racist considerations are involved. It may be interesting to note that in his play, *The Octoroon* (1859), Dion Boucicault had his heroine, who loved and was loved by a white man, kill herself to evade the issue. But the play was based upon Mayne Reid's English novel, *The Quadroon*, in which, though the girl had just twice as much "Negro blood" as her American counterpart, the lovers were permitted to marry.

19 See Rudolf and Clara M. Kirk, "Abraham Cahan and WDH, The Story of a Friendship," *American Jewish Historical Quarterly*, LII (1962), 27–57.

20 Two passages in the serial version of *Silas Lapham*, bearing on the effect on property values of the Jewish invasion of a Boston neighborhood, were dropped after H had received objections from Jewish readers. Having tried to make it clear that neither he nor the Laphams sympathized with the ideas expressed, he told one correspondent, "Perhaps also you owe me an apology for making an unjust accusation." See George Arms and William M. Gibson, "*Silas Lapham, Daisy Miller*, and the Jews," *NEQ*, XVI (1943), 118–22. For anti-Semitism in Boston of the Golden Age see Kermit Vanderbilt, "H among the Brahmins," *NEQ*, XXXV (1962), 291–317, and his book, *The Achievement of WDH*, pp. 116 ff., 188. In *Seven English Cities*, commenting on the treatment of Jews in mediaeval York, H remarks: "In New York the Christians have grown milder, and now they only keep the Jews out of their clubs and their homes."

21 This comes pretty close to the reaction of the Chicago *Tribune* to the "Union with Britain Now" movement around World War II. This could be achieved, the newspaper pointed out, should Great Britain apply for admission as a state of the Federal Union!

22 See Cady, *The Road to Realism*, p. 27.

23 In *A Woman's Reason*, Robert Fenton wishes to quit the navy after his marriage but finds no other employment. Just what H meant to convey by this I am doubtful, but the last page of the novel seems to indicate that in 1883 he thought the navy was unhappily being allowed to fall into ruin and neglect. The "Study," *HM*,

LXXIII (1886), 965–66, has a moving review of a biography of Judge Richard Reid of Kentucky, who failed to follow the code of the region in which he lived by refusing to kill a man who had unjustly assaulted and horsewhipped him. "Whatever the public interest in wrong may be, there can be no end to it but forgiveness between him who suffers and him who injures." In *NAR*, CLXXIII (1901), 883–85, H praises a pacifist novel, *Lay Down Your Arms* (*Die Waffen Nieder*) by the Baroness von Süttner. Cf. "EC," *HM*, CXXIII (1911), 796–99.

24   In *Seven English Cities*, however, H calls Cromwell's Commonwealth a "pseudo-republic," "a state as wholly without liberty, equality, and fraternity as in the king-capped oligarchy they had before and have had ever since." The Quakers "invented the only form of Democratic Christianity the world has yet known, unless indeed the German Mennonites are the same as the earlier English Quakers were in creed and life."

25   If Joe should be drafted, H wrote his father from Venice, August 28, 1862, "you must get a substitute, and shall have every cent I've saved, to help you do so. . . . It will cost me no effort to part with the money, though the loss of it will postpone my coming to see you, indefinitely, and will put off another event which I had hoped was to happen next summer. . . . In regard to Sam I don't know what to say. I hope if the chance fell upon him, he would be willing to go. If he should be very unwilling, then my offer remains the same for him as for Joe—I could not forgive myself otherwise; though if both should happen to be drafted, the substitute must be got for Joe." But on November 4, 1863, when he heard that Sam was in the army, he was shocked. "Poor Sam! He puts us all to shame, and I pray God keep him safe through the war." On H's reluctance to fight, see also Edd Winfield Parks, "A Realist Avoids Reality: WDH and the Civil War Years," *SAQ*, LII (1953), 93–97, an article of which I cannot, however, accept all the implications.

26   See Wagenknecht, *Nathaniel Hawthorne, Man and Writer* (OUP, 1961), pp. 124–30.

27   *Atl*, XVIII (1866), 125–26.

28   Even much later, in *Stories of Ohio*, H takes pride in Ohio's contribution to the war. "Remembering that General Grant, General Sherman, General Sheridan, the three greatest soldiers of the war, were all Ohio men, we might be tempted to claim that without these

the war would not have been won for the Union, but it is safer to claim nothing more than that Ohio gave the nation the generals who won the war." In his campaign biography of Hayes, he lauds both his hero's Civil War record and his support of the radical Republicans during Reconstruction, and speaks of "the late Mr. Vallandigham (whose course, only more open than that of Mr. Tilden, in the war it is merciful not to remember). . . ." Vallandigham gets fairer treatment in *Stories of Ohio* however. He was "a very able man" and "not malignant, however mistaken"; even 3,000 soldiers in the field voted for him.

29 See Owen Wister's interesting paragraph on the use of the Civil War in Howells's fiction in his article about him, *Atl*, CLX (1937), 704–13.

30 "L&L," *HW*, XL (1896), 6–7.

31 Which Cleveland and his secretary of state, Richard Olney, had invoked in this crisis, interpreting its provisions more broadly than had hitherto been attempted.

32 H's friendliness toward England may have been influenced by the fact that at this time, and until he was disillusioned by the Boer War, he was inclined to feel that British overlordship held out more hope to the oppressed peoples of the earth than any other possibility available. "A positive good both to the Turks and the Chinese would have been English rule, and it is this which Americans ought to hope and pray for in the interest of the suffering populations on the eastward and the westward of the suffering population of Russia. It would indeed be the greatest possible good to the Russians if they were under British rule too."

Howells's attitude toward revolution makes an interesting footnote to his attitude toward war; see, especially, Louis J. Budd, "Twain, H, and the Boston Nihilists," *NEQ*, XXXII (1959), 351–71. In 1891 H was friendly with Sergius Stepniak, but he did not join the Society of American Friends of Russian Freedom. Budd thinks Stepniak influenced H's leftward swing but is unable to document the impression. When in 1893 the Senate began debating a treaty that made attempted assassination of the Czar or any member of his family a nonpolitical crime, thus decreasing the likelihood of American asylum for any such offender, H, like Edward Bellamy, George Kennan, and Samuel Gompers, served as honorary vice-president for a proposed meeting in Carnegie Hall. H did not attend the meeting, but he sent an open letter calling the treaty "grotesquely one-sided" and "out of keeping with American principles and traditions." The New York state legislature condemned it, and H tried to stir up feeling against it in Ohio. In an interview in the Boston *Herald*, he compared it to the Fugitive Slave Law, and when it had been ratified he hoped that since the United States had "made a compact with the Devil, the good God will help us dodge it!" But when Gorky came to the United States, H would not sign an appeal for funds and later declared that while Mark Twain had been attracted to Gorky as a revolutionist, he himself had been drawn as a realist to the writer's art.

33   See William M. Gibson, "Mark Twain and H, Anti-Imperialists," *NEQ*, XX (1947), 435–70.

34   LXVIII (1904), 321.

35   Reprinted in *Sixty American Opinions on the War* (T. Fisher Unwin, 1915).

36   In Edith Wharton's *The Book of the Homeless* (S, 1916), published for Belgian relief.

37   Letter to Prof. W. H. Schofield, Dec. 9, 1916, in pamphlet, *Tributes to Canada* (Np, Nd).

38   See Clara M. Kirk, "Reality and Actuality in the March Family Narratives of WDH," *PMLA*, LXXIV (1959), 137–52, especially pp. 137, 152.

39   See Kirk and Kirk, *WDH, Representative Selections*, p. clviii, and Hough, *The Quiet Rebel*, p. 66.

CHAPTER FIVE: MR. HOMOS

1   Arthur Sherburne Hardy, *Things Remembered* (HM, 1923).

2   Occasionally he does "write like Clemens," never more so than in a paper called "I Talk of Dreams" in *Impressions and Experiences*. He catches Mark Twain's trick of exaggeration and mock-ferocity; there are many illustrations in their correspondence.

3   "On Coming Back," *Atl*, LXXVIII (1896), 562–65.

4   In *The Americanization of Edward Bok* (S, 1920), Bok quoted from an amusing letter written when H was publishing in *The Ladies' Home Journal*, and presumably not intended to be taken quite seriously.

The requests for my autograph have of late become so burdensome that I am obliged either to refuse all or to make some sort of limitation. Every author must have an uneasy fear that his signature is "collected" at times like postage-stamps, and at times "traded" among the collectors for other signatures. That would not matter so much if the applicants were always able to spell his name, or were apparently acquainted with his work or interested in it.

I propose, therefore, to give my name hereafter only to such askers as can furnish me proof by intelligent comment upon it that they have read some book of mine. If they can inclose a bookseller's certificate that they have bought the book, their case will be very much strengthened; but I do not insist upon this. In all instances a card and a stamped and directed envelope must be inclosed. I will never "add a sentiment" except in the case of applicants who can give me proof that they have read all my books. . . .

5 "The Pearl," *HM*, CXXXIII (1916), 409–13.

6 Both pieces are in *A Daughter of the Storage.*

7 Swedenborgian doctrine as James understood it is well summarized in Howells's review of James's book, *The Secret of Swedenborg, Atl,* XXIV (1869), 762–63.

8 H has been said to have been a member of the Church of the Carpenter, which developed out of the Society of Christian Socialists in Boston, and was organized as an Episcopal mission in 1890. "We especially invite those who do not believe in the Church, be they rich or poor." The Reverend William Dwight Porter Bliss was closely associated with Henry George, Laurence Gronlund, and Edward Bellamy. H was friendly to all of these, but there seems to be no evidence that he actually joined the church, though he did attend meetings and told his father that "it was like seeing the old faith renewed. . . ." See Clara and Rudolf Kirk, "H and the Church of the Carpenter," *NEQ,* XXXII (1959), 185–206.

9 As argued by Arnold B. Fox, "H as a Religious Critic," *NEQ,* XXV (1952), 199–216. Fox says that Matthew Braile's answer to Dylks's claim to be God "is an obvious attack upon the very basis of Biblical religion." Can Mr. Fox possibly think that a believing Christian must have *granted* Dylks's claim? In any case, he does not seem to have read the novel very carefully. As if deliberately guarding against Fox's misinterpretation, H has Braile say that "there isn't a *false* prophet in the Old Testament that couldn't match experiences with you!" (italics mine). Surely Mr. Fox is not so unfamiliar with the Old Testament as to be unaware that Braile is here making a distinction between false prophets and true. Can he possibly believe that the reference is to Isaiah, Jeremiah, etc.? Nor does it follow from Braile's

reference to "all the impostors in the world, from Mahomet up and down" that H rejected the Divinity of Christ, though, to be sure, there is other evidence to indicate that he did. H always speaks of Christ with great reverence, and he would have been quite incapable of such a sneak attack upon him as Fox here imagines.

10   Both Carrington's book on H and Richard Foster's article, "The Contemporaneity of H," *NEQ*, XXXII (1959), 54–78, are very able but one-sided presentations of the view that the world of H's fiction is essentially an agnostic world. The play, *The Night Before Christmas*, presented farcically, is a devastating examination of the way Christmas is and ought not to be, comparable in its way to Edna St. Vincent Millay's "To Jesus on His Birthday."

11   See two 1902 articles in *HW*—"A Suggestion from the Boer War" (XLVI, 747) and "Some Modest Misgivings" (XLVI, 946)— for ironical reflections on war and calamity as ministers of God's justice. Cf. "EC," *HM*, CXVII (1908), 957, for a satirical expression of the primitive idea riddled in the Book of Job, that prosperity is a token of God's reward for righteousness. When, in *The Son of Royal Langbrith*, Mrs. Enderby asks her clerical husband whether Langbrith's case must go over to the Day of Judgment, he replies: "You know that I never like to say those positive things. But if we suppose that there is a day of judgment in the old sense, what else could it be except for those sins on which justice has apparently been adjourned from the earthly tribunals?"

12   Both his book reviews and his fiction show that H had some interest in and knowledge of contemporary Biblical scholarship; see the Saratoga clergyman's consideration of the utterances of Jesus on marriage (*The Day of Their Wedding*, Ch. VII) and the discussion of the possibility of Egyptian influence on Hebrew ideas of the afterlife (*The Landlord at Lion's Head*, Ch. XXVI).

13   When Winifred Howells was born soon after H's grandmother had died, he thought it might perhaps be "part of her heavenly life" to watch over the baby. In 1889 he wrote of Winny to his father, "Her Angel doth always behold the Face of our Father." He also tried to think of the second anniversary of her death as her second birthday.

14   Vol. LVI, December 14, 1912, pp. 9–10.

15   *HM*, CXXX (1915), 472–75.

16   See also H's views on H. M. Alden, *A Study of Death*, "LL,"

HW, XXXIX (1895), 965, and of A. R. Wallace, *Man's Place in the Universe*, "EC," *HM*, CVIII (1904), 640–44.

17 See Cady, *The Road to Realism*, p. 117.

18 On February 15, 1891, H wrote his father of a séance held in a farmer's house at Concord, where "the most wonderful things happened. The floor and walls were shaken, and the table lifted and banged with blows from a hammer, and tappings galore. Most of the things were done in the dark, but some of the blows were given in full lamplight. I don't know what it was, and it all sounds absurd when you tell it, but I was badly rattled at the time, and I don't want to see any more of the performance."

19 H also had a very rich dream life: see "I Talk of Dreams" in *Impressions and Experiences*, *Mark Twain-H Letters*, 469, 763–66, and much besides. He spent one night with King Edward VII and his mother Queen Victoria, "who was not dead, but had abdicated to oblige him." He dreamed of some of the places he had loved in Venice as long as he lived, and apparently he never lost his dream-hold on those who had died.

The most interesting thing about H's dreams, however, is that he was apparently often out of character in them. One can understand why he should have dreamed of himself in battle and always running away, of being on the stage without knowing his part, and of receiving social snubs. He had too the very common dream of being naked in public, and once he was "in the hands of a barber, who added to the shaving and shampooing business the art of removing his customer's heads in treatment for headache." But why should he have dreamed of himself as a criminal? His own explanation was that "the soul is mostly absent" in dreams, and that there is no inner monitor to check. "By them we may know what the state of the habitual criminal is, what the state of the lunatic, the animal, the devil is. In them the personal character ceases; the dreamer is remanded to his type."

20 *A Traveler from Altruria* (1894) and *Through the Eye of the Needle* (1907). Eleven "Letters of an Altrurian Traveler" appeared in *Cosmopolitan*, Vols. XVI and XVII, between November 1893 and September 1894. The first two of these were never reprinted by H; the next three were altered in *Impressions and Experiences*; the rest became Part I of the *Needle*. All were reprinted in *Letters of an Altrurian Traveler*, edited by the Kirks. All the Altrurian material is reprinted in Volume 20 of "A Selected Edition of WDH." See also

Clara and Rudolf Kirk, *WDH, Traveler from Altruria* (RUP, 1962).

21   It is interesting that among those who meet Mr. Homos and talk over Altrurian and American conditions with him, H makes the college professor very hidebound while the banker is surprisingly liberal. H gives the banker his favorite idea that if you want social change, you must vote, not fight; he also allows him to deny that socialists are "un-American"; instead, they are the only ones "who propose to vote their ideas into laws, and nothing can be more American than that."

22   See William F. Eckstrom, "The Equalitarian Principle in the Fiction of WDH," *AL*, XXIV (1952), 40–50. I do not know what H would say to the claim of modern nudists that they have established true equality, but I cannot help being amused by Barker's experience with the Boston vagrants, whom he first encounters nude in the washroom. In their nakedness "the worst of them had the alienable comeliness of nature, and their faces, softened by their relation to their bodies, were not so bad." The next day, when he sees them clothed, his reaction is quite different!

23   It is interesting that John Humphrey Noyes, one of the founders of the New York Oneida Community, was an uncle of Elinor Mead, whom Howells was to marry.

24   E. H. Cady, *OAHQ*, LIII, 41. The same slant appears in H's admiration for "Citizen" (William M.) Corry, state representative, in Cincinnati *Gazette* days; see Louis J. Budd in the same periodical, LXII, 338–39.

25   Phelps, *Autobiography with Letters* (OUP, 1939), p. 504.

26   See the less serious treatment of the same problem in the play *The Impossible*.

27   The Howells Collection at the Houghton Library contains refusals from Whittier, George William Curtis, and Edward Everett Hale. This is made the more inexplicable in view of the protests by William Morris and others abroad and by the fact that in Chicago itself, such solid citizens as the banker Lyman H. Gage, Marvin Hughitt, president of the Northwestern Railroad, and the merchant Potter Palmer were working to have the death sentences commuted. As a sample of the abuse to which H was subjected, one may cite the query of *Life*: "Has our Boston friend followed Tolstoï so far as to have become a non-resistant? If so, how long may we expect him

to keep personally clean and wear boiled shirts?" *Life* ran a brutal cartoon, showing seven bodies hanging from a gallows with the caption

SEVEN UP

A Game That Will Be Played in Chicago Next Month

which caused the Boston *Transcript* to cry "shame." The Boston Catholic paper, *The Pilot*, declared that H had performed an action which few of his "milk-and-water critics will have the honorable impulse to think of or the independence to carry out," and Lowell, who did not agree with him, wrote in 1890: "You know I don't share some of your opinions or sympathize with some of your judgments, but I am not such an ass as not to think better of a man for saying what he thinks and not what I think. Though I thought those Chicago ruffians well hanged, I specially honored your courage in saying what you did about them. You can't make me fonder of you, but I am sure you will make me prouder of you."

28 For Howells and the Haymarket affair, see Cady, *The Realist at War*, pp. 67–80, which includes H's second unprinted and possibly unsent letter to the New York *Tribune*; Everett Carter, "The Haymarket Affair in Literature," *AQ*, II (1950), 270–78; John W. Ward, "Another H. Anarchist Letter," *AL*, XXII (1950–51), 489–90; Howard A. Willson, "WDH's Unpublished Letters about the Haymarket Affair," *Journal of the Illinois State Historical Association*, LVI (1963), 5–19. According to a letter to Aurelia in the Houghton Library, October 24, 1899, H met Altgeld on his midwestern lecture tour.

29 J. W. Getzels, "WDH and Socialism," *Science and Society*, II (1938), 376–86, tried unsuccessfully to trace H's Socialism directly to Marx. Conrad Wright, "The Sources of Mr. H's Socialism," same, pp. 514–17, isolated Gronlund as the channel. George Arms, same, III (1949), 146–48, accepted Gronlund and showed his affinity to Bellamy's Nationalism. W. F. Taylor, "On the Origin of H's Interest in Economic Reform," *AL*, II (1930), 3–14, parallels H and Bellamy.

30 H perceived that the poor Negroes who expected "forty acres and a mule" apiece after the Civil War had "a truer ideal of a civilized state than the manufacturers who want more and more tariff but won't raise their workmen's wages a cent." If we had given them

forty acres a mule, we might have gone far toward solving what is now called "the Negro problem." Instead, Congress preferred to give millions of acres to railroad builders and industrialists, who gutted it and used it for selfish advantage.

31   See W. F. Taylor's article, cited in n. 29.

32   In *HW*, XLVI (1902), 811 ("Without our Special Wonder"), H expressed the hope that, upon his accession, King Edward VII would pardon Mrs. Maybrick, which he did. His apparent belief in her innocence is shared by such modern students of the Maybrick case as Joseph Shearing and Trevor J. Christie.

33   Vol. XXXII, 23.

34   H's last discussion of capital punishment, so far as I am aware, was in an "EC" of 1915, *HM*, CXXX, 634–37, which reaches no conclusion. Whether this has any significance I am unable to say. (In earlier times he was not supposed to discuss the subject in *Harper's*.) In the story "The Angel of the Lord" (*Questionable Shapes*), Rulledge calls capital punishment "that barbarity." *The Son of Royal Langbrith* contains a reference to the Russian penal colony off the northeast coast of Japan, where nonpolitical murderers are kept. Judge Garley says: "We generally kill off our murderers before they have time to show remorse, but the Russians keep them, in a kind of cold storage, up there in the latitude of Siberia, and they have opportunities of studying effects that we precipitately deny ourselves the knowledge of." In *The Seen and Unseen*, the custom of giving the prosecution the last word is attacked as "barbarous."

BIBLIOGRAPHY

William M. Gibson and George Arms, *A Bibliography of WDH* (New York Public Library, 1948) is standard. Since this is a work of 182 large pages, I cannot reproduce it here. I have read everything listed in it with the exception of some of the early Ohio material.

There is no collected edition of H. Ha once projected one in the "Library Edition," but only six volumes were published (1911). "H's Unpublished Prefaces" to some of the other volumes have been edited and published by George Arms, *NEQ*, XVII (1944), 580–91.

A "Selected Edition" in 36 volumes, under the general editorship of E. H. Cady (IUP) is in progress.

Clara M. Kirk and Rudolf Kirk, eds., *WDH: Representative Selections*, Revised Edition (Hill and Wang, 1961), containing selections, a very useful bibliography of writings about H, and an extensive biographical and critical introduction, is perhaps the best introduction to H.

A list of H's book-length publications follows. The publisher is Ha except where otherwise indicated. Under FICTION, volumes marked with an asterisk are collections of short stories. Of these *The Daughter of the Storage* also contains some poems. The most desirable edition of *Criticism and Fiction* is now the one edited by the Kirks and published by NYUP (1959), in which many other critical articles have been included. A modern edition of the Lincoln book, reproducing Lincoln's corrections in facsimile, was published by IUP, 1960. Marilyn Austin Baldwin published a modern annotated edition of *My Mark Twain* through Louisiana State University Press, 1967.

FICTION

Annie Kilburn (1889); *April Hopes* (1888); **Between the Dark and the Daylight* (1907); *A Chance Acquaintance* (HM, 1873); **Christ-*

317

mas Every Day and Other Stories (1893); *The Coast of Bohemia* (1893); **The Daughter of the Storage* (1916); *The Day of Their Wedding* (1896); *Doctor Breen's Practice* (HM, 1881); **A Fearful Responsibility and Other Stories* (HM, 1881); *Fennel and Rue* (1908); *The Flight of Pony Baker* (1902); *A Foregone Conclusion* (HM, 1875); *A Hazard of New Fortunes* (1890); *An Imperative Duty* (1892); *Indian Summer* (HM, 1886); *The Kentons* (1902); *The Lady of the Aroostook* (HM, 1879); *The Landlord at Lion's Head* (1897); *The Leatherwood God* (Ce, 1916); *Letters Home* (1903); *Letters of an Altrurian Traveler*, ed. Clara M. Kirk and Rudolf Kirk (SFR, 1961); *The Minister's Charge* (HM, 1887); *Miss Bellard's Inspiration* (1905); *Mrs. Farrell* (1921); *A Modern Instance* (HM, 1882); *New Leaf Mills* (1913); *An Open-Eyed Conspiracy* (1897); **A Pair of Patient Lovers* (1901); *A Parting and a Meeting* (1896); *The Quality of Mercy* (1892); **Questionable Shapes* (1903); *Ragged Lady* (1899); *The Rise of Silas Lapham* (HM, 1885); *The Seen and Unseen at Stratford-on-Avon* (1914); *The Shadow of a Dream* (1890); *The Son of Royal Langbrith* (1904); *The Story of a Play* (1898); *Their Second Wedding Journey* (1899); *Their Wedding Journey* (HM, 1872); *Through the Eye of the Needle* (1907); *A Traveler from Altruria* (1894); *The Undiscovered Country* (HM, 1880); *The Vacation of the Kelwyns* (1920); *A Woman's Reason* (HM, 1883); *The World of Chance* (1893).

Poems

Poems (HM, 1873); *Poems of Two Friends*, with John J. Piatt (Columbus, Follett, Foster and Company, 1860); *Stops of Various Quills* (1895).

Plays

All H's plays have now been collected by Walter H. Meserve, ed., *The Complete Plays of WDH* (NYUP, 1960).

Travel

Certain Delightful English Towns (1906); *Familiar Spanish Travels* (1913); *Hither and Thither in Germany* (1920); *Italian Journeys* (HM, 1867, 1896); *A Little Swiss Sojourn* (1892); *London Films* (1906); *Roman Holidays and Others* (1908); *Seven English Cities* (1909); *Tuscan Cities* (HM, 1886); *Venetian Life* (HM, 1866, 1907).

Miscellaneous

A Boy's Town (1890); *Criticism and Fiction* (1891); *A Day's Pleasure and Other Sketches* (HM, 1881); *Heroines of Fiction*, 2 vols. (1901); *Imaginary Interviews* (1910); *Impressions and Experiences* (1896); *Literary Friends and Acquaintance* (1900); *Literature and Life* (1902); *A Little Girl among the Old Masters* (HM, 1884); *Lives and Speeches of Abraham Lincoln and Hannibal Hamlin* (Follett, Foster & Co., 1860); *Modern Italian Poets* (1887); *My Literary Passions* (1895); *My Mark Twain* (1910); *My Year in a Log Cabin* (1893); *Sketch of the Life and Character of Rutherford B. Hayes* (HM, 1876); *Stories of Ohio* (ABC, 1897); *Suburban Sketches* (HM, 1871); *Three Villages* (HM, 1884); *Winifred Howells* (privately printed, 1891); *Years of My Youth* (1916).

In 1877–78 H edited a series of "Autobiographies" for HM and contributed long biographical introductions: *Memoirs of Frederica Sophia Wilhelmina* (2 vols.); *Lives of Lord Herbert of Cherbury and Thomas Ellwood*; *Life of Vittorio Alfieri*; *Memoirs of Carlo Goldoni*; *Memoirs of Edward Gibbon, Esq*; *Memoirs of Jean François Marmontel* (2 vols.). In 1888, for Ha, he edited *Library of Universal Adventure by Sea and Land* with Thomas Sergeant Perry. In 1895 he introduced *Recollections of Life in Ohio from 1813 to 1840* by his father, William Cooper Howells (Cincinnati, The Robert Clarke Company, 1895).

His prefaces to books by other writers have been collected in *Prefaces to Contemporaries, 1882–1920*, ed. by George Arms, W. M. Gibson, and Frederic C. Marston, Jr. (SFR, 1957). Albert Mordell has collected H's criticisms of Henry James in *Discovery of a Genius; WDH and Henry James* (Twayne, 1961); H's 1899 lecture, "Novel-Writing and Novel-Reading: An Impersonal Explanation," has been reprinted by W. M. Gibson, *Bulletin New York Public Library*, LXII (1958), 15–34. See, also, H's "An Editor's Relations with Young Authors," *Youth's Companion*, LXVIII (1895), 418–19; "Meetings with King," in *Clarence King Memoirs: The Helmet of Mambrino* (Putnam, 1904); "Part of Which I Was," *NAR*, CCI (1915), 135–41; and H with Henry James and Frank A. Sanborn, "Literary Recollections," *NAR*, CXCV (1912), 550–66.

The largest collections of letters so far available are Mildred

Howells, ed., *Life in Letters of William Dean Howells*, 2 vols. (Doubleday, 1928) and H. N. Smith and W. M. Gibson, eds., *Mark Twain-H Letters* (HUP, 1960). For other letters, see George Arms, " 'Ever Devotedly Yours'; The Whitlock-H Correspondence," *JRUL*, X (1946), 1–19; James G. Austin, *Fields of* The Atlantic Monthly: *Letters to an Editor, 1861–1870* (Huntington Library, 1953); Moncure D. Conway, *Autobiography, Memories and Experiences*, 2 vols. (HM, 1904); Leo P. Coyle, "H's Campaign Biography of Rutherford B. Hayes: A Series of Letters," *OAHQ*, LXV (1957), 391–406, and "Restoration of a H Letter," *Mark Twain Journal*, Vol. XI, No. 2, Summer 1960, pp. 12, 15; Richard Crowder, "American Nestor: Six Unpublished Letters from H to Ade," *Bucknell Review*, VII (1958), 144–47; Jean Downey, "Atlantic Friends: H and Cooke," *American Notes and Queries*, I (1963), 132–33; Charles Duffy, "An Unpublished Letter: H to Stedman," *AL*, XXX (1958), 369–70; Kimball C. Elkins, "Eliot, H, and the Courses of Graduate Instruction, 1869–71," *HLB*, X (1956), 141–46; George S. Hellman, "The Letters of H to Higginson," *Twenty-Seventh Annual Report of the Bibliophile Society, 1901–1929*, pp. 17–56; Clara and Rudolf Kirk, "Letters to an 'Enchanted Guest': WDH to Edmund Gosse," *JRUL*, XXII (1959), 1–25; Marc L. Ratner, "H and Boyesen: Two Views of Realism," *NEQ*, XXXV (1962), 376–91; Joseph Schiffman, "Mutual Indebtedness: Unpublished Letters of Edward Bellamy to WDH," *HLB*, XII (1958), 363–74; J. B. Stronks, "An Early Autobiographical Letter to WDH," *NEQ*, XXXIII (1960), 240–42; James L. Woodress, Jr., "The Lowell-H Friendship: Some Unpublished Letters," *NEQ*, XXVI (1953), 523–28.

George Arms and William M. Gibson have reprinted "Five Interviews with WDH," *Americana*, XXXVII (1943), 257–95. For other interviews, see Clifton Johnson, "The Writer and the Rest of the World," *Outlook*, XLIX (1894), 580–82, and "Sense and Sentiment," *Outlook*, LI (1895), 304–5; Clara M. Kirk, "Toward a Theory of Art: A Dialogue between WDH and Charles Eliot Norton," *NEQ*, XXXVI (1963), 291–319; A. S. van Westrum, "Mr. H on Love and Literature," *The Lamp*, XXVIII (1904), 27–31. "A Tribute to WDH, Souvenir of a Dinner Given to the Eminent Author in Celebration of his Seventy-fifth Birthday," *HW*, LVI, May 9, 1912, pp. 27–34, was reprinted in part in *NAR*, CCXII (1920), 1–16, with "An Appreciation" by William Lyon Phelps, pp. 17–20.

The only book about H published during his lifetime was Alexander Harvey's worthless and eccentric *WDH: A Study of the Achievement of a Literary Artist* (B. W. Huebsch, 1917). This was followed shortly after his death by two immensely superior works: Delmore G. Cooke, *WDH, A Critical Study* (Du, 1922) and O. W. Firkins, *WDH, A Study* (HUP, 1924).

Since the H revival began, we have had a considerable number of books. Two volumes by Edwin H. Cady mark the closest we have come to a definitive biography—*The Road to Realism: The Early Years, 1837–1885, of WDH* and *The Realist at War: The Mature Years, 1885–1920, of WDH* (Syracuse University Press, 1956, 1958). Of the other books, Brooks is mainly biographical, but the critical interest predominates in all the others. They are listed here alphabetically by the names of their authors:

George N. Bennett, *WDH: The Development of a Novelist* (University of Oklahoma Press, 1959); Van Wyck Brooks, *H, His Life and World* (Du, 1959); George C. Carrington, Jr., *The Immense Complex Drama: The World and Art of the H Novel* (Ohio State University Press, 1966); Everett Carter, *H and the Age of Realism* (Lippincott, 1954); Olov W. Fryckstedt, *In Quest of America: A Study of H's Early Development as a Novelist* (HUP, 1958); William M. Gibson, *William D. Howells*, "University of Minnesota Pamphlets on American Writers," No. 63 (UMP, 1967); Robert L. Hough, *The Quiet Rebel: WDH as Social Commentator* (University of Nebraska Press, 1959); Clara M. Kirk, *WDH and Art in his Time* (RUP, 1965) and *WDH, Traveler from Altruria, 1889–94* (RUP, 1962); William McMurray, *The Literary Realism of WDH* (Southern Illinois University Press, 1967); James L. Woodress, Jr., *H and Italy* (DUP, 1952). See also *Public Meeting at the American Academy and the National Institute of Arts and Letters, in Honor of WDH* (American Academy of Arts and Letters, 1922).

Kermit Vanderbilt's *The Achievement of WDH* (Princeton University Press, 1968) did not appear until after I had finished my book, but I have added a few references to it in the notes.

In addition to what is cited in the notes the following may be listed among books and articles containing useful H material. It must be understood, however, that this is not a complete bibliography in any sense.

Harry Hayden Clark, ed., *Transitions in American Literary History* (DUP, 1953); Alexander Cowie, *The Rise of the American*

Novel (ABC, 1948); Hamlin Garland, "H," in John Macy, ed., *American Writers on American Literature* (Liveright, 1931), *Roadside Meetings* (M, 1930) and *A Son of the Middle Border* (M, 1917); Robert Grant, "WDH," in M. A. DeWolfe Howe, ed., *Later Years of the Saturday Club, 1870–1920* (HM, 1927); J. Henry Harper, *The House of Harper* (Ha, 1912) and *I Remember* (Ha, 1934); Robert Underwood Johnson, *Remembered Yesterdays* (Little, Brown, 1923); Alfred Kazin, *On Native Grounds* (Reynal and Hitchcock, 1942); John Macy, *The Spirit of American Literature* (D, 1913); Frank Norris, *The Responsibilities of the Novelist* (D, 1903); Vernon L. Parrington, *Main Currents in American Thought* (Harcourt, 1930); William Lyon Phelps, *H, James, Bryant and Other Essays* (M, 1924); John Paul Pritchard, *Return to the Fountains* (DUP, 1924); Arthur H. Quinn, *A History of American Drama from the Civil War to the Present Day* (ACC, 1936) and American Fiction (ACC, 1936); Forrest Reid, *Retrospective Adventures* (Faber and Faber, 1941); John M. Robertson, *Essays Toward a Critical Method* (Unwin, 1889); Laura Stedman and George M. Gould, *Life and Letters of Edmund Clarence Stedman*, 2 vols. (Moffat, Yard, 1910); John A. Steuart, *Letters to Living Authors* (Sampson Low, 1890); Walter F. Taylor, *The Economic Novel in America* (UNCP, 1942); Caroline Ticknor, *Glimpses of Authors* (HM, 1922); Leonard Trilling, *The Opposing Self* (Viking Press, 1955); Carl Van Doren, *The American Novel, 1789–1939* (M, 1940); Edward Wagenknecht, *Cavalcade of the American Novel* (Holt, 1952); William Wasserstrom, *Heiress of All the Ages: Sex and Sentiment in the Genteel Tradition* (UMP, 1959); Carl J. Weber, *The Rise and Fall of James Ripley Osgood* (Colby College Press, 1959); Edith Wharton, *A Backward Glance* (ACC, 1934); William Allen White, *Autobiography* (M, 1946); Brand Whitlock, *Forty Years of It* (ACC, 1914) and *The Letters and Journal of Brand Whitlock*, ed. Allan Nevins, 2 vols. (ACC, 1936); Stanley T. Williams, *The Spanish Background of American Literature*, 2 vols. (Yale University Press, 1955); Edith Wyatt, *Great Companions* (ACC, 1917).

Henry M. Alden, "WDH," *Bkm*, XLIX (1919), 549–54; George Arms, "H's New York Novel: Comedy and Belief," *NEQ*, XXI (1948), 313–25; Annette K. Baxter, "Caste and Class: H's Boston and Wharton's New York," *MQ*, IV (1962–63), 353–61; George J. Becker, "WDH: The Awakening of Conscience," *CE*, XIX (1958), 283–91; Scott Bennett, "A Concealed Printing in WDH," *PBSA*,

LXI (1967), 56–60; Arthur Boardman, "Social Point of View in the Novels of WDH," *AL*, XXXIX (1967), 42–59; Louis J. Budd, "WDH's Defence of the Romance," *PMLA*, LXVII (1952), 32–42; E. H. Cady, "H in 1948," *UKCR*, XV (1948), 83–91, "WDH in Italy: Some Bibliographical Notes," *Symposium*, VII (1953), 147–53, "H and Twain: The World in Midwestern Eyes," *Ball State Teachers College Forum*, Vol. III, No. 2, Winter 1962–63, pp. 3–8, and "The H Nobody Knows," *Mad River Review*, I (1964–65), 3–25; Paul J. Carter, Jr., "The Influence of WDH upon Mark Twain's Social Satire," *University of Colorado Studies, Series in Language and Literature*, No. 4 (1953), pp. 93–100; Harry Hayden Clark, "The Role of Science in the Thought of WDH," *TWASAL*, XLII (1953), 263–303; Stanley Cooperman, "Utopian Realism: The Futurist Novels of Bellamy and H," *CE*, XXIV (1963), 464–67; Leo P. Coyle, "Mark Twain and WDH," *GR*, X (1956), 302–11; Kenneth E. Eble, "The Western Ideals of WDH," *Western Humanities Review*, XI (1957), 331–38; John Erskine, "WDH," *Bkm*, LI (1920), 385–89; Waldon Fawcett, "Mr. H. and his Brother," *Critic*, XXXV (1899), 1026–28; Annie Howells Fréchette, "WDH," *Canadian Bookman*, Vol. II, July 1920, pp. 9–12; James Gargano, "*A Modern Instance:* The Twin Evils of Society," *TSLL*, IV (1962–63), 399–407; Hamlin Garland, "Sanity in Fiction," *NAR*, CLXXVI (1903), 336–48; W. M. Gibson, "Materials and Forms in H's First Novels," *AL*, XIX (1947–48), 158–66; Henry Gifford, "WDH: His Moral Conservatism," *Kenyon Review*, XX (1958), 124–33; Clare R. Goldfarb, "From Complicity to Altruria: The Use of Tolstoy in H," *UKCR*, XXXII (1966), 311–17; Edmund Gosse, "The Passing of WDH," *Living Age*, CCCVI (1920), 98–100; Virginia Harlow, "WDH and Thomas Sergeant Perry," *Bulletin Boston Public Library*, I (1949), 135–50; Clara and Rudolf Kirk, "H's Guidebook to Venice," *AL*, XXXIII (1961), 221–24, and "H in Caricature," *JRUL*, XXI (1958), 69–70; E. S. Martin, "WDH," *HM*, CXLI (1920), 165–66; Michael Millgate, "The Emotional Commitment of WDH," *Neophilologus*, XLIV (1960), 48–54, "WDH: A Bibliographical Amendment," *PBSA*, LVI (1962), 254–57, and "WDH: A Bibliographical Amendment," *PBSA*, LVIII (1964), 468–69; David H. Noble, "WDH: The Discovery of Society," *MQ*, III (1961–62), 149–62; Alma J. Payne, "The Family in the Utopia of WDH," *GR*, XV (1961), 217–29; Douglas R. Picht, "WDH, Realistic-Realist," *Research Studies Washington State University*, XXXV (1967), 92–94;

Donald Pizer, "The Ethical Unity of *The Rise of Silas Lapham*," *AL*, XXXII (1960–61), 322–27; Lawrence E. Scanlon, "*The Rise of Silas Lapham*: Literalism or Art?" *Discourse*, V (1961–62), 212–25; B. A. Sokoloff, "WDH and the Ohio Village: A Study of Environment and Art," *AQ*, XI (1959), 58–75; James B. Stronks, "Paul Laurence Dunbar and WDH," *OAHQ*, LXVII (1958), 95–108; Sr. Mary Petrus Sullivan, "The Function of Setting in H's *The Landlord at Lion's Head*," *AL*, XXXV (1963–64), 38–64; G. Thomas Tanselle, "The Architecture of *The Rise of Silas Lapham*," *AL*, XXXVII (1965–66), 430–57; Booth Tarkington, "Mr H," *HM*, CXLI (1920), 346–50; W. F. Taylor, "WDH, Artist and American," *Sewanee Review*, XLVI (1938), 288–303; Frank Turaj, "The Social Gospel in H's Novels," *SAQ*, LXVI (1967), 449–64; Kermit Vanderbilt, "*The Undiscovered Country*: H's Version of American Pastoral," *AQ*, XVII (1965), 634–55; W. de Wagstaffe, "The Personality of Mr. H," *Book News Monthly*, XXVI (1908), 739–41; Robert W. Walts, "WDH and his 'Library Edition,'" *PBSA*, LVII (1963), 453–59; William Wasserstrom, "H's Mansion and Thoreau's Cabin," *CE*, XXVI (1965), 366–72; Max Westbrook, "The Critical Implications of H's Realism," *UTSE*, XXXVI (1957), 71–79.

INDEX

818   WAGENKNECHT
4   WILLIAM DEAN
HOWELLS HOWELLS, FRIENDLY
         EYE 70-05917

Date Due

		STORAGE	

FINKELSTEIN
MEMORIAL LIBRARY

of

Ramapo Central School District No. 2
Spring Valley, New York

G9

PRINTED IN U.S.A.